Popular
Government
in an
African Town

Popular Government in an African Town

Kita, Mali

Nicholas S. Hopkins

The University of Chicago Press
Chicago and London

The University of Chicago Press, Chicago 60637
The University of Chicago Press, Ltd., London

© 1972 by The University of Chicago
All rights reserved. Published 1972
Printed in the United States of America

International Standard Book Number: 0–226–35173–4
Library of Congress Catalog Card Number: 70–162528

to the
memory
of
Carl Withers

Contents

CONTENTS

Contents

Illustrations

Tables

Preface

My initial arrival in Kita was inauspicious. The train that was carrying me there gave out about ten miles short of its destination, and, after a six-hour wait for a new locomotive to be sent out from Bamako, we arrived in Kita at 2 A.M. Some kind souls directed me on the half-mile walk to the local rest house, then—as now—a rather casual affair. On the way we were stopped by a patrol from the Brigade de Vigilance whose members wanted to check our papers; but no one was astir at the rest house except a wakeful member of a National Union delegation that was spending the night there. I collapsed exhausted on the bed he located for me.

But all beginnings are difficult, and the inauspiciousness of this one was amply compensated for by my experiences in two years of living in Kita. In October, 1961, I was going there to spend ten months teaching English to boys in the local secondary school. I had received some prior training in anthropology, as an undergraduate at Harvard and during most of a year in Paris, and I already had it in mind to carry out field research in anthropology in Mali. So I made it a point to take an interest in the social structure and the flow of events in this town of eight thousand people. I had many long talks with some of the older men in town, notably the former canton chief, who was then out of a job, and I spent a lot of time with the young men of my own age—schoolteachers, clerks, merchants, mechanics, and others. I also spent much time with my pupils and had the great joy of seeing many of them, after only a year of instruction, acquire the ability to carry on a simple conversation in English; actually some of them used English as a secret language, and were inspired in their study for this reason. During that year of 1961–62 I was able to visit many parts of Mali, from Gao to Kayes, including particularly the Dogon country and Segou, although owing to lack of any local transport other than an untrustworthy bicycle I saw almost nothing of the rural areas around Kita.

Following this most challenging and rewarding year in Kita, I returned to the United States to attend graduate school in anthropology at the University of Chicago. I spent two years there meeting the various requirements for the degree, and in the summer of 1964 I left again for Mali, supported by a fellowship from the National Institute of Mental Health, this time to carry out field work on the formation of the national culture in Mali, while based in Kita. My ideas of what I was going to find were founded on my experiences there three years earlier, which was shortly after Mali's independence. At that time it seemed to me that Mali's single party, the Union Soudanaise-Rassemblement Démocratique Africain, and its government were working effectively to spread modern ideas and organization throughout the entire country. It was this process that I proposed to study under the heading of the national culture, which I defined as the system of values and behavior of those people who are committed to the new state. The reality that I discovered in Kita in 1964–65, and which I attempt to describe in this book, was a good deal more complex, for it was obvious that there was no simple distinction between the national culture and other cultures. Yet I think that I remained fairly faithful to my original conception.

Before leaving Chicago I secured permission from the Malian government, through its Washington embassy, to carry out the field work; this permission had to be reconfirmed in Bamako and again in Kita. At both levels authorities gave me to understand that they were not enthusiastic about my schemes; they gave me what help they could, however, and in general our relations were correct. In Kita it was decided that I was the functional equivalent of a civil servant, and thus that whenever I left Kita I had to inform the local administrator, the Commandant de Cercle, where I was going. As there were periods when I was leavng Kita for one or more of the nearby villages practically every day, I soon developed the pattern of dropping off a note for the Commandant once a week. I also had access to government census reports—tax rolls, really—and to the National Archives at the Institut des Sciences Humaines in Bamako. The census reports serve as the basis for the population figures given in this book. As they were well done and in a way that corresponded to the social structure of the family (they could almost serve as a model for anthropological census-taking) , they also proved extremely useful in checking genealogical information, especially in ensuring that everyone got included in the genealogy. I was not, however, allowed to circulate a questionnaire on personal background among the civil servants, many of whom were non-Kitans. This refusal was founded on the fact that the questionnaire amounted to a census, and only the government had the right to conduct censuses.

My relations with the party hierarchy were also correct, even cordial at a personal level. The major deficiency from the point of view of my research was that I was not allowed to attend any party meetings, on the grounds that I was not a member. This rule was politely but firmly enforced on those few occasions when, through ignorance, I overstepped the bounds. On the other hand, I was able to attend the series of information meetings described in chapter eight, because, through a fluke in the organization of the party, these were technically not party meetings, though every indication suggested that they were in fact just as much party meetings as any of the committee and section meetings from which I was excluded. Party personnel provided me with various kinds of assistance, particularly with lists of the membership of most of the party, union, and cooperative bureaus in Kita; these lists are the basis of the analyses presented in chapter five. Since party offices were so widely distributed among the population, I had good friends at all levels of the party.

In dealing with the administration and the party, I was able to build on the good relations I had established while I was teaching English. I also had many contacts among the population at large, and I sought out many new informants as well. I interviewed a large number of old men who were experts on genealogy, local history, and traditional patterns of social organization. Some of these men I met only once, but others, who were more articulate, more helpful, or who seemed better informed, I saw frequently throughout the fifteen months that I spent in Kita. From these men I learned about the traditional history of Kita and of the Maninka in general, and I learned about the traditional view of life in Mali. I also learned a great deal about gentility, humility, and nobility. Some of my fondest memories of Mali are of the time spent with these men. They were frequently poor even by Malian standards, yet our relations were always on a gift exchange basis. Usually I took them a small gift of ten kola nuts or one hundred francs (40 cents), considered to be "kola nut money," though everyone knew that the money would be used for something else. I normally took nuts on a first visit, when it was imperative to stress the full implications of the traditional respect pattern, and later reverted to the more useful gift of money.

Some of these men were in Kita, but the greater number of them lived in the villages of the ex-canton of Kita (the canton had been replaced by the arrondissement, with slightly different boundaries, at the time of independence). I travelled around to see them, almost invariably taking as many passengers as my "deux-chevaux" car would carry in addition to my interpreter-assistant and myself; in other words, two plus as many small children as could be squeezed in. The roads around Kita are not good, often having been run over rocky terrain deliberately so that they would be passable even in the rainy season, and these forays into the bush were frequently as physically exhausting as they were humanly rewarding. The rigors of the drive were always forgotten when the hot and dusty travellers would be served with the traditional refreshment for travellers: milk fresh from the cow into which pounded and dried millet (*couscous*) is poured, and to which sugar is added. Sometimes there might be millet beer or, more rarely, palm wine.

After several months in the field, I decided to direct my forays into the bush to one group of villages. I chose a group of nine villages which had been joined together to form a rural precooperative association, but which also had a series of traditional links between them as well. Among these villages, I went most frequently to Bendougouba, the "capital" of this small area, where a market was held every Wednesday. By focusing in great detail on the social and economic structures of these villages, I was able to acquire a deeper understanding of the patterns of social organization in the rural areas.

In Kita I gathered most of my information, including the bulk of the statements concerning recent political history and of those stating values and attitudes, from participant observation and informal interviews. This meant that I hung around the men's loafing areas, such as the tailor shops, barber shops, smithies, and stores to listen in on the conversations and to try to steer them in a direction interesting to me. I visited friends in their homes, and they visited us in ours. I also attended numerous life-crisis rites, of which the most frequent and most important were naming ceremonies, held when the infant was one week old. These ceremonies were especially important to the young and middle-aged men who were my chief informants on modern politics, for they were frequently the fathers. Most of this research was done directly, either in French with those who were French-speaking, or in my fledgling Maninka, which, while it did not permit me to converse on any but the simplest of issues, did allow me to "overhear" some of what was being said.

We lived in an adobe house on the outskirts of Moribougou, one of the seven quarters, or wards, of Kita. On a slight rise, this house had a terrace from which we could survey most of Kita town. The house was at the same time definitely in the town, and yet somewhat secluded for privacy. This relative seclusion did not prevent numbers of visitors from collecting on our terrace in the evening, especially on those occasions when one of the local musicians or storytellers was making a professional call. Generally, during the day I visited the old men who were my informants on genealogy and history, or the younger men who were my informants on contemporary politics and social structure or just on Kita life in general. Sometimes I worked on transcribing texts with my assistant or copied tax rolls or worked on my notes, which I kept largely in diary form. Unless there was a public occasion of some kind, I generally spent the evenings at home, working on my notes and talking with visitors.

My debts of thanks for aid and counsel in this enterprise are numerous. The research itself was carried out under Grant #8964 from the National Institute of Mental Health. The early research in Paris and my first acquaintance with Mali were made possible by the Augustus Clifford Tower Fellowship from Harvard University. Archival research in Paris during the summer of 1963 was made possible by an N.I.G.M.S. grant through the Department of Anthropology of the University of Chicago. Some of the costs of preparing the manuscript were covered by the Graduate School of Arts and Sciences of New York University.

In my early training in anthropology I was chiefly inspired by Clyde Kluckhohn, Douglas Oliver, Carl Withers, and Laurence Wylie. I am very grateful to my dissertation committee at the University of Chicago. Clifford Geertz, Robert LeVine, and especially the committee's chairman, Lloyd A. Fallers, gave freely of their time, advice, and encouragement. I had many stimulating conversations about Mali, Africa, and the nature of politics with Aristide R. Zolberg of the University of Chicago, and William A. Foltz of Yale. In Paris I learned a great deal from Mme Germaine Dieterlen, Pierre Idiart, and Claude Meillassoux. Paul Delmond and Paul Barlet, both former French colonial administrators in Kita, were kind enough to answer in great detail my questions about life in Kita in the 1930s and 1940s, offering an enchanting view on Kitan life then. In Bamako I talked at great length with Youssouf Cissé, Abdoulaye Sissao, and Moussa Oumar Sy of the Institut des Sciences Humaines, and I received help and encouragement from Amadou Hampaté Ba, one of Mali's most distinguished gentlemen, both when he was the director of that Institute and afterwards. While in the field I was able to compare notes with other researchers: Charles Bird, William A. Brown, Charles Cutter, and Grace and Eric Pollet. David and Sandra Burns, Charles Sadler, and Charles and Julie Steedman offered their assistance and hospitality in Bamako, and Lawrence and Kathryn McNeill opened their house in Sirakoro to us. While I was working on the various stages of this manuscript, talks with many friends in America helped me to clarify my ideas: T. O. Beidelman, John Janzen, William I. Jones, Peter Rigby, Martin Silverman, and William Sytek were chief among these.

How can one adequately thank the people among whom one does research? Field research is at least as much a process of self-discovery as it is a process of discovery of the other. I learned a great deal about myself, and I matured a great deal, as a result of my two years in Kita. I became a guest and a friend, and I became conscious of how much more I was learning than I was giving. For this, for the information that this book contains, and for the ideas that their experiences stimulated, I have to thank the people of Kita. Although it is always invidious to single out individuals, it is also in the best Kita tradition to mention publicly those whom one wishes to thank. Aliou Coulibaly and his wife Fanta Traoré were our gracious hosts in Kita, and Mamadou Kanté filled the same role in

Bendougouba. My loyal assistant was Moussa Kanté, and he and Faguimba Keita provided unfailingly cheerful company. Siméon Traoré helped me with the language and helped translate some of the oral texts. I was fortunate that Simbon Keita, one of the wisest and most respected men in town, befriended me and took an interest in my work from the beginning. My good friends Sayon Coulibaly, Oumar Barou Touré and Marc Traoré, teachers all, taught me a lot. Those in official positions who helped me, and whose assistance I gratefully acknowledge, include Baba Ba, Mamoutou Coulibaly, Hamidoun Dia, Djigui Diabaté, Mamadou Dramé, Gaoussou Keita, Bakary Ouologuèm, Seydou Sy, Amadou Sow, and Aliou Tall. Among the younger men I would like to make special mention of Baba Fagaye Coulibaly, Tiéba Daffé, Djibril Diallo, Baba Kamara, Michel Kamara, Yaya Kane, Célestin Keita, Fakourou Keita, Oumar Keita, Abdoulaye Kodio, Mathurin Koné, Diango Kouyaté, Habou Magassouba, Yaya Maiga, Malick Sangaré, Daba Tounkara, and Abdoulaye Traoré. Among the older men, to whom I feel a special debt and for whom I have a special affection, I would like to thank Diamadouba Diabaté, Dielimadi Diabaté, Kélémanson Diabaté, Yoro Diallo, Famory Diawara, Hilarion Keita, Marifou Keita, Sylvestre Keita, Solo Kouyaté, Makandian Tounkara and his wife Fili Souko, and Solo Tounkara. To offer this book in return for all the assistance cheerfully given is small enough recompense, and too late for some, but it is all that it is within my measure to do. Would it were more!

Needless to say, no one but me is responsible for the opinions, interpretations, and shortcomings of this book.

Popular
Government
in an
African Town

1

Popular Government and Modernization

What kind of government best assures the happiness of the people living under it? Is the answer to this question the same as the answer to another—what kind of government do people want? How does the solution to these problems affect centrally elaborated and sponsored schemes for social change and economic development? How can one balance the values and desires of one community against the imperatives of running or even creating a nation? Is it possible to move towards modernization without sacrificing the intimate, personal quality of local self-government? These are the kinds of question that I find myself raising as I reflect on the meaning of the study that I present here.

One set of answers to these questions has been that the proper basis for government lies in the participation of all the members of the community in question. This line of thought has particular relevance today, when it is being suggested as a basis for reform in university, church, and factory as well as being proposed as the prior condition for development in the underdeveloped countries. Yet exactly what this principle means in practice is not always clear, and there are few studies directed to exploring the nature and implications of participation. One of the contributions that anthropology can make to our understanding of contemporary societies and the directions in which they might move is to investigate the various attempts to create new social institutions, to show what in them has worked and why, and to explain why some noble principles have led to unfortunate results.

3

POPULAR GOVERNMENT AND MODERNIZATION

This book examines the case of an African town to see what balance was struck, at a particular point in its history, between participation and a bureaucracy that channeled instructions and schemes from the capital. This investigation leads to reflections on the implications of popular participation for the nature of the political system and for the direction that it may take in the future. Kita, in the Republic of Mali, as it was in the mid-1960s, seems a particularly favorable place to illustrate these problems. In Kita a genuine local democracy, supported by local values and traditions, was combined with national, modern government which was also populistically oriented, that is, based on the principle that political authority emanates from all the people and that consequently the major if not unique concern of government should be to work for the good of all the people. Kita and Mali are not extremes in these respects, but the combination is illustrative of the kind of problems that can result.

Kita, the locale of this study, is a town of some eight thousand people located about 120 miles west of Mali's capital, Bamako, on the railroad that leads from Bamako down to the ocean at Dakar. The town is situated at the foot of a flat-topped mountain that rises some eight hundred feet above the surrounding plain. Kita town can be said to have begun when the French established a fort there in 1881, though its initial growth and urban character were due to an influx of African traders. By Malian standards the town is neither large nor small. Today Kita consists of seven quarters, or wards, each with its own tradition, bound together by the economic and administrative functions of a small town. There is an active market surrounded by a ring of stores and workshops. On the eastern edge of town there is a large area in which the offices of the administration are scattered: the offices of the circle, the agriculture service, the police, the judge, the post office, most of the schools, and so on. A little bit further in the same direction is the railroad station, the major symbol of Kita's connection to the rest of Mali. In the town most of the houses are constructed, urban-style, as rectangular adobe blocks with tin roofs, but there are still many examples of the local rural style of round adobe huts with conical thatched roofs. Kita stands out socially from its rural hinterland as well, for there is a greater ethnic and occupational diversity in the town.

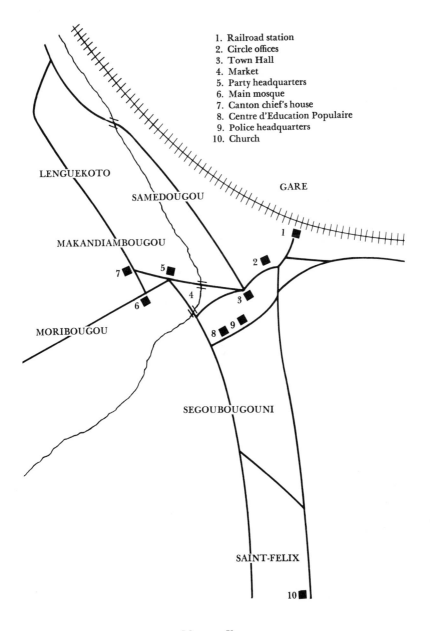

1. Railroad station
2. Circle offices
3. Town Hall
4. Market
5. Party headquarters
6. Main mosque
7. Canton chief's house
8. Centre d'Education Populaire
9. Police headquarters
10. Church

LENGUEKOTO

SAMEDOUGOU

GARE

MAKANDIAMBOUGOU

MORIBOUGOU

SEGOUBOUGOUNI

SAINT-FELIX

MAP OF KITA

POPULAR GOVERNMENT AND MODERNIZATION

The case of Kita and the kind of social organization that existed there in the mid-1960s adds to our sense of the variety of patterns of organization that is humanly possible, and contributes to our understanding of the process of government not only in Africa but throughout the world. Today leaders can no longer be content just to govern, they must further the development of their countries and communities (Fallers 1963:205). The dilemma of reconciling a positive leadership based on a coherent program for this development with a system that genuinely allows the expression of popular sentiment is not limited to Kita. The discussion of the way these processes worked in Kita, and of what their consequences were, may throw some light on similar circumstances elsewhere in the world. Of first importance are the dangers that may occur when the pendulum swings too far in the direction of bureaucracy or too far in the direction of participation. On the one hand, bureaucrats have a tendency to extend their control indefinitely; on the other, local popular government tends to the formation of a strong local identity which in turn is less frequently expressed in accomplishing social change than in fending off central government initiatives for the modernization and development of the country as a whole.

In this book I focus on the experience of Kita in politics in the first years following the independence of Mali in 1960. Some background is essential to the understanding of this situation, and the first part of the book is devoted to that. Chaper 2 describes Mali, giving particular emphasis to the kind of policies and structures that were encouraged by the national government and to the implications of an interventionist government for local politics. Chapter 3 discusses the social, economic, and political structures characteristic of Kita before independence, for from these grew many postindependence institutions. Chapter 4 analyzes contemporary Kitan society, stressing the ways in which people identify themselves or may be characterized by outsiders.

The second part of the book is devoted to the analysis of the political system that existed in Kita at the time of my field work in 1964–65. Chapter 5 describes the institutions of government, particularly the administration, the party, the cooperatives, and the unions. The accent here is on the way that Kitans naturalized these institutions and used them for settling their own affairs. In chapter 6 I present an extended case study of the ebb and flow of personalities in Kita politics from the Second World War to the time of the study. In addition to showing the maneuvers and tactics of Kita politicians, the chapter shows the process whereby Kita politics moved away from a traditional idiom to one based on universalistic principles and the role of the individual. Drawing on chapter 6 for case material, chapter 7 shows how the dialectic of political competition, despite the existence of a pattern for unequal patron-client relations, led to the involvement of large numbers of people in the political process. Would-be leaders needed supporters; this simple fact encouraged a kind of demagogic politics, and it allowed simple individuals, however low they might have been in the status hierarchy, to participate by allotting their support to one or another of the factions surrounding the would-be leaders. In chapter 8, turning away from competition for office, I illustrate what the role of public opinion was in the processes of coming to agreement and settling disputes—those key processes in which too acute a polarization threatens the unity of a community. In chapter 9, I discuss the ideological and cultural basis for these political processes in terms of the existence of two alternative models for a political system, which I call the ideological and the pragmatic. Both place the requirement of maximum possible participation in politics among their key values. In conclusion I attempt to analyze the strengths and weaknesses of this kind of political system, relating it to the fall, in 1968, of the government that had brought Mali to independence eight years earlier, and discussing its implications for the future.

Whether seen from the point of view of the formal institutions of party and cooperative, from that of the processes of political rivalry and decision-making, or from that of the underlying values and assumptions, extensive participation by all segments of the community was one of the cornerstones of Kita's political system. Public opinion and consensus played a large role in determining the course of events. A high value was placed on having people participate in the making of decisions that affected them, and, conversely, attempts to give orders or instructions without this prior participation were sharply resented. Many Kitans held offices in the party and related organizations. The general assembly, where any citizen could speak his piece and participate in the deliberations and attempt to manipulate public opinion, was a key and recurrent feature. Due to the disappearance of traditional links between men, politicians had increasingly to rely on issue-based support, and so were led to make increasingly universalistic appeals in attempts to attract this support. These are the features of Kita's political system that have led me to characterize it as "popular government," and it is these features, their interactions and their implications, that this book is about.

2

Mali:
Socialism
and Popular
Government

Popular government is only possible when there is a community with a strong sense of its identity and a more or less generally accepted set of values and of patterns of behavior to guide people's actions. This book focuses on this sense of identity, these values and patterns of behavior, in one town, Kita. But Kita's structures only make sense when the national society is considered. Mali stands out among the countries of Africa because of its relatively pronounced sense of unity, based in large part on the historical sense of the people. The choice of the name of the country, derived from a medieval kingdom, is indicative of this. Further, Mali's was one of the few African governments actively committed to socialism and to the idea that it was the responsibility of the government to direct social change so as to encourage economic development and bring prosperity to all. This philosophy made the government of Mali particularly interventionist, and it is important for the analysis of Kita's self-government to evaluate the consequences of this interventionism. The framework of the nation is basic to an understanding of popular government in Kita.

Mali

The heart of Mali is situated along the upper reaches of the Niger and Senegal rivers in the savanna belt of West Africa, although the country also includes a sizeable portion of the Sahara Desert. It has no outlet to the sea. The climate is the monsoon climate characteristic of interior West Africa, with a single rainy

9

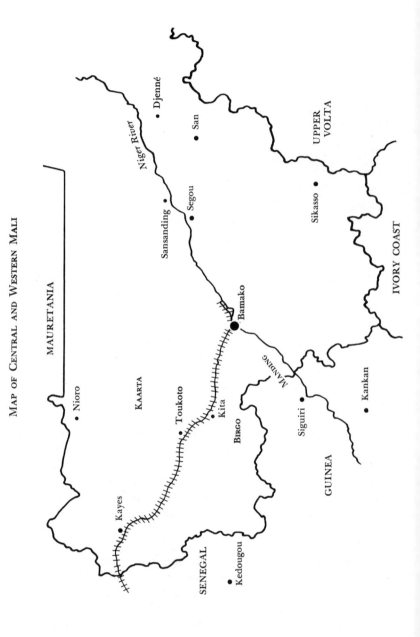

season occurring between June and September. Except for some escarpments, Mali is generally flat, although some areas, like Kita, manage to combine a substantial amount of rough terrain with little change in altitude.

The economy of Mali is largely agricultural; industry is embryonic, engaged mainly in processing agricultural products (see Amin 1965, anonymous 1967, de Wilde 1967, Jones 1969). The main exports are peanuts, livestock, and dried fish. The most pressing economic problems are those of stimulating sufficient exports to pay for imports and generating enough revenue so that the government can pay its bills (including a large amount for civil servants' salaries) without causing inflation (Jones 1969). In many ways, Mali seems to be among those countries which are destined to be unable to hold their own in the world's economy. There is room for improvement, but little hope that it will progress in relation to other countries.

The vast majority of Mali's population of about five million is rural, with less than 10 percent living in towns the size of Kita or larger. Bamako, the capital, with a population of 150,000 is several times larger than the next largest towns, such as Kayes, Ségou, Sikasso, San, Mopti, and Gao, which range from 15,000 to 30,000 inhabitants. These towns are important centers for interregional commerce, and Bamako, Kayes, Ségou, Sikasso, Mopti, and Gao are the capitals of the six regions into which Mali is divided. As a center for regional commerce and the capital of one of Mali's forty-two circles, the key administrative subdivisions of the country, Kita is in the middle range of Malian towns. Despite their small size towns like Kita stand out sharply in the rural environment and have taken on a definite urban character.[1] Inhabitants of these towns consider themselves to be urban, and, to paraphrase Pirandello, urban you are if you think you are. Such towns play an important role of intermediary between the cities, where the national style is elaborated (cf. Meillassoux 1968), and the rural areas, where most of the population lives. These towns play a key role in the process of economic development and modernization. They are also important in terms of individual mobility: migrants to these towns frequently shift their self-identification to suit local prejudices and their new circumstances (Gallais 1962:120–23).

1. See various studies on West African small towns: Brokensha (1966); Chirot (1968); Delmond (1953); Kamian (1959); Miner (1965); Tardif (1965).

11

About half of Mali's population belongs to the various ethnic groups covered by the heading of Mandé: the Maninka, the Bamana, the Soninké, and so on.[2] The other major ethnic groups are the Fula (17 percent); the various Voltaic groups, such as the Bobo, the Minianka and the Senufo (12 percent); the Sahara peoples, including the Tuareg with their sedentary "slaves," the Bella, and the Moors or Arabs (9 percent); the Sonrai (6 percent); and the otherwise unclassified urban (6 percent) (Brasseur and le Moal 1963). Despite the profusion of ethnic names, the way of life is essentially similar (Grandet 1957). Gallais (1962) has shown how the ethnic designations sometimes correspond to a historical reality, sometimes to an occupational speciality, sometimes to the influence of an urban center, sometimes to religion, and sometimes to the ability of a group to organize itself in space. Bamana, which is mutually comprehensible with Maninka and other related dialects, is the vehicular language in all the country save the Niger Bend area, where Sonrai plays that role.

If ethnic identities are fluid, local identities are very strong. The town of Kita has generated a distinct identity; and despite the apparent ethnic heterogeneity of the population, if one looks only at labels, the main primordial tie is to the town itself. People think of themselves as Kitans before they think of themselves as belonging to any other category or group. This parochialism, which is characteristic of Malian towns, is most strikingly expressed in the fervor generated by football matches or theatrical competitions involving Kita and other towns (Hopkins 1965:188). The basis for this Kitan identity is Kita's distinctive culture, which is a microvariant of Maninka-Bamana culture which in turn is a variant of a wider regional culture common to the Western Sudan.

The area included in present-day Mali was the seat of some of the most famous of the premodern West African states, beginning about fifteen hundred years ago with the Ghana empire, centered on the edge of the Sahara along the present Mali-Mauretania border. Ghana was followed by Mali, whose heartland was the upper reaches of the Niger in what is now Guinea and Mali. Next was Sonrai, located in the Niger Bend area. In the eighteenth and nineteenth centuries there were the Bamana kingdoms of Segou and the

2. The Maninka are also known as the Malinké, Mandinka, and Mandingo. The Bamana are also known as the Bambara. The Soninké are also known as Sarakollé and Marka. The Fula are also known as Fulani and Fulbé.

Kaarta, the Fula theocracy of the Macina, the Toucouleur kingdom based on the Tijaniyya Muslim brotherhood, and numerous lesser states. In between these political heights in time, and in areas beyond state control, peasants continued to live, farm, and fight. Kita seems to have been in such a low-pressure zone. The most important of the states for Kita and Mali is the Mali empire (cf. Ch. Monteil 1929; Mauny 1959; Niane 1960), from which the present state drew its name and much of its imagery. The theme song for Radio Mali's news broadcasts in 1965 was a tune said to hark back to the time of Soundiata Keita, the semilegendary founder of Mali. The stories of Soundiata and Mali are still important in their traditional contexts as well, for many of the local traditions of origin refer to them.

The extreme western part of Mali was in contact with French and Portuguese gold seekers very early, but the final French penetration did not start until the middle of the nineteenth century, when a post was established at Medine in 1855. Even after this, there was a pause of twenty-five years before the march inland began in earnest towards 1880. Between the occupation of Bafoulabé in 1879 and Sikasso in 1898, the bulk of what is now Mali passed under French control (Méniaud 1931; Hargreaves 1963, 1967; Kanya-Forstner 1969). Kita was one of the earliest sites to be occupied, in 1881. Military rule soon turned into a kind of indirect rule based on the canton, held to be a traditional unit. By World War I the situation was more or less stabilized, though there were some uprisings in the Bélédougou, in Minianka country, and among the Tuareg in 1915–16 (Suret-Canale 1964:183–86; I. Traoré n.d.). During the period following World War I, the first Malians educated in the Western style began to appear and to make their influence felt (Snyder 1965).

Starting with the triumph of the Free French in the various colonies of Africa, a chain of political activity began which led to national independence for these colonies some fifteen to twenty years later (cf. Zolberg 1964). This is a story that has been told for Mali many times (Delval 1951; Morgenthau 1964; Hodgkin and Morgenthau 1964), and does not need to be repeated here, except for one or two points that will clarify what follows in this book. In Mali soon after politics "began" in 1946 there were two parties. One was more conservative and in general had the support of the French administration, the traditional chiefs, and the African clerks who worked for the colonial administration. This was the Parti Soudanais du Progrès (known as the PSP or "Progressistes"). The other was more radical, nationalistic, and even revolutionary; its original support came largely from the younger civil servants and, especially, the teachers, and from African merchants and peasants. This was the Union Soudanaise, the Sudanese section of the Rassemblement Démocratique Africain. It was usually referred to as the RDA. In the early elections, the PSP won more votes than the RDA; as the radical propaganda and organization of the latter began to take effect and as the electorate was expanded to include new classes of voters, the RDA gradually began to catch up, and eventually, in the elections for the territorial assembly in 1957, it won a majority. From being a party in "double opposition" (to the colonial administration and to the PSP), the RDA became the party in charge of forming the first African cabinet. This period of rivalry between the two parties was one that Kitans often looked back to with some nostalgia, in 1965, and it was the source of many myths about who stood where.

The events surrounding Mali's final step to independence were complicated (Foltz 1965). First, in June, 1959, the French Sudan constituted itself the Sudanese Republic and joined with the Senegalese Republic to form the Mali Federation. The Mali Federation became independent from France as a unit in June, 1960, the first French African territory after Guinea to do so. In August, 1960, due to various political difficulties, Senegal and the Sudan split apart; in September, 1960, the Sudanese Republic declared itself independent under the name of the Republic of Mali. At this time, Mali proclaimed that it had chosen the "socialist option": it was henceforth going to follow socialist principles and become a socialist state.

As a further measure of independence, Mali withdrew from the franc zone and established its own currency in July, 1962; shortly afterwards there were riots in Bamako, apparently instigated by merchants afraid of commercial ruin. In 1964, there was some trouble, halfway between banditry and rebellion, with the Tuareg in the extreme northeast of the country, which the Malian army put down after a few months of fighting. Up to this point, the various threats to Malian unity and to the integrity of the RDA regime had been absorbed. But gradually discontent over economic difficulties began to build up, and eventually these difficulties forced the government to take drastic measures. Mali signed a financial agreement with France in February, 1967, which reversed the earlier policy by accepting some degree of French influence in return for financial assistance. The Mali franc was devalued to half its former value and became convertible. The policy of Malian financial independence had been so frequently justified in political terms that its abandonment was bound to raise questions about the survival of the regime. The July, 1967, Youth Week in Bamako was followed by the outburst of a Malian version of the Chinese "cultural revolution," with troupes of young men investigating the misdeeds of their elders in a search for evidence of corruption and lack of ideological purity. The many changes in organization since 1967 are too complex to describe in detail and take us beyond the situation discussed in this book. Eventually, on November 19, 1968, a military coup led by junior officers overthrew the RDA government of President Modibo Keita. The officers proclaimed that they had acted in order to set Mali's affairs in order (Comte 1969; Snyder 1969). Although some solid gestures were made in the direction of the merchants, the military government announced that it was prepared to follow through on the effective programs begun under the RDA.

MALIAN SOCIALISM

The Kita that this book is about is the Kita of 1964–65, a period which in some ways can be considered the high point of Malian socialism. The time of adjustment following independence was over, and the discouragement due to unfilled promises had not yet sapped the system profoundly. During this period much of Kita's politics was focused on the problem of reacting to the schemes of the central government. But what were these schemes? What were the policies that the Malian government wanted to apply in the towns and rural areas of Mali during the first few years of independence?

Many writers have discussed what the goals and plans of Malian socialism were, but few have tried to see what plans were actually attempted and what the nature of the society was in which they were attempted (cf. Amin 1965; anonymous 1967; Badian 1965; Diallo 1968; Grundy 1963; Hazard 1967; Hodgkin and Morgenthau 1964; Hopkins 1969b; Jones 1969; Snyder 1967; Zolberg 1967b). The general directions of Malian central government policy were, first, to build a national political society; second, to guarantee the political independence of Mali through policies designed to ensure its economic independence; and third, to change the social and economic structures of the various elements of Malian society so that they would correspond to an abstract ideal of a socialist society. The idea was to create a new society, on a scientific basis, and a new Malian man to go with it. The way in which the government carried out these goals brought it into contact with the various local units throughout the country, and thus the enactment of these schemes was bound up with the nature of the relations between the nation and its constituent parts.

The major instrument through which the Malians tried to build a national political society was the party. Mali's single party, the RDA, was a mass party, and it was assumed that all citizens belonged to it. It was organized into a series of levels with several units on each level joining to form a unit at the next level. The basis for most party units was territorial, and this basis was reinforced after independence when the party was reorganized to correspond to the administrative divisions of the country. All those who lived in a certain administrative unit—village, circle, and so on— were considered to belong to the party unit corresponding to that level. Those who were most active in the party held offices in the political and executive bureaus that were the center of party activity. Members of these executive bureaus were elected by general assemblies at the lower levels and by congresses at the higher ones. The chief policy-making body in the country was the national political bureau (BPN), of which Mali's president was the secretary-general. The party apparatus allowed a great many people at all levels to hold offices and to take part in general assemblies and other meetings. It also provided channels for the communication of ideas and desires upwards from the base, and for instructions and orders downwards from the BPN. There was a perhaps inevitable tendency for the latter movement to be more consistent and more insistent than the former.

By being extended and systematized after independence, the party apparatus was made a more flexible instrument. It absorbed a good part of the political energies of the people, and its local branches were the prime institutions of self-government in most communities. In all these ways the party as a national institution, localized and naturalized in every community throughout the country, became a noteworthy force for national integration. It worked to change local political and social structures by soliciting the exclusive participation of people in its structures, for in the political realm the introduction of new structures tended to imply the abandonment of the old.[3] In the towns and the larger villages, self-government through the party apparatus came to take the place of self-government through the hierarchy of chiefs that the French had put in place, or through the play of a lineage system.

The existence of a common administrative hierarchy was a second factor of unity. To a great extent the administrative hierarchy was inherited from the French, but there were two major changes after Malian independence. All of the officials were Malian, and this meant that they had an involvement in the local community that no European could have. And there was a concerted effort to bring the administration closer to the people. Small towns and villages had their first administrator, teacher, male nurse, or agricultural agent. These people, almost invariably Malians from other parts of the country, brought home to the villagers that they were part of a new kind of entity.

Thus the first step of the Malian government was to involve villagers and townspeople more closely in the new nation, and this meant establishing a series of new institutions of local government. People who felt themselves to be Malian, as Kitans did, considered that these institutions were Malian and thus legitimate. This feeling was based on Malian nationalism: these institutions set Mali off from its neighbors or were seen as guarantees of Malian independence. Applying the principle of the virtue of self-government at all levels, Kitans were as jealous of Mali's right to govern itself as they were of Kita's right to do so without interference from the national level.

The RDA government took credit for the independence of Mali, and a great deal of its legitimacy derived from that fact and from its responsibility for maintaining that independence. But this emphasis on its chief past accomplishment, and the continuing task of defending national integrity, though important, were not the only bases of legitimacy. Another source of legitimacy was the ability of the government to supply the daily wants of the people. In general, this meant being able to raise the standard of living; in particular, to maintain prices and buying power, and to extend the network of educational and health services. The RDA government

---

3. In contrast to the situation with medicine and education, where the old and the new complemented one another. People with a stubborn illness would try both traditional and modern medicine; parents sent their children to Koranic school before they started the state school.

tried to meet the expectations of the people in these matters, but for a variety of reasons it was less and less able to do so successfully. Mali's considerable poverty as a nation had much to do with this, and mismanagement and directing of resources into long-term projects accounted for the rest. The people of Kita, however, like most Malians, tended to judge the government by what it was doing for them in the short run. In these terms, the government was not overly successful, and so this basis of legitimacy was weakened.

To counter the tendency on the part of the people to judge it according to short-run material benefits, the RDA government attempted to base its legitimacy on its monopoly over the establishment of goals for the society as a whole. In other words, it tried to base its legitimacy on what it was going to do as well as on what it had done; in each case, however, the vocabulary used was elaborated at the national and general levels rather than the local and specific ones. An important part of this claim to legitimacy was founded on the idea of socialism as a favored path to development and prosperity. The RDA government justified what it was doing in the name of socialism and expected people to subordinate their desires for material goods to the program of building a socialist society in Mali. This raised the problem of persuasion, for insofar as the state's goals did not include the private goals of most citizens (though the state did not deny these goals, its programs tended to postpone satisfying them until collective goals had been achieved) it could not depend on the spontaneous support of the citizens. It had, therefore, to devise ways of gaining that support through the use of argument and reason.

In Malian terms a government's legitimacy is also based partly on how it governs. Malians (and the material presented here will show this clearly) have very firm ideas about what manner of government they prefer. The legitimacy of any particular government is reevaluated constantly in terms of how its latest actions have met these standards. In brief, Malians prefer popular government. The problem that faced the RDA government was how to achieve the national goals it had set while still governing in a way that was acceptable to the people. The arguments that the RDA offered in favor of its programs were that they fostered national independence, that they would increase prosperity (although only in the long run), and that they were correct in terms of scientific socialism. The weak point in this argument was the absence of many short-term successes to encourage people to think that the government might be right. If the RDA gave up persuasion and consultation, finding that their appeals were increasingly ignored, the only recourse was to force. Apart from the fact that the Malian state did not possess the resources to use force on any large scale to compel changes, any actions in this direction only worsened the government's image in the eyes of the people, for by these actions it was forswearing the traditionally legitimate patterns of government.

The major area of social reform which affected Kitans was that of economics, specifically marketing and retailing.[4] Although the RDA had enjoyed the support of most Malian merchants—including many in Kita—during the struggle for independence, one of the major thrusts of RDA policy during the 1960s was to eliminate the network of merchants in favor of a network of cooperatives. In the rural areas, the village was to form a cooperative and market its cash crops and purchase its capital equipment and consumer needs through it (Hopkins 1969a). Thus no longer would there be a role for merchants scouring the villages for peanuts, or for the petty merchant hawking cloth and small consumer items from village to village; all this would be handled by the cooperatives.

In the towns the main cooperative organization was the consumers' cooperative. Again, the main object was to replace the network of retail merchants by a network of consumers' cooperatives based on wards. But both in the towns and in the rural areas, the immediate effect was to deprive merchants of a role. There was no serious attempt to change the basis of production in the village, although each village was encouraged to start a collective field which would eventually have formed the basis for a collectivization of agriculture.

The nearest approach to a change in the manner of production was the human investment system *(fasobara)*. This system called for the people to offer their labor for projects such as clearing fields, working on roads, building schools, and the like. Together with the collective fields in the villages, the human investment system could have represented the beginnings of a collectivization of production, but Mali was a long way from that. In the meantime, human investment had become a way of organizing a community to accomplish

---

4. I have not attempted to deal with the state corporations, so obvious in Bamako, because they had little effect in Kita. See Jones (1969).

the kind of task where many hands were needed and where the community was to benefit.

There were also attempts to affect the personal status of categories of people who were considered to be underprivileged: chiefly women and members of castes. A new marriage code, presented in 1962, was supposed to go further towards guaranteeing women's rights. It stipulated that the consent of the bride was a prior condition to marriage; that divorce could only be granted by a court and for sufficient reason; and that monogamous marriage should be a legally recognized option, although polygyny with up to the Koranic limit of four wives continued to be allowed (and widely practiced). The code also limited the bride wealth, and this was the element to which the men reacted most favorably. The government periodically became concerned with the situation of the members of castes (*nyamakala;* see chapter 3 below), especially the *dieli,* alternatively considering the castes to be underprivileged groups whose status should be raised and overprivileged groups whose privileges needed to be reduced. The drift of the government in these matters of personal status was to eliminate the variety of personal statuses which had characterized traditional society in favor of a single status, that of citizen.

Malian socialism was reflected in Kita largely by changes in the political system, in the distributive system, and by sporadic efforts to change the nature of personal status. The way in which these changes were furthered by the central government had important implications for local government and for relations between Kita and the nation. It is to this problem that I now turn.

MALIAN INTERVENTIONISM AND KITA'S GOVERNMENT

Government programs aiming at radical changes in the political, economic, and social structures of Mali ran into problems in the towns and villages where government was seen less as a means of creating a new society than as a means of managing the one that already existed—an attitude towards government that Malian socialism wanted to change. The overt actions of the central government towards the various localities always assumed that there were no differences in personal status to keep in mind and that everyone already had the proper socialist, modern orientation toward government and the implementation of party programs. One of the pressures on the local system was the constant structuring of the situation along these lines by the central government.

The attitude of the government toward all aspects of Malian society was that they were malleable, that social structures are subject to rational human reflection and judgment, and furthermore that many of the Malian structures should be changed because they were incompatible with the kind of modern, socialist society that the government wanted to build (Snyder 1967). The way in which these changes would be effected was for the government to establish programs—for cooperatives, political structures, and the like—and then to bring these programs to the people, explaining the programs and showing how they should be operated. The programs were to be scientifically elaborated by the technicians at the center, who could exercise control over them and make sure that everything was coherent. Such programs were presented to the people through the medium of governmental institutions, the administration and the party.

Placing the programs for change within a bureaucratic framework where they could be applied by an expanded personnel was only one of the kinds of pressure that the central government could bring to bear on local situations. By the force of their ideas the national leaders could hope to convince people at the local level that these programs were correct and thus gain voluntary support for them. This presupposed an ability to persuade and required not only patience, tact, and insight, but also intelligent programs to support and the means through which the government could reach the people. The government also had important material resources at its command, from control of the media to the ability to place its money in certain ways. It also had the power to abolish alternatives, as when it encouraged the formation of cooperatives by eliminating the network of merchants. And it had the power, within certain limits, to reward its supporters and punish those who opposed it. This power to discipline enabled the government to exercise at least a kind of limiting control on local communities such as Kita: although it might be hard to make people do something, it was relatively easy to prevent them from doing anything else. Similarly, although the central government might have a hard time imposing its preferences for local leaders on Kita, it could prevent those it considered undesirable from holding prominent positions.

The central government had considerable power to intervene in local communities, and its policies of radical change led it to want to intervene. But such action appeared to Kitans as an attempt to run their lives and their town; one of the prime political values in Kita is that of self-government at all levels. Whatever Kitans might have thought of the government's programs for change—and the reaction was not totally hostile—any attempts to apply these programs were resented as dictatorial moves that interfered with local political and social realities. The central government, on the other hand, did not appear willing to let its programs be implemented by local governments because that might threaten the central planning that was considered to be essential. I return to these ideas about the powers and duties of governments in chapter 9.

The RDA stated that adaptation to local conditions (a kind of local self-government) was a necessary precondition to the successful implementation of its programs. But it seems that efforts in this direction were rarely made. What happened instead was that programs were indeed adapted to local conditions, but in an atmosphere of conspiracy against the central government. Local leaders knew that they were obliged to implement the programs and that the success of their political careers depended to some extent on how well they did so; but at the same time they knew their local position depended on their adherence to local political values. The attempts of politicians to avoid falling into either of these traps meant that the programs were applied with the kind of ad hoc adjustments that weakened them from the technicians' point of view. Thus it was that the new institutions only came to be a part of the local scene if they were in some sense naturalized by coming under local control. The party branches were excellent examples of this principle: they were successful institutions of local government only insofar as they could detach themselves from the task of implementing central government policies, which they might even on occasion work against. It seems in Kita that insofar as an institution was under effective central control it could not be an institution of local self-government; insofar as it adapted to local conditions it escaped from central control.

The pressure for reform was not the sole link between the governments of Mali and Kita; there were also personal links between politicians. Factions and alliances are an omnipresent feature of Malian politics. Leaders of factions at the national level had supporters in each of the towns throughout the country, and these national and local factions were mutually supportive. A local leader would turn to his patron in Bamako for assistance, and the patron would look to his local ally for support. A network of influence and support thus linked the polities of the various towns and villages in Mali with that of the capital (in this context it is less the national system that is involved than the political system peculiar to the capital). In this network, a town like Kita played an intermediate role, for there were smaller towns and villages with their own factions which were linked to the capital system through Kita's politics. The party structure encouraged this, for the representatives of the smaller towns and villages in the circle of Kita had a say in the selection of Kita's political bureau, and thus alliances with these representatives were important to Kita's leaders, just as alliances with Kita's leaders were important to some national leaders.

Kita's involvement in the political and social system of the nation was close. There were links of both traditional and modern kinds between Kita and the other areas of Mali. One of the chief institutions that linked the various parts of Mali together was the central government, in its twin manifestations of administration and party. The government tried to mold the society of Kita and the surrounding area; people reacted to these government attempts by finding that they amounted to outside interference in the sphere of local government. The national government was committed to populistic government, yet sometimes found it difficult to admit the principle of a kind of local self-government that might be used against the centrally planned development schemes. Thus local popular government and national populistic government turned out to be opposed concepts. Nevertheless, the desires and plans of the central government, as well as the requirements of central government figures for political support, meant that the central government played a very large role in Kita's local popular government.

3

Kita: The Structures of the Past

Popular government in Kita has roots that reach back to the precolonial social system, although the dynamics of this government were somewhat modified under colonial rule. The traditional system underwent prodigious changes during the eighty years of the colonial period as the previously self-sufficient Kita system was integrated into political and economic systems that reached not only the limits of the colony but beyond, to world empires and markets. While political power was concentrated in the role of the canton chief, an entirely new economic system developed, based on the exploitation of a cash crop for the world market and involving changes in rural life and the growth of a community of merchants in the town. The town itself was born, as "Kita" changed from a conglomeration of villages into a small town with typically symbiotic and asymmetrical relations with its surrounding villages. A politics based on hierarchy and intercession—with tendencies towards clientage—evolved during this period.

Detailed information on the political and economic aspects of the precolonial and colonial systems is hard to get, because the early French observers were not sensitive to the functioning of the indigenous systems. The statements of contemporary informants about the past are colored by their feelings on what the contemporary system ought to be, or by their participation in structures that have now disappeared. The picture of what the government and economics of Kita were like before the arrival of the French and during the colonial period is somewhat fuzzy. But it is convincing enough to show that the kind of government Kita had a few years after independence was in many ways not the result of that independence. Although there was undoubtedly in many ways a kind of liberation of forces that had been suppressed during the colonial period, the postindependence government was more the result of the reaffirmation of deeply rooted values modified by the developing economic institutions.

THE TRADITIONAL SOCIAL SYSTEM

Before the French occupation in 1881, the name "Kita" referred to a series of villages strung out around the triangular mountain of Kita. During the colonial period, this name came to refer to the town, based on several of these villages, that grew up around the French fort and administrative center. The country of Kita was one of the many units, known as *kafo* or *diamana* in Maninka and as *canton* in French, which were the territorial and social basis of Maninka social organization. It was perhaps somewhat more isolated than most of these units, for its nearest neighbors were Fula intruders who occupied the territory between Kita and the closest canton with which it had genealogical ties. The Maninka of Kita and the Fula were organized in much the same way, but there was no kinship and thus no basis for a rhetoric of association between them.

Within the canton the emphasis was on differentiating one person from another. The patrilineages were ranked according to their order of arrival in the country and to their role in the events recounted in the myths of origin.[1] Internally, age and generation differentiated their members. There were also horizontal divisions which especially concerned the *nyamakala,* or members of castes. These castes were occupationally defined, hereditary, endogamous social groups which were generally considered to be of inferior status. The chief ones, in Kita and throughout this area, were the

1. The chief lineages in Kita were the Kamara, the Tounkara, the Kasumasi Keita, the Niamakansi Keita, and the Coulibaly. The Kamara and the Tounkara claimed to have settled in Kita first; the Niamakansi were also early arrivals; but the chiefship was held by the Kasumasi Keita to whom credit was given for Kita's independence from the Traoré of neighboring Bafing. The Coulibaly were powerful refugees from the Saboula, the *diamana* adjoining Kita on the north.

dieli (wordsmiths) and the *numu* (smiths). The population included other special categories, notably the slaves and the Muslims (*mori*). Traditional Maninka society consisted of a number of different groups, each with a different role. All roles were equally important to the maintenance of the body politic. The importance of this symbiosis is stressed in the great legends surrounding the figure of Soundiata, common to the Maninka, the Bamana, and others, and also in the legends surrounding the founding of Kita.[2]

Although lineage and village no longer form the basis of the political system, they are still relevant for the social system in the rural areas and, to a great extent, in Kita town as well. For those with roots in the country (and that meant most people), the essential identifications were with the various genealogical segments, with the village of origin, and with the caste. The model of social relations provided in Kita's mythical charter, where relations between the lineages are symbolically presented, still represented a possible model to many people.[3] The kind of role played by leaders in the precolonial system, the emphasis on inequality of status combined with equal participation by all in public discussions, are among the bases for present political patterns.

The Precolonial Government of Kita

It is impossible to say to what extent precolonial politics in Kita were lineage politics; certainly politics during the colonial period was often lineage-based. A report from early in the colonial period suggests that the lineages of that time (roughly the same as those that I discovered eighty years later) saw themselves as political blocks within the *diamana*. Chanteaux (1884) describes four main "families" in Kita: the Keita, the Tounkara, the Kamara, and the Coulibaly. The Keita were divided into three sections: the Tandunka, the Galunka, and a third group in the villages of Diaramadji, Fodébougou, and Makandiambougouni.[4]

2. See Hopkins (in press) for further details. For Kita see also Sidibé (1932) and Jaeger (1951). For other descriptions of Maninka social organization, see Labouret (1934), Montrat (1935), Strasfogel (n.d.), Bernus (1956), Leynaud (1961:119–33), and Meillassoux (1963). For Soundiata, see Sidibé (1959) and Niane (1960).

3. I intend to argue this point in a future article; a very brief summary is given in note 1 above.

4. The name given to this third group by Chanteaux was on a section of the manuscript eaten by insects; the legible part did not resemble any name I came across in my field work, although the grouping makes sense.

Much more important for an understanding of the political system of precolonial Kita are the institutions of leadership and the process of government. The titular leader of the *diamana* was the *diamana tigi*, the projection onto a larger scale of the household head, who is the steward of the common family property, and of the village chief. This leader is the senior man in the *diamana*'s chiefly lineage, which in Kita was the Tandunka branch of the Kasumasi lineage of the Keita, who have the credit for freeing Kita from the domination of the Bafing Traoré king in legendary times. As in many other Maninka and Bamana areas, the chiefly lineage was not the first lineage to settle the area, for everyone agrees that the Tounkara and the Kamara were there first (cf. Jaeger 1951; Niane 1960: 130; Tellier 1898:32–34). In Kita, the Tounkara are *dugu kolo tigi,* the ritual chiefs, comparable to the earth priests often found elsewhere in West Africa. The Tounkara alone may make sacrifices to the spirits of the earth and of the mountain; they are also said to have had a special ability to cause rain to start and stop. The Tounkara, the Kamara, and a lineage of Keita who had also arrived before the Kasumasi were entitled to "choose" the chief and played a key role in his installation. The last chief to be installed (in 1942) told me:

> Three groups had a role in the installation of a *diamana tigi:* the Tounkara, the Kamara, and the Kanisi. Although they no longer had any role in the actual choice, it was said that no one could really be *diamana tigi* if he didn't have the approval of the Tounkara and the Kamara. These groups had a right to customary presents at the installation of the chief, such as slaves (later changed to money), but especially a good, adult bull. The bull was slaughtered, and when the skin was laid out the *diamana tigi* would sit on it, and slaves would raise him three times, saying, "People, here is your chief." Then the Tounkara and the Kamara would make speeches approving the choice and perform rituals. Then the new chief would be conducted home, and there would be a celebration.[5]

Despite the emphasis which contemporary informants place on the manner of choosing a chief, the evidence suggests that the precolonial chief had very few powers and was rarely the leading personality in the country. French observers of Kita in the period of

5. Most other informants identified the Keita lineage as Niamakansi rather than Kanisi. In 1942 the chief was in fact chosen by a vote of all the village chiefs in the canton. The man chosen—my informant, a Muslim and a former schoolteacher—professed not to know what the rituals involved.

27

penetration (Piétri 1885:133; Bayol 1888:40) and present-day Kita informants insist that the chief had little coercive power. Penel (1895:22ff) says that the chief "has the right to do what he is able to do," though he cites local theory as holding that the chief can "do what he wants." One of my informants said:

> Before the arrival of the French, one man was at the head of the country, but he didn't command anyone. It was the French who named a *diamana tigi* in Kita. The old man in the post was named to it as a sign of respect for him, but this didn't mean the whole country belonged to him. . . . No one paid anything to the *diamana tigi*, either villages or households, and household heads paid nothing to village chiefs.[6]

The emphasis on choosing the senior man in the core lineage meant that considerations of wealth, ability, or influence were neglected so that the chief might in fact be one of the poorest men in the community. The chief whom the French found in 1881, for instance, was an old man with little power or influence (Bechet 1889:169).

The *diamana tigi* was often old or ineffectual, and the *dugu kolo tigi* had purely ritual functions, so the effective leadership of the community fell to those who by reason of wealth, number of followers, or oratorical skills could exercise some influence. Such "big men" were referred to as *togo tigi:* men with a name or reputation. The power of such a man was based neither on his genealogical position nor on his ritual position, but essentially on his wealth, and particularly on the number of fighting men and guns at his command.

Kita country was dominated by such a man in 1881. Tokontan Keita was of the chiefly Tandunka branch of the Kasumasi, and lived in Makandiambougou, of which he was chief. One of my informants described his position as follows:

> Tokontan was a *togo tigi*, not a *diamana tigi*. At that time, no one could say they owned the entire country. All were equal. He who had a reputation of wealth was the most powerful. Tokontan started by farming. Marka merchants came from the Kaarta; they all stopped at Tokontan's house and he fed them. Tokontan married a woman from the Kaarta. All the Kaarta merchants knew him. He gained his reputation through his

---

6. The informant comes from a small but high status Keita lineage and is considered to be an authority on traditional customs. The idea that no one "commanded" anyone else before the French came was a favorite one with him and was not unrelated to his views on the current political situation.

hospitality. But he was not a [canton] chief. Tokontan was chief of Makandiambougou.[7]

Additional elements of strength came from his large number of sons (Bayol 1881:56), and his numerous slaves and clients, many of whom had sought out his protection precisely because he was already powerful. The more influential he became, the larger his retinue; the larger his retinue, the more influential he became. Bayol (1888:40) noted, "Each chief is master of his village; old Makadougou presides over the palavers; but Tokontan is the man most listened to."

Part of Tokontan's role was to represent the community to the outside. He organized military expeditions and he took the lead in arranging a modus vivendi with the Toucouleur empire of El Hadj Oumar Tall. It is commonly said in Kita that Tokontan sent gold to the French to persuade them to destroy the nearby fortified village of Goubanko, whose people had been raiding Kita mercilessly; whether he did or not, the village was destroyed in 1881. The French army officers who visited Kita in 1880 and set up a fort there in 1881 treated him as the effective leader of Kita; it was to him that they turned to sign their treaty of protectorate in April, 1880.

The "big man" was in a position to exert his influence because of his wealth and retainers, but even he could not always act without consulting others. Thus when Tokontan signed the treaty with the French, it was only after public opinion had clearly shifted to favor the treaty (Galliéni 1885:146; Hopkins 1964:59). He might also lose his position by contravening crucial norms. One of Tokontan's predecessors as "big man" in Kita was chased out when he abused his position by attempting to enslave people from other villages in the country.

The pressure of public opinion was an important aspect of social control and decision-making. Public opinion could, of course, be expressed in many circumstances, but the chief institutional context was that of an assembly of all the men of the country, which met to consider important business affecting the whole country, such as warfare, and to settle quarrels involving two different vil-

7. This is the same informant. The Kaarta is the area around Nioro, several hundred miles north of Kita.

lages. One informant described the meetings (which would have occurred before his birth) as follows:

> If a serious matter came up, all the country gathered for a *kuma*, which was held, not at the *diamana tigi*'s place, but at Kéniéba, under a large tree. The floor was given to one person at a time; he had the right to talk. In those days, no one could beat another, unless he caught him seducing his wife or stealing something. If this happened, the household heads would be convened to discuss the affair. . . .
>
> If two villages quarrelled, the *mogoba* would sit down and talk it over until a settlement was reached. The old men themselves didn't quarrel. In those days, a quarrel didn't go far. If two men were fighting, the combatants would come together to talk things over. . . . If an old man said to stop, they would. . . .
>
> The meeting place was under a suru tree in Kéniéba. When the word was given, all the people of Kita would come. The meetings were held at Kéniéba because people respected its chief. The chief's *dieli* made the opening speech, setting forth the reason for the meeting, then the chief would say the rest, with the *dieli* repeating it for the crowd. From then on, the others spoke directly rather than through the *dieli*. Agreement was reached after all the *dugu tigi* and the *nyamogo* had said their piece.[8]

Leadership in precolonial Kita was based on wealth derived from agriculture and trade; on having good relations with outside powers; and on having a large household of patrilineal relations, clients, and slaves who could farm and provide a military force. The formal position of chief was essentially a way of providing a human symbol for the community. The lineages very probably acted as blocks behind their leaders, who were not always their titular heads. Leaders also courted public opinion; this required considerable skill, since opinion could turn against them as Tokontan discovered in 1881 when he was attacked and beaten by men with sticks (Hopkins 1964:64). Public opinion and consensus were important to the "big men," who could hope to build support through a manipulation of public opinion but whose attempts to take a more authoritarian leadership role would be hampered by it. This public opinion was most legitimately expressed in the assemblies open to the entire country.

---

8. Once again, the same informant. Kéniéba is his home village. *Kuma* means "talk"; *mogoba* and *nyamogo* are two words for referring to the "important people"; a *dugu tigi* is a village chief.

The Chiefship under Colonial Rule

The imposition of French colonial rule on Kita was the first step in the shift in Kita's political system towards a more bureaucratic orientation. The changes that resulted in the manner of governing Kita were far-ranging, especially during the colonial period itself, when the maintenance of peace and order were the bywords of the administration and where consequently some of the freer aspects of the traditional system of government were disallowed. For the first time the idea of a chain of command, and of an organization that had to do things to justify its existence, were introduced into Kita. The institution of the chiefship, which had apparently been a relatively unimportant element in the precolonial government, became the keystone of Kita's government during the colonial period.

In order to understand what happened to the institution under colonial rule, the circumstances of the early colonial period must be taken into account. During the first ten years of French administration, Kita was an important military base, and this determined French needs and outlooks. Their first task was to build a fort to resist attacks by Africans; the army also needed African auxiliary troops, especially porters. When the French first occupied Kita in 1881, their position was based on the treaty of protectorate that Galliéni had signed with the leaders of Kita on April 24, 1880, a treaty signed by a representative of the *diamana tigi* as well as by Tokontan.[9] But French requirements very quickly led them to move away from any policy of indirect rule in Kita (Barlet 1942:25). The early French commanders wanted a local leader to work through; the confusion between a legal but ineffective chief and an effective nonchief, neither of whom had much coercive power, baffled and frustrated them. Perhaps their military training led them to expect a neat chain of command; whatever the reason, they began to use various degrees of force to get the Kitans to work on the construction of the fort, to supply food for the army, to act as porters, and even to send their children to school.

---

9. The details of the negotiation for the treaty are given in a letter from Galliéni in Makandiambougou to the governor in Saint-Louis (Senegal), dated April 25, 1880 (Archives de la France d'Outre-Mer, File Mission 16). For a copy of the treaty, see *Journal Officiel du Sénégal et Dépendances*, August 9, 1888, pp. 263–64.

But soon the concept of a chief who would act as intermediary between his people and the French administration was worked out, apparently by Vallière, one of Galliéni's aides, in 1888. In the geographical area that Vallière knew best, which is the area that concerns us here, the *diamana* or *kafo* was a traditional institution. Vallière proposed to make this institution the basis for the French administration of the area, which was to be known as a "canton." He argued that villages should be linked together as they had been traditionally, under a traditionally chosen chief who would be the intermediary between the French administration and the populace. To those who feared that providing for organization of this kind might create a basis for opposition to French rule, Vallière responded that the chiefs would compromise themselves by becoming intermediaries, that it was hard for people within even a single canton to unite, and that one canton could always be played off against another.[10]

The cantons that were established in the circle of Kita corresponded to the traditional *diamana* (cf. Tellier 1898; Delmond 1941:12). The villages that formed the country of Kita became the canton of Kita under the traditional chief. This organization gradually evolved during the 1890s, for the canton chief could not become an important person overnight. Tellier, who was commandant in the late 1890s, refers to the administrative roles of village chiefs, but not to the canton chiefs. Pérignon (1899) refers to the canton chief as an intermediary between the commandant and the village chief, while showing that the village chiefs still dealt directly with the French administration. A few years later, another commandant, Roos (1903–4), refers to the canton chiefs as "simply intermediaries between their people and the administration. They make sure that the orders they receive from the circle are obeyed, and they settle native family affairs with their notables." By this time, military needs were no longer relevant.

In the early days the administration dealt directly with the Africans, especially when it came to collecting taxes or rations, finding laborers, or settling quarrels. In the 1880s and 1890s there was a shelter just outside the entrance to the fort (which only a few

10. See Vallière, "Rapport politique sur le Grand Bélédougou," February 1, 1888, and "Mémoire sur le Cercle de Bamako," March 25, 1888 (both in Archives de la France d'Outre-Mer, File Sénégal IV.90 bis [a]).

trusted Africans could enter) where meetings were held between African leaders and French administrators (Barlet 1942:53). But gradually some of this responsibility began to be shifted onto the Africans. In the early 1900s there was a "native court" in Kita which met every Monday. It was composed of all the local chiefs, most of whom were old men "whose principal preoccupation was to preserve the uses and customs of the country intact" (Roos 1903–4).

But gradually during the colonial period the position of canton chief acquired importance. The canton chief began to outshine the village chiefs, and there began to be considerable competition for succession to the post, especially in 1925 when, thanks in part to the blunders of an incompetent commandant, the dispute reached Dakar. Eventually, during the 1930s and 1940s, there was talk of making the chief more of a civil servant and less of a traditional chief. The ultimate step would be to make him transferable from one post to another; this step was taken in the Ivory Coast, where the institution had less roots, but not in the French Sudan (cf. Zolberg 1964:22).

Each canton chief had a representative at the circle seat who kept the French administrator up-to-date on his canton and transmitted orders and mail from the circle seat to the canton chief back home. This pattern was true even of Kita, where the canton chief resided within a few minutes' walk of the circle offices. The representative to the circle was known as the *lasigi den,* meaning someone who is sent to remain next to the chief. Each of the villages in Kita canton also had a *lasigi den* in Kita town who performed the same functions vis-à-vis the canton chief. The chief had a *ki den,* a messenger, who ran errands for the chief, including summoning people to Kita. There was also a secretary, usually a young literate relative. Tokontan Garan (chief in 1939–42) used his son, Seydon Garan, who worked as a clerk in the circle offices and doubled as *lasigi den.* The secretary helped the chief in the paper work—keeping up the census rolls, collecting taxes, issuing "carnets de famille," and corresponding with the administration—or did it all if the chief was illiterate. When there was too much work for the secretary (as when new census rolls had to be made every four or five years), additional clerks might be sent out from the circle offices.

The influence and importance of the canton chief depended on his background and competence. From 1925 to 1939 the chief was an old, unsophisticated man who had always lived deep in the bush before being chosen chief and obliged to move to Kita. The result was that the de facto chief was Tokontan Garan Keita of Makandiambougou, the son of the Tokontan mentioned in the preceding section. When the old man died in 1939, Tokontan Garan was formally chosen to replace him, but he himself, though still in full command of his faculties, was an old man by then.

He was succeeded in 1942 by Fatogoma Keita[11] who, as a former school teacher, was the first literate chief. He was the first chief chosen outside tradition, although even he belonged to the chiefly lineage (see figure 1). He was elected by all the village chiefs in the canton; the only other candidate was a lieutenant from the French

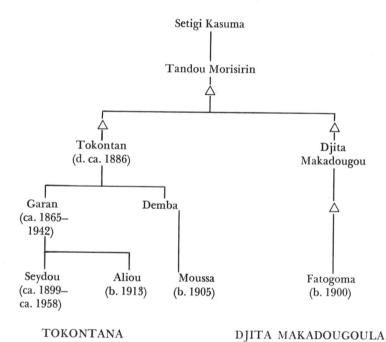

TOKONTANA   DJITA MAKADOUGOULA

FIGURE 1. GENEALOGICAL CONNECTIONS OF KEITA OF THE CHIEFLY LINEAGE

11. Much of what follows comes from interviews with this man. See chapter 6 for a discussion of his political role. All names in this and the following chapters are pseudonyms, except for Tokontan. Where the *diamu* (clan name) had political importance (for example, Keita, Tounkara, Diallo, or Sidibé) it was kept. An attempt has been made to have the pseudonyms reflect the same ethnic and religious impression as the real names.

army with even less of a traditional basis for his ambition to be chief. Fatogoma tried to act within tradition in his administration and at the same time to be the modern chief wanted by the French. When a question came up he would convene the old men, especially those with traditional positions of their own as lineage and clan heads. He would get them talking, while playing a discreet part in the discussion. Eventually he would try to guide the decision, for instance by pointing out that times had changed, and that old methods were no longer relevant. Thus he tried to modernize the canton gradually, and with the approval of the old men.

Fatogoma toured his canton regularly to maintain contact with the villagers. He would divide the canton up into groups of villages which shared clan or lineage membership. He would spend two or three days in the main village of each lineage and convene all the chiefs of that lineage there. When he was on tour he moved with a certain pomp, never travelling without a retinue that included his favorite wife (Barlet 1966). In this, also, he was faithful to a particular interpretation of tradition.

When people wanted to petition the canton chief to intervene on their behalf, or to grant them a favor, they would usually work through an intermediary, as is the time-honored custom in the Sudan. They might use a *nyamakala* although Fatogoma says that he tried to discourage the use of *nyamakala* as they have a tendency to exaggerate matters and worsen them. Or they might first approach someone known to be on good terms with the chief. Thus a kind of court would be built up around the chief.

Fatogoma continued to be paid as a school teacher after he became chief, for a teacher earned a higher salary than a chief. He was officially a teacher seconded to the administration. Fatogoma also got 3 percent of the taxes collected in the canton, which amounted to a sum of 150,000 to 200,000 CFA francs ($600–800) annually. Part of this, however, he redistributed among the old men of the canton: not necessarily the village chiefs, who got their own statutory share of the taxes collected in their villages, but the old men who advised him and on whose support he counted. Fatogama considered that this served to retain the support of these men.

Fatogoma was also concerned with the economic well-being and progress of the canton. He was involved in setting up a peanut producers' cooperative in the late 1940s (which I discuss below), and he was interested in developing new strains of plants.

Looking back on the chiefship, Kitans saw the position as one that allowed its holder to do individuals favors or disfavors, often in exchange for a bribe (known as a *su ro fen,* or "night thing," because it traditionally changed hands under cover of darkness), and to issue more or less arbitrary orders ostensibly on behalf of the administration. There was still active resentment against Seydou Garan Keita, who had exercised power on behalf of his father Tokontan Garan from 1939 to 1942, and against Fatogoma, because it was felt that they had abused their position. In Kitan theory, anyone occupying a post of public authority was bound to cause resentment in some quarters, for one could not be just to everyone. Nonetheless, the position of chief had become an attractive position to occupy, and the man who occupied it became thereby an influential person.

Economic Patterns in Colonial Kita

The main activity in Kita before the advent of the French was agriculture. Millet, sorghum, peanuts, and rice were the main field crops; cotton, melons, tomatoes, tobacco, and some vegetables were grown in gardens (Mage 1868:100). The economic unit was the household, although this unit varied a great deal in size, from the equivalent of a nuclear family to a large lineage with clients and slaves. Each household produced for itself; only a man like Tokontan had the resources to raise horses, grain, and cotton for the market, or to free some of his household's adult males from productive activity. Each household operated as a small enterprise; the more fortunate ones were able to build an ongoing operation while others were reduced to clientage. Woven cloth was the only good regularly produced for trade (Tellier 1898:218).

The French occupation changed the economic context by creating conditions of peace so that the farmers were able to farm fields further and further from the protection of the mountain. As a consequence, the villages at the foot of the mountain began to spawn daughter settlements in the surrounding plain. This process, which seems to have gotten underway in the 1890s, was hastened by a famine at the time of World War I and, doubtless, also by the desire to get a little further away from the center of authority. By 1934, the inhabitants of the twenty-four administrative villages lived in more than two hundred settlements (Delmond 1966:2). In the late 1930s many of these separate settlements were made independent villages, and it became usual to raise a settlement to the status of a village if it was large enough and stable enough (Barlet 1966:4). The population of the canton grew steadily, especially after 1920 (see table 1).

TABLE 1

POPULATION OF KITA CANTON AND TOWN, 1884-1965

Year	Canton	Town	Town Includes[a]
1884	2,692	855	Ma, Mo, Le
1890	4,035	1759	Ma, Mo, Le, Ko
1899	5,828	2939	Ma, Mo, Le, Ko, Se
1903	8,266	3694	Ma, Mo, Le, Ko, Se
1934	19,782	3400 (est.)	Ma, Mo, Le, Ko, Se, Ga, Ba, SF
1953	28,481	5197	Ma, Mo, Le, Ko, Se, Ga, SF, of, Eur
1965[b]	38,872	7930	Ma, Mo, Le, Se, Ga, SF, Sa, of

a. Ma = Makandiambougou   Ba = Bangassi-Liberté
    Mo = Moribougou   SF = Saint-Félix
    Le = Lenguékoto   Sa = Samédougou
    Ko = Kofoulabé   of = officials
    Se = Ségoubougouni   Eur = Europeans
    Ga = Kita-Gare

b. The figures for the canton and the town have been compiled from the census rolls, more or less brought up to date, for the wards of Kita town and for the villages which had been part of the canton, itself abolished in 1959.

SOURCES: Chanteaux 1884 (1884); anonymous 1890 (1890); Roos 1903–4 (1899 and 1903); Delmond 1967 (1934); the Kita circle archives (1953 and 1965).

The French occupation also caused a shift in trade routes and introduced new trade items, the idea of a cash crop, and a new organization of trade. Before the arrival of the French, Kita had been an important stop on the trade route that ran from Kankan in Upper Guinea to Nioro on the edges of the Sahara Desert. Horses and salt went from north to south (Mage 1868:100) in exchange for gold and slaves. Galliéni reported that in the period from April 20 to 26, 1880, three caravans with two hundred traders passed through Kita bound from the Bouré, a gold-producing center in the south, to Nioro.[12] Kita itself was simply a way station and did little trading of its own in either direction.

The immediate result of French occupation was to cut Kita off from its traditional trade routes, as Upper Guinea did not come under French control until the late 1880s, and Nioro until 1891. In the early 1890s, when the northern route reopened, there was an influx of Moorish merchants from Nioro, Néma, and Oualata. They came in the dry season and stayed with one of their number who had permanently settled in Kita. This commerce was mostly in the traditional commodities of salt, cloth, livestock, kola nuts, and gold.[13] But soon the commercial pattern shifted to an interest in the Europeans as trading partners, for the old army supply route was rapidly becoming a channel for the introduction of European goods. The first French traders established themselves in Kita in the late 1890s, and there were four companies by 1900 (Barlet 1942:65).

Kita's golden age came during the two years from 1902 to 1904, when it was the eastern terminus of the railroad line from Kayes. In 1904 the railroad reached Bamako, whose natural advantages were greater, and Kita was supplanted. Old men in Kita who lived at this time still spoke of it in 1965 as the best period Kita had ever known. In 1903 there were twenty-one European firms doing business in Kita, and over twenty thousand African merchants came to trade with them. This was also the period when cash crops and other natural resources began to be exported. In 1903, 300 tons of peanuts, 315 tons of rubber and 4 tons of ivory were exported (Barlet 1942:76).

Kita's population grew rapidly from 1885 to 1905. This is the period when Kita first became a town, a different kind of settlement from the villages round about. There were changes in the population, with farmers moving out to villages and merchants, railroad workers, and colonial employees arriving. It was a period when trading and the administration grew, and even the physical appearance of the town changed with the laying out of streets and the construction of a market and of two-story stone buildings in the colonial style for the administration. After 1905, the population

---

12. Letter no. 13 of April 26, 1880, from Galliéni in Makandiambougou to Governor Brière de l'Isle in Saint-Louis (Senegal) (Archives de la France d'Outre-Mer, file Mission 16).

13. The Moors' commercial patterns are described by Meillassoux (1963:208).

levelled off or perhaps even declined slightly and did not begin to grow again until after 1945.[14] Barlet (1944:8) noted that the population of the canton of Kita had doubled between 1914 and 1944 while that of the town remained steady.

The future of Kita's economy lay in the cash crops, especially in peanuts, rather than in the transit trade which was soon lost to Bamako and other better situated points. The 300 tons of peanuts exported from the circle in 1903 grew to 8,000 tons in 1913 (GGAOF 1921:924), before the trade was interrupted by World War I. Production again rose to 8,000 tons in 1938 and 1939 (Barlet 1944:34) but it dropped to 200 tons by 1943 because of World War II. After the war, production in the Sudan as a whole rose slowly (Amin 1965:24). Table 2 shows the producton for the circle

TABLE 2

PEANUT PRODUCTION, CIRCLE OF KITA, 1959-65

Year	Tons
1959-60	10,114
1960-61	16,615
1961-62	18,193
1962-63	less than 17,000
1963-64	17,345
1964-65	about 10,000

of Kita during the six years after internal self-government. The importance of this production for the economy of the circle is shown by the fact that 17,000 tons at 13 francs a kilo (the price paid to the producer in 1964 and 1965) would have resulted in a payment of 221,000,000 Malian francs (about $900,000 at the rate of exchange of that time).

Peasants did not become completely dependent on peanuts for their income. Most men farmed roughly equal amounts of peanuts and millet, usually in alternate years in the same fields, while the women grew rice and fonio and kept gardens, and maize was grown on the land surrounding the compounds. People living near Kita grew vegetables for the market that was held there every day. Women might come from as far as fifty kilometers with fruit and

14. Meillassoux (1965:127) makes a similar observation for Bamako.

vegetables for the market. Cattle were kept for slaughter in the villages or for sale to the town's butchers; milk was also sold. In the rural areas the economy was essentially one of subsistence agriculture with the addition of peanuts as a source of the cash needed to pay taxes and to buy store goods.

There was not a great deal of variation in the standard of living in Kita town. On the whole, everyone got enough to eat, the standard food being grain with various kinds of meat and vegetable sauces. Even those who were relatively well off did not live conspicuously better than their neighbors. Their diet might include more rice, considered a luxury, and more meat and milk; but practically everyone in Kita followed the same basic menu. This does not mean that some people did not live better than others, or that there were not some people who had a hard time keeping body and soul togther. Those in real difficulty were mostly families without working adults—elderly people living alone, a mother with children, school children from out of town with no relatives or family friends.

The evolution of the economic system during the colonial period led to a much greater degree of economic role differentiation, if not to a wider distribution of incomes or increased overall wealth. But the important factor was the development of a town and of a characteristic pattern of town-countryside relations. This was chiefly expressed in the commercial relations between merchants and peasants.

The Social Organization of Peanut Marketing

The commercialization of peanuts gradually led to the development of a distinctive commercial structure in which African merchants, for the most part living in Kita, played a major role. The peasants grew the peanuts in isolated fields, hard to find and hard to reach because of the poor road network. The buyer had the problem of locating the peanuts, and the peasant had the problem of transporting them to Kita or some other collection point. The European export houses were not equipped to scour the bush for peanuts, and the peasant preferred to sell his peanuts in the field or in his village so as to avoid the trouble of transporting them. So a middleman role developed. African merchants, who knew the country and often had personal relations with the peasants whose peanuts they were buying, would roam the countryside looking for peanuts and would return to places where they customarily bought them. They would often offer consumer goods at the same time. They usually worked on commission for Lebanese merchants, who advanced them money and goods. The Lebanese would then sell the peanuts to one of the European trading companies.[15] Slight fluctuations in peanut prices gave the middlemen the opportunity to outbid one another, and thus gave the peasant the chance to feel that he exercised some control over the situation. The middlemen were also in a position to offer credit to the farmers, but no systematic indebtedness of the peasantry developed, perhaps because the merchants themselves were only agents. Another reason is that no land is owned individually, and so a peasant's only possession is his produce. In consequence it seems that the merchants preferred to "encourage" the peasants to work harder and to attempt to bind them commercially, rather than to dispossess them or otherwise establish control over them.

The relations between a Kita-based merchant and his peasant partner were said to involve *teriya* ("friendship"). The merchant offered credit to the peasant during the hungry season; the peasant repaid the loan and bought his goods from the merchant's store. The merchant thus established a lien on the peanut crop, and the peasants felt they were getting a friend in Kita who could sponsor them in dealings with the administration (Barlet 1944:34). This relationship was very close to the one involving hosts and guests (see chapter 4 below), and in fact the merchant usually acted as host to his "friends" when they were in Kita. Sometimes this relationship, like the host-guest one, was reinforced by marriage, usually between a town boy and a village girl. Families living in Kita often considsidered it worthwhile to have affines living in the villages (and

15. In the area around Ségou, in central Mali, the buyers bought peanuts, millet, kapok, and shea nuts. Robert Pageard (1958:298) has left a description of these buyers, as they appeared at the end of the colonial period: "The buyer controls sub-buyers, and is the master of a vast network, which is limited only by competition. A man from the bush is as likely to seek him out as the canton chief when he needs something in town. The buyers, who are usually transporters as well, represent a commercial bourgeoisie born of the trade system that hardly existed outside Sansanding and Djenné before our arrival. Their power rests on the trust of the commercial houses (CFAO, SCOA, Chavanel, Vézia, and Maurel and Prom especially), which itself depends on that of the banks (Crédit Lyonnais in Ségou). The buyers send their sons and daughters to the French school, but also frequently to the Koranic school. Their trucks and their money help restore life to the bush for several months a year."

besides, country girls had a reputation for good morals and steady personalities). When two families were linked in this way mutual help was considered normal. This meant that the village family would turn to the town family to intercede for them in official matters, to procure for them the items that came through the national commercial network, and to provide food and lodging for any of their children who might be attending school in Kita and for themselves when they visited town. The town family looked to the village family to keep cattle for them (pasturage was better, and it was easier to avoid taxation), to supply them with grain in times of shortage and with honey and other special items from time to time. The demands for grain placed by town families on the rural families associated with them went up sharply during the 1965 rainy season when there was a grain shortage throughout Mali and the town was being poorly supplied through regular channels.

Starting in the postwar period, there were attempts to circumvent this system with its many stages from peasant to exporter and its emphasis on patronage relations at each stage. The chiefs of Kita canton and neighboring Birgo canton, both former school teachers, formed a producers' cooperative in 1949. This cooperative was originally founded for the entire circle, but when that proved to be too clumsy, the Birgo chief withdrew from the cooperative and founded another one for the Birgo alone. The original cooperative continued to operate in the rest of the circle. These cooperatives were based on the principle that if the buyers could be cut out, a higher price could be paid to the peasants. The cooperatives tried to sell directly either to one of the large export houses, or, eventually, to a soap factory in Marseille. Members paid a fee of one hundred francs to join, and were then entitled to receive a bonus of a half-franc a kilo the first year and one franc a kilo in later years.

The cooperatives had varied success. The original cooperative did not succeed too well; according to one of the founders they were too ambitious and stretched themselves too far in their early days (by purchasing two trucks, for instance, when one would have done) and never recovered from that financial strain. They also tried to cover too wide an area: the whole circle except for the Birgo. The Birgo cooperative, on the other hand, worked quite well and continued to prosper until 1961 when it was absorbed into the government cooperative structure. People in Kita said that the government cooperatives of the 1960s had been particularly successful in the

Birgo because of the familiarity gained with the similar institutions of the Birgo cooperative of the 1950s.

The success of the Birgo cooperative led to a conflict with African buyers around 1951 (Pâques 1954:41). Government rules at that time limited the regular commercial buyers to the stipulated "trading centers" (*points de traite*) to which the peasants had to bring their peanuts. The cooperatives were not thus restricted. This gave the Birgo cooperative an advantage that led to protests by African buyers. When the buyers, who had extended credit to the peasants during the rainy season, tried to circulate in the villages in order to recoup their debts in the form of peanuts, they were punished by the government. In 1951, the amount of peanuts bought by commercial buyers dropped 80 percent in the Birgo. How much of this conflict was economic and how much was political cannot be known, for those who ran the cooperative were PSP and the buyers were largely RDA, and the two parties were then in bitter competition. The founder of the Birgo cooperative was at that time Kita's delegate to the Sudan Territorial Assembly.

During the 1950s the peanut trading season, from January to April of every year, was the time when the town was lively and exciting, for it was full of people. Many people came from Bamako and elsewhere—merchants, truckers, unskilled laborers from Mauretania—and many villagers came to town once their crops were sold, for there is no agricultural work at this time of year. The bigger Kita merchants made most of their annual income (perhaps in the range of $1000 to $1500) during the trading season, for the rest of the year presented few opportunities. No Kita merchants were as wealthy as the Bamako long-distance merchants described by Meillassoux (1965) and Amselle (1969). Not all Kita merchants were involved in the peanut trade. Some sold goods imported into Kita, such as European manufactured goods, African cloth, and kola nuts. But everyone prospered when the peanut season brought money into town.

The town of Kita was the commercial center for a large part of the circle of Kita. Kita and its hinterland were bound together in an economic structure based on the production of peanuts. From the villages peanuts came in to Kita, and consumer goods went out to the villages from Kita. Merchants depended on their personal ties with villagers to enhance their economic position, for there was active competition between African buyers to purchase peanuts, and the establishment of personal ties added another dimension to the competition. Such ties included marriage links and acting as intermediaries for peasants in town, as well as the extension of credit. During the period when two parties competed in Mali, these ties also had a political dimension, as the example of the locally founded cooperatives makes clear. On the whole the relationship between town merchants and rural peasant producers was symbiotic, for the merchants were just as dependent on a good peanut crop as the peasants were. The situation had moved a long way from the self-sufficient villages of the period before 1880.

If the broad pattern of town-country relations did not change after independence, the economic roles of the merchants and the civil servants changed radically. After independence, the leading citizens were no longer the wealthier merchants and the members of the chiefly lineage. Instead they were the high civil servants and party officials, now all Malian and vastly more numerous. The civil servants, receiving a salary, were not dependent on personal ties in the villages or on the overall size of the peanut crop for their income. The major source of money in the town was no longer the spinoff from private commercial involvement in the peanut season, but the salaries of the civil servants and other government expenditures, including government purchases of peanuts. But Kita continued to depend on its hinterland for its prosperity; Kita remained close to rural problems and attitudes; and Kita's politics continued to reflect this symbiosis.

4

Communities, Identities, and Statuses

The metamorphosis of Kita from village to town described in the last chapter entailed many changes in the community's social organization. Old ways of classifying people became irrelevant, while new ones developed, derived in part from the changes in the town. The emergence of the town itself as a major form of identity, the growth of Islam and the shift in its nature, the feeling of belonging to one or another of Kita's wards, the contrast between old inhabitants and new arrivals, and the development of new occupational patterns: these were the major directions of change which affected the social organization of postindependence Kita. These new elements reflected some traits of the older patterns of Maninka social organization, but above all they reflected the economic and social changes that followed from the transformation of Kita from a series of self-sufficient villages to a town with a regional political and economic role. These changes laid the groundwork for the shift from one kind of participatory government to another.

ETHNICITY AND TOWN IDENTITY

Ethnicity in Mali has never been a major basis for organization, either in the traditional rural areas or in the towns. The kind of role which ethnicity might play in a national framework is played in Mali by regionalism, each region being summed up by its principal town. Malian towns have always exerted a strong influence on the ethnic identity of people living in them, either changing their identity to a more urban one (Gallais 1962) or absorbing it into a town identity. This latter process seems to have occurred in Kita, where ethnic affiliation counted for little, but belonging to the town—being a Kitan—counted for a great deal.

In sharp contrast to the surrounding countryside, which is virtually entirely Maninka, the town of Kita contains people claiming to belong to some two dozen ethnic groups. The home territories of these ethnic groups are scattered over Mali and adjacent countries. Table 3 gives the complete breakdown of the ethnic groups in the population of the town. The individual ethnic groups have been grouped according to their affinities, based on language and common identity for the major groups, and on geographical contiguity of their home territories for the smaller ones. Thus Maninka, Bamana, Soninké, Kasonka, and seven others, have all been grouped under general heading of Mandé; they represent about two-thirds of the population.[1] The small Fula-speaking groups of Toucouleur and Diawambé have been added to the Fula; together these groups represent about one-fifth of the population. The other groups are splintered and are negligible numerically. The four largest groups are the Maninka, the Fula, the Bamana, and the Soninké. Together they represent 80.8 percent of Kita's population.[2]

The presence of these major ethnic groups is linked to the historical development of Kita. The Maninka are the original population of the villages from which the town grew, and they are still the basic population in the villages immediately surrounding Kita. The Fula represent in part immigrants from nearby areas (some as close as ten kilometers) inhabited by Maninka-speaking agricultural Fula, and in part the descendents of the Toucouleur settlers of Ségoubougouni. The core of the Soninké are the Cissé and other merchants who settled in Kita at the turn of the century; other such merchants are listed as Moors, Dioula, and Sonrai-Djennenké. The Kasonka, whose home base is around Kayes, further west on the railroad, mostly came to Kita to work on the railroad. There seems

1. In calculating these population figures I have assumed that all members of a household are of the same ethnic group as the household head. This is demonstrably not always the case, though it usually is; I feel that the exceptions will cancel each other out—for every Fula wife married to a Maninka husband, there is a Maninka wife married to a Fula husband. This also honors the local convention whereby a child inherits not only his father's clan and lineage affiliations but also his ethnic category.

2. The same four groups represent 67 percent of Bamako's population, though the internal proportions are somewhat different (Meillassoux 1965:128).

TABLE 3

ETHNIC GROUPS IN KITA: TOTALS AND AMONG
OFFICEHOLDERS (1965)

Ethnic Group	Population		Officeholders	
	Number	Percentage	Number	Percentage
Maninka	2,640	33.3	80	37.9
Bamana	1,203	15.2	23	10.9
Soninké	1,044	13.2	24	11.4
Kasonka	202	2.5	5	2.0
Dioula	100	1.3	4	1.9
Kagoro	70	.9	1	.5
Samoko	53	.7	—	—
Dogon	28	.4	2	.9
Bozo	22	.3	—	—
Somono	18	.2	—	—
Dafing	11	.1	—	—
Total Mandé	5,391	68.1	139	65.9
Fula	1,512	19.1	40	19.0
Toucouleur	58	.7	3	1.4
Diawambé	4	.05	1	.5
Total Fula	1,574	19.8	44	20.9
Mossi	151	1.9	1	.5
Bobo	30	.4	—	—
Tourka	18	.2	—	—
Minianka	17	.2	1	.5
Senufo	7	.09	—	—
Total Voltaics	223	2.8	2	.9
Moors	98	1.2	3	1.4
Wolof	41	.5	5	2.0
Sonrai and Djennenké .	40	.5	2	.9
Guineans (Kissi, Toma and Soso)	16	.2	1	.5
Mulatto	3	.04	—	—
Unknown	544	6.9	15	7.1
Grand Total	7,930	100.04	211	99.2

to be no single reason to account for the Bamana. Some are merchants, and others are the descendents of freed slaves who settled in Kita.

The economic position of Kita at the turn of the century attracted immigrants from various towns and ethnic groups. Over a period of several generations, these immigrants were subject to the unifying force of the town and were "naturalized." People who lived together, traded with each other, married each other, competed against one another in politics, gradually evolved a certain way of doing things, a set of expectations, which are typically and specifically Kitan. The Kitan town style of life came to be a badge to distinguish town dwellers from people living in nearby villages. This assimilation of Maninka peasants and immigrant merchants into a common culture is closely linked with the development of a specific dialect for urban Kitans, distinct both from the Maninka spoken in the surrounding rural areas and from the Bamana spoken in other towns.

Around Kita marriage customs are another excellent symbol of the distinctiveness of a local community, and the town's marriage customs differ in detail from those of the villages round about. The differences lie in such details as the number of visits a would-be groom must make to the family of his intended, how many kola nuts he must take, how much the bride wealth should be (though this was fixed by the Malian government in 1962), and similar details of the ceremony. There are endless discussions of how people marry elsewhere, and how these customs differ from those of Kita. Kitans talk about their marriage customs the way Englishmen talk about their accents.

The assimilation of immigrant and native families to a common culture did not have to bridge any tremendous cultural gaps. Ethnic groups in Mali in general have a long tradition of living together and being associated within a single political framework (Zolberg 1967a). We know that there were Moors, Diawambé, and Soninké living and trading peacefully in Kita before the colonial period. Furthermore, all the major groups share what is to all intents and purposes a common culture. All were patrilineal and polygynous, had castes and slavery, recognized chiefs recruited on the basis of genealogy whose power was greatly limited unless reinforced by wealth, had similar religious conceptions, shared the same historical legends such as that of Soundiata, and were used to living in pluri-ethnic environments. Finally, the creation of a single community in Kita was facilitated by the presence of patterns for absorbing strangers into the community. The most notable of these patterns was the possibility of evoking a tie between host and guest, cutting across ethnic distinctions, which is discussed below.

The development in Kita of a distinctive urban culture, owing something to the ethnic groups which predominated in its growth and something to knowledge of a pattern of an urban way of life based on trade and Islam, is far from unique in Mali. It has happened in precolonial times and during the quite different conditions of the colonial period. In some towns, a special term developed for the bearers of this urban culture, such as the Djennenké of Djenné (Ch. Monteil 1932) or the Markadialan of San (Kamian 1959:228). Other towns, where there is no such singular name, have probably gone as far in the development of a particular culture. In Timbuctoo, where the Arma may represent the core bearers of the urban culture (Miner 1965), in Sofara (S. Traoré 1959), and in Bamako (Meillassoux 1968) this seems to have happened. In modern Mali people are far more frequently classed according to their home town or area than according to their often ambiguous ethnicity. Malians have stereotypes based on towns: the people of Ségou are said to be subtle and refined, those of San to be cold and unfriendly, those of Bamako to be overpoweringly self-confident, and those of Kita to be intriguers.

The fluidity of ethnic designations is itself a sign of the relative lack of importance of ethnic affiliation. The indications given in the town rolls, on which the figures presented here are based, are founded on common understandings. Thus all Keita are Maninka, all Cissé are Soninké, and so on. In cases not covered by the traditional attributions, the person involved was simply asked to identify himself. The figures in tables 3 and 4 should be interpreted in the light of this understanding.

When strangers assimilate to an "indigenous" group in Kita, they switch their allegiance to Maninka, because there is no such category as the "Markadialan" of San to express something more precise, namely, that the people are Kitans. The following anecdote illustrates this. Three generations ago a man came to Kita from Djenné and founded a family. The family was classified locally as Soninké (many people from Djenné are supposed in Kita to be Soninké; besides, their hosts in Kita were Soninké), although the family tradition is that they are in fact Arma (the core ethnic group in Timbuctoo, which was always closely linked with Djenné; this family's clan name is an illustrious one among the Arma). When school opened in Kita in the autumn of 1964, a grandson of the original immigrant, a schoolteacher, was enrolling his younger sister for her first year of school. This was being done in the presence of many other Kitans, also waiting to enroll their children

49

and siblings. As he was filling out the papers, he came across a question asking the "*race*" (meaning "tribe") of the girl. He looked up and asked, addressing no one in particular, "Well, what are we?" at which everyone laughed. He wrote down "Maninka" and justified this cho ce on the grounds that they had been so long in Kita that they had become Maninka. Later he complained of the irrelevance of the question in the modern context.

Despite the uncertainty that affects people's conceptions of the ethnic group to which they belong, it is possible to hear people identified by their ethnic affiliation, and one does find individuals who are self-conscious about which group they belong to. The Keita and the Tounkara in Kita sometimes refer to themselves as Maninka in contrast to the outsiders. One educated Tounkara *dieli* claimed that his family were really Soninké, which is true, according to the Soundiata story, but that would have been 750 years ago. He was probably reacting more to the idea that Tounkara is considered in some circles to be a Soninké clan name (he had served in the army in Soninké country). Whatever his reasoning, he was trying to adopt what he imagined to be a Soninké life style, while the rest of his family never thought they were anything but Maninka. One young schoolteacher of an "old" Kita family told me that since his family were Wolof they followed slightly different marriage customs. Fula are occasionally addressed as "Pulo" (meaning "little Fula") or some derivative of this word, but usually in a joking manner, as occurs between friends. One man expressed the opinion that Kita would be better off if the commandant were a Maninka;[3] another man, that the president of Mali would necessarily have to be a Maninka or else there would be trouble:[4] though it is hard to know how seriously to take such comments. Some members of the older generation would prefer a marriage within the ethnic group, but members of the younger generation tend rather to follow

3. The first three African commandants de cercle in Kita were a Toucouleur from Ségou, a Toucouleur from Timbuctoo, and a Soninké from Nioro.

4. Mali's first president, Modibo Keita, was usually considered to be a Maninka because of his clan name. But he was born in Bamako, and his father was a civil servant from a family that came from Guiré in northern Mali and considered itself Soninké (Marty 1920:107). Culturally, he was more a product of urban Bamako than of any ethnic group. Another person in Kita criticized him for being in spirit a Bamana!

their fancy where it leads them—and particularly among the mobile educated class it is likely to lead them a long way. These attitudes and comments are exceptional—the exceptions that prove the rule.

If the history of Kita were any guide, the deepest split in the population ought to be between the Kita Maninka and the Fula from the Birgo, adjoining Kita to the south, for these two groups were engaged in mutual raiding when the French pacified the area in 1881 by destroying the Fula fortified village of Goubanko. One frequently hears people refer to the raids carried out by the Fula against Kita, and the general opinion even among Maninka is that the Fula would have dominated the Maninka completely if the French had not arrived when they did. The Birgo Fula are prone to tease the Maninka about the cowardice and stupidity they showed at that time. Yet this conflict between Maninka and Fula has not survived as a basic rivalry in the politics and everyday life of Kita. When political alliances were formed they cut across this distinction. During the period of two-party politics, the canton chiefs of both Kita and the Birgo were former schoolteachers re-garded as usurpers by traditionalists. Both were early members of the PSP. Conversely, their opponents on the traditional level both joined the RDA and so were associated there, although there was nothing to indicate that they were actually more radical; quite the contrary, they were the upholders of the "proper" tradition against usurpers. Here the common interests resulting from the conflict of "ins" and "outs" were more important than ethnic distinctions in determining political alliances.

Origin from the same area or town offers a firmer base for political alliances than affiliation with a single ethnic group. People from the same town, even if of different ethnic groups, often estab-lish fictive kinship relations. A more purely political example in-volved a Soninké *dieli,* Sylla, from Mopti, who was one of the leading figures in Kita politics during the early 1960s (see chapter 6). Under attack by his enemies (mostly people from Kita, includ-ing both Soninké and *dieli*), he appealed for aid to a Toucouleur noble from Mopti, at that time a schoolteacher in Kita, on the grounds that they were both from Mopti and ought to help one another. The appeal was listened to, and the alliance helped Sylla retain his position. This same Toucouleur noble had as one of his closest friends in Kita a Fula *numu* from Mopti, also a schoolteacher. Thus members of three different ethnic groups and three different castes were linked in Kita because they were all from the same town.

In Kita solidarity based on residence or religion is more relevant for identity than the real or imagined differences between the various ethnic groups. These groups in Kita are neither social groups nor relevant social categories; it is sometimes uncertain to which one a person may be said to belong. There are no corporate ethnic group interests which must be defended; ethnic groups have no organized existence (as, for instance, a chief for each ethnic group) ; and they are not distinguished to any significant degree by their customs or their language. It is not ethnicity which is the basis for the internal organization of Kita, but the wards and people's occupations. The point is not to say how well the different ethnic groups get along together, but to point out that they really do not exist as such any longer in the town, but instead have fused into a common Kita identity.

RELIGION AND TOWN UNITY

The religious situation of Kita has changed considerably since the beginning of the colonial period. At that time, Islam was a matter for small groups of religious specialists, the *mori,* and the bulk of the population followed the local variety of the traditional Maninka religion. The major community rituals were associated with the earth and antiwitchcraft cults (Brun 1907; Sidibé 1932; Jaeger 1951). Since then, Islam has become the majority religion, and its annual round of ceremonies have become the principal expressions of the unity of the town. As a predominantly urban religion, Islam also serves to bolster Kita's urban identity by distinguishing town from country, the civilized from the savage. The divisions of Islam into rival brotherhoods, so characteristic of Western Sudan Islam, have been attenuated in recent years; the only self-conscious group whose identity has a religious basis is the small community of Catholics. But the Catholics are so few that they pose no threat to the Muslims and so do not alter the observation that Islam primarily serves to strengthen town solidarity.

If Kita town has a pronounced Muslim character, this is a fairly recent development. In 1912, the circle as a whole was just over 1 percent Muslim (Delafosse 1912 (i) :163). The town must then have been about 15 or 20 percent Muslim. However, there have always been Muslims in Kita, and Muslim influence has been felt among people who were not themselves Muslims. One of the early Catholic missionaries in Kita wrote (Marcot 1892:306) :

> The Maninka all claim that they will never want to accept the Crescent and yet, some days, one would think oneself in the midst of a Muslim country. Under the name of "sowing festival" they celebrate the end of Ramadhan and Tabaski ['Id el-Adha]. Friday is set aside; it is the main day for dancing and for drinking *dolo* [millet beer]; it is the day on which one gives alms; the day chosen for circumcising children, and so on. And yet there are only a few Muslims in Kita.

Another early observer noted (Tellier 1898:152) : "The fetishists have adopted all the Muslim feasts, while retaining their own as well." Kita undoubtably shared in the Maninka pattern of a symbiotic relationship between a small group of Muslim religious specialists, the *mori,* usually defined on a hereditary basis like the castes, and the bulk of the population (cf. Smith 1965a,b). The legends of Kita's founding suggest this by their emphasis on cooperation between Muslim and pagan magic. But in the past century the pattern has shifted from one of symbiosis between two distinct groups to one where most people claim to be some kind of a Muslim, for being a Muslim has become a mark of high status.

Around Kita, as generally in West Africa, Islam is regarded as a typically urban phenomenon. Nowadays there are, of course, many Muslims in the villages, but the essential identity of Islam and urbanity remains. The Muslim looking down on the pagan is the same man as the townsman looking down on the villager. The chief symbol of the difference between urban-Muslim and rural-pagan behavior is the way in which a polygamist treats his wives: a proper Muslim will follow a regular rotation (two days to each wife in succession), while a non-Muslim will allegedly prefer some wives to others.

Islam in the Western Sudan is associated with brotherhoods. The two main ones in Kita are the Qadriyya and the Tijaniyya, but the social and philosophical distinctions between these two groups is quite uncertain; the people themselves say that there is no longer any real difference between them. They are both regarded as "conservative," involved with magical and superstitious elements and structured along hierarchical lines unacceptable to the modernist element. The modernist goal is to establish a pietistic, simple Islam free from superstition and charlatans (cf. Ba and Cardaire

1957). In this self-consciousness it corresponds to the shift that Geertz (1968:61) has characterized as a change from "religious-ness" to "religious-mindedness." The direction of change here is parallel to the trend toward the concept of citizenship in the social realm. The modernists are essentially a group composed of young men, often French-speaking and thus "modern" in other ways, and of returned pilgrims for whom a change in religious posture conse-crates their new religious status.

In Kita there has theoretically never been more than a single main mosque, located in Moribougou and associated with the Cissé family. The Toucouleur who settled in Ségoubougouni al-ways had their own mosque, too, but it never rivalled the Moribou-gou mosque. Because this main mosque seemed unduly linked with the Cissé family and Moribougou, there was for some time a scheme to build a new Friday mosque on vacant land between the two tra-ditionally Muslim wards of Moribougou and Ségoubougouni where the great collective prayers at the end of Ramadhan and on the 'Id el-Adha are held. In addition to these two older mosques, and the new main mosque, two more were being built in 1965, in the peripheral wards of Lenguékoto and Gare. The distance to the main mosque was given in both cases as the main reason for con-struction, but there was a lot of opposition from those who felt that the unity of Kita's Muslims should be symbolized by a single mosque. This issue resembles the debate on whether there should be one party branch for the whole town, or a branch for each ward (see chapters 5 and 6).

The two main Muslim festivals are occasions of great activity in Kita. The fast of Ramadhan is followed by many Kitans, from schoolboys to old men, and the hardship is generally regarded as a good and purifying thing. The symbol of fasting is to spit out one's saliva, for the local belief is that the prohibition on food and drink extends even to swallowing one's saliva (cf. V. Monteil 1964:111). During Ramadhan the markets, offices, and schools are full of people spitting more or less ostentatiously. The end of Ramadhan is celebrated with fervor. There is a communal prayer to which practically the entire male population of the town comes (small boys come carrying their father's prayer rugs) as well as many women, especially the older ones. The ceremony is repeated at 'Id el-Adha ("Tabaski") when the slaughter of a ram in emulation of Abraham is the central part of the ceremony. Both these feasts, but especially the end of Ramadhan, are occasions to purchase new clothes and to have special dances, sometimes over a period of two or three days. Tailors work late every night for several weeks beforehand, readying everyone's finery, and on the day people parade through town in their new clothes, and small boys and girls circulate from house to house in the hope of getting small presents from adults. These are also the occasions for formal visiting. The commandant de cercle and the party head paid a joint visit, for instance, on the imam of Kita at Ramadhan, 1965. There is a delicate balance between those who visit and those who are visited; people's sociopolitical status is on the line.

There has been a French Catholic mission in Kita since 1887. It was manned by the Holy Ghost Fathers until 1901, when the Holy Ghost Fathers and the White Fathers traded mission posts under instructions from the Vatican to consolidate their respective territories. The result of this mission activity is that there is a Catholic ward in Kita where most of Kita's Catholic population (6.3 percent of the total population) lives and that there are six or eight villages near Kita with small Catholic populations. It seems that the height of Catholic strength in Kita was in the 1920s and 1930s; both in Kita town and in the villages it has receded since then. A major motive for affiliation to the Catholic church in earlier generations was the protection that people thought the priests could afford them from the French administration; this has not been a motive in the last generation. Conversions to Catholicism are rare (in fact the church is not actively seeking new converts), while conversions from Catholicism or avoidance of both major religions are more frequent. Name changes are a frequent symbol of changes of religious stance. A schoolteacher who had been known as "Marc-André" (a Catholic name) announced that he wanted henceforth to be known as "Karamoko" (a Muslim name). People teased him but respected his wishes. Another man, living in a village some nine kilometers from Kita, had been baptized "Pierre" and had served as an altar boy in his youth. More recently, however, he has switched his name to "Mamadou." Both Karamoko and Mamadou emphasized that they were returning to the religion of their ancestors.

The Catholics of Saint-Félix have certain symbols of their distinctiveness. In contrast to the rest of the population of Kita, both Muslim and pagan, they ostentatiously keep pigs and eat pork.

They also specialize in the brewing of local alcohols (millet beer, palm wine, and mead) and keep a number of bistros many of whose customers are Muslims from the other wards of Kita, custom being especially heavy Sunday afternoons.

A further example of interaction between the two communities is the interest that many Muslims had at one point in enrolling their children in the Catholic schools because they had a reputation for stricter discipline than the state schools and because they had more European teachers. There are also marriages between Catholics and Muslims, in both directions. One of the reasons for this is that young men like to find their sweethearts in other, exotic wards, where the youths think they are escaping from parental surveillance. The Catholics are disturbed by the tendency of their young people to marry outside the community, for they feel that this will lead to the disappearance of Catholicism. Some blame Catholic parents for raising their daughters so strictly that Catholic boys are obliged to go to Muslim wards to flirt.

Mutual participation in ceremonies is slight, except for naming ceremonies.[5] One Catholic civil servant held a traditional naming ceremony for his son which attracted large numbers of Muslim civil servants; ultimately even a Muslim prayer was said. This same Catholic served as the "sponsor" for a child born to a Muslim *dieli*,[6] and the naming ceremony of this child was the occasion for explicitly stating the ties that bind the Catholics to the rest of Kita. Another Muslim *dieli* acting as the spokesman for the Catholic civil servant stressed that "We are all one."

Another incident illustrative of Catholic-Muslim relations occurred on Christmas Eve. The Catholic youth group was sponsoring a theatrical evening at which the main play was based on the story of the Uganda martyrs.[7] Many of the leading citizens of Kita were present, including the commandant, the secretary-general of the

---

5. A child is named a week after his birth, and the ceremony at that time is a small but important one in the life of a family.

6. This role is very like that of a godfather. The *dieli* honors the man by asking him to sponsor the child, and the civil servant is expected to make frequent presents on behalf of the child. This particular *dieli* was not particularly Muslim, as the chief link between him and the civil servant was that they were drinking partners. But the context of the naming ceremony was Muslim.

7. These were Baganda converts to Catholicism who were killed by the Kabaka of Buganda in 1886. They were collectively canonized in 1964; they are the first modern African saints.

party, the former canton chief—all Muslims. Before the play began, a Muslim *nyamakala* resident in Saint-Félix made a speech in which he emphasized that there were two equally good paths to God, the Christian and the Muslim, and that the audience should now observe the presentation of the Christian path. After the play was over, a large part of the crowd present, including the Muslims, went to the nearby church to attend the Christmas Eve mass.

The Catholics feel themselves to be a distinctive minority in Kita and are afraid of discrimination. The feeling of separateness is illustrated by the comment that one made to a friend, who had been chosen secretary of a rural cooperative: "You must do your job well, because we are in the minority, and whenever the majority chooses us for posts of responsibility, we must do the best job we can."

In fact Catholics participate in Kitan life on the same footing as other people, in the civil service, sporting and recreational activities, commerce and politics. In politics there seemed to be an unwritten rule that every Kita-wide bureau should have one Catholic member. The Catholics are such a small group in Kita that their suspicious attitude towards the Muslim majority is not reciprocated. The presence of Catholics is not an issue for the Muslims; there can be no thought that the few Catholics can compete as a group on terms of equality with the Muslims. The Catholic task is not to force their views on others, but to maintain their integrity in a largely Muslim population. In religious terms there is a great deal of tolerance, for the idea is widespread that Islam and Christianity are two alternative but equally valid paths to God.

The traditional Maninka religious beliefs underlie both Islam and Christianity. But these beliefs do not lead to the open practice of "pagan" rituals in the town, nor do they provide the basis for cult groups or other categories within the population, with the single exception of a possession cult, the *djiden* (Chéron 1931), most of whose few adherents are strangers. The relationship between paganism, Islam, and Christianity is symbolized by the pattern of personal names. Everyone in Kita has a *maninka togo*, a Maninka name. If a person is a good Muslim or a good Christian, his Maninka name will not be widely known. In addition, each person will have a *mori togo*, a Muslim name, or a *kretien togo*, a Christian name, whichever is appropriate. Some individuals with more complex personal histories may have both. At the Muslim naming ceremony, the Muslim name is formally announced while the Maninka name is whispered to the participants.

One can perhaps summarize the situation by saying that the traditional Maninka beliefs provide the popular substratum of religious belief while Islam provides the religious framework that allows people to validate their status as members of the community by demonstrating the external signs of Islam such as prayer and fasting. Islam also provides the religious justification for the present sociopolitical arrangements through the institutions of village, ward, or town mosques as focuses of community feeling, and through a set of symbols which distinguish "civilized" urban dwellers from "uncouth" villagers. Underneath, the traditional beliefs largely remain; above, most are Muslims but a few are Christian. In becoming the religion of the majority, Islam has ceased to be an affair of specialists and has, by admitting everybody, come to furnish a language for expressing the symbols of community unity as well as for reaching beyond the community to the world and the afterlife.

The Wards

The importance of the town's territorial divisions, the wards, reflects an emphasis on territoriality in traditional Maninka social organization. This importance was also greatly reinforced by the bureaucratic patterns under the colonial and independent regimes, which treated the ward, like the village, as the basic unit for administration. Prior to the establishment of the municipality in 1959, the wards were independent villages, each with its own chief and internal organization. Independence made the wards the basis for the party and the cooperative organizations; with their functions reinforced, the wards retained much of the independence and spirit of villages. At the same time, the growth of the town led to an increased urban consciousness, based on the town's economic role and relative sophistication.

In 1965 the town of Kita was divided into seven wards. They were an important focus for people's loyalties, and rivalry between them was on occasion intense. Each ward had a distinct character, for each reflected the specific historical circumstances of its founding and development. Two of Kita's wards were villages before the French occupation. A third is a split from one of those, dating back to 1912. The other four originated in the period from 1885 to 1905 when Kita took on its present form (see table 4 for population figures).

TABLE 4

POPULATION OF KITA BY WARD AND ETHNIC GROUP, 1965

	Maninka	Fula	Bamana	Soninké	Other	Unknown	Total
Gare	188	132	99	92	220	72	803
Lenguékoto	244	15	44	14	76	6	399
Makandiambougou	749	232	256	296	308	23	1,864
Moribougou	688	547	403	559	186	187	2,570
Saint-Félix	192	103	196	—	15	27	533
Samédougou	375	24	9	28	21	10	467
Ségoubougouni	204	521	196	55	99	219	1,294
Total	2,640	1,574	1,203	1,044	925	544	7,930

Makandiambougou is an old Keita village, belonging to the Tandunka branch of the Kasumasi Keita. This was Tokontan's village, and when the French decided to put a fort in Kita they chose to put it not far from his village. Most of the canton chiefs during the colonial period were from Makandiambougou, which thus had the double advantage of being near the seat of colonial power and having the canton chief. The core of the ward is still formed by the Keita and their dependents, but many Dioula, Soninké, and Manin-kamori merchants, some civil servants, and others, have also settled there, and many of the Keita and their dependents have moved out to the bush. The rivalry between the two Keita lineages of Djita Makadougoula (the branch of Fatogoma) and Tokontana for the canton chiefship has become a petty rivalry for preeminence in the ward.

Lenguékoto, or Tounkarala, is the other of Kita's wards to have been one of Kita's original villages. The original inhabitants of Lenguékoto were Tounkara, but very few still live there as most have moved out to farming villages. Lenguékoto today is populated largely by overflow from Makandiambougou, many of whom are either strangers to Kita altogether or trace their ancestry back to other Kita villages. Considered a part of Lenguékoto for adminis-trative purposes is the proto-ward of Kossilabougou, another of Kita's original villages, inhabited by Keita. Kossilabougou was totally abandoned at one point, and has been reoccupied in recent years by the same kind of overflow from Makandiambougou that has populated Lenguékoto, together with some descendants of original inhabitants who have moved back to Kita from the bush.

Samédougou is divided into two parts, of which the larger consists mostly of Keita who live at Yilimalo, some fifteen kilometers away. This ward was founded about 1912 by members of a Keita lineage which had previously lived in Makandiambougou, although they were not especially closely related to the Keita of Makandiambougou. They asked the French commandant for permission to establish their own village; he granted permission provided they could find one hundred people, which they did. Although the population of Samédougou is larger on the rolls than that of Lenguékoto—with which it was united in a single party committee—more of that population lives in Yilimalo so that the portion actually resident in Kita is smaller.

Moribougou was settled by the Cissé clan in the 1880s on land given to the clan by the Makandiambougou Keita. The name of the village means "Village of the Muslims," and Moribougou is traditionally Kita's Muslim ward. The main Friday mosque is in Moribougou and is associated with the Cissé family. The early inhabitants were mostly Muslim merchants attracted to Kita by the commercial possibilities deriving from the French conquest. Moribougou is also the ward where the *nyamakala* settle; it has large numbers of *dieli, numu,* and others. In recent years, particularly, Moribougou has grown because many Maninka from the area south and west of Kita have settled in an extension of Moribougou known as "Niafala" from the name of one of the original Maninka villages. Moribougou is proud of having been the center for the RDA in Kita, and attributes this to its generally progressive quality: Islam, commerce, and the RDA are linked.

Ségoubougouni was first settled shortly after 1890 by Toucouleur who were returning to Senegal from Segou after the defeat of Ahmadou Tall in 1890. The French had decided to repatriate them, but they got no further than Kita. So they could be properly watched, the French administration settled them on land that was then some distance from the center of Kita but near the administrative headquarters. The Toucouleur established their own mosque; their village chief was chosen from the Diallo clan. The ward didn't begin to grow until it became the "civil servants' ward" following World War II. The government started the trend by building some houses for civil servants in the ward, and subsequently many Africans also built houses, which were often rented to the administration for civil servants. When the town was organized in 1959, the center of political power was in Ségoubougouni, and some territory that had previously been part of other wards was added to Ségoubougouni. At present, most of the clerical and executive civil servants live in the ward, around the core of Toucouleur.

Saint-Félix is the Catholic ward, somewhat apart from the main part of Kita and hidden in a mango grove. It grew up in the last ten or fifteen years of the nineteenth century as the place of residence of the freed slaves and other displaced persons who had accepted the protection offered by the Catholic mission. Saint-Félix is the site of the Catholic church, the Catholic schools, and the Catholic dispensary. Two other small villages in this area, called Kofoulabé and Bangassi-Liberté, have been absorbed into Saint-Félix and Ségoubougouni. Beyond Saint-Félix is a new proto-ward of migrants from the villages south of Kita, including many Catholics. This proto-ward is known as Dounba-koura (New Dounba) because many of the people are from the village of Dounba, eight kilometers to the south.

Kita-Gare is separated from the rest of Kita by the railroad tracks, which cannot be crossed by car. The ward is the only one to which it is impossible to drive a car and the only one with no roads inside it. It grew up starting around 1900 as the ward where the railroad workers (first construction, then maintenance) lived. Even more than Saint-Félix it is a ward of "strangers," and has never really felt as much a part of Kita as the other wards have. Most of the Kasonka in Kita are alleged to live here, though if that is so, they are not on the census rolls. At any rate, the Gare is referred to as a "Kasonka ward." It remains the ward of the railroad workers, most of whom live here. Because of this, it has the highest proportion of wage earners among Kita's wards.

The various wards that make up Kita thus have diverse origins and specific characters. People tend to identify strongly with the ward they live in—or rather, with the ward they are associated with either through being born into it or because they first settled there. Few people change their residence from one ward to another.

When Kita's "urban renewal" plan was instituted,[8] people who had to leave their homes tried very hard to stay in the same ward when relocating. People who do move from one ward to another usually retain their primary association in the first ward. Even villagers think of themselves as "belonging" to one or another of the wards, usually the one that they reach first when coming into Kita from their home village. Moribougou is the ward for all those who approach Kita from the southeast, and Saint-Félix and Ségoubougouni are the wards for those who come from the south. The pull of the ward is also shown by the choice made by Catholics from villages deriving from Kossilabougou when they move to Kita; rather than move to the Catholic ward, they have settled in the territory occupied by their ancestors, some two kilometers from Saint-Félix on the other side of town, even though some of them go back and forth two or more times a day.

The wards provide the units for competition of many sorts in Kita. In the middle 1950s, a type of dancing society known as the *gumbé* (cf. Meillassoux 1968:116-130) became the major focus of interest on the part of the youth. It was organized on a ward basis; there was one *gumbé* society for Makandiambougou and another for Moribougou, in which Ségoubougouni also participated. These two were tremendously competitive, each trying to outdo the other in conspicuous spending. A series of football matches held in 1965 between teenage boys (the "Pioneers," see chapter 5) from the different wards excited a great deal of interest and emotion (there were, for instance, quarrels over whether two boys who were "from" Makandiambougou but lived in Gare ought to play for one or the other of these teams—they played for Makandiambougou, but Gare protested). The strength of the emotion aroused by these schoolboy football games suggests that Kitans do not exaggerate when they say that football games involving adult players would cause too much division to be allowed.

Competition also sometimes involves politics. Thus it is possible to hear people say that ward X has run things long enough, it is time for a change. The wards are proud of their political role—Moribougou of having been the first RDA ward, Makandiambougou of having been the seat of the canton chiefs, Ségoubougouni of

8. A plan to impose a grid layout on Kita to facilitate supplying people with public utilities.

having been the first ward to implement a grid pattern in its layout (a sign of progressiveness). More direct conflicts have occurred over boundaries. Ségoubougouni and Saint-Félix, and Ségoubougouni and Moribougou, have outstanding quarrels over their boundaries (see chapter 8) : both quarrels are officially settled, but resentment lingers. The border between Moribougou and Makandiambougou has never been drawn, for people attached to the two wards live intermingled at the border (attachment being more sociological than geographical), and it would be impossible to draw a line such that all those who are of Makandiambougou would be on one side, and all those of Moribougou on the other. In a transition from a social to a territorial basis of membership too many people would be obliged to "change" wards for the transition to be accomplished easily.

The identity of each ward was symbolized in the colonial period by each having a separate *dugu tigi* (village chief), who had some reasonable traditional claim to the post: the chief in Makandiambougou was a Keita, in Lenguékoto a Tounkara imported specially from the bush for the role, in Samédougou a Keita, in Moribougou a Cissé, in Ségoubougouni a Diallo. In Saint-Félix there is a tradition that the ward chief must come from a family that has known the Holy Ghost Fathers: in other words, there is a kind of pseudolineage, also connected with the settlement of the ward. Only in Kita-Gare is tradition so weak that a man was chosen on his technical qualifications alone (he is a public scribe and thus literate). These chiefs were not abolished when the municipal government was set up, though their attributions were much reduced (see below, chapter 5).

After the establishment of the municipality, when the villages were changed into wards, there were committees of the party in each ward, except that the two smallest, Lenguékoto and Samédougou, were fused. The existence of these committees, with their attendant youth organizations, women's organizations, Pioneers, and so on, tended to strengthen the ward bonds, for it made the ward a highly respectable and influential unit in Kita politics. People living in a ward belonged to the ward committee and had to operate through its leadership if they wanted to deal with higher levels (always in theory and often in practice). It became the practice in Kita to see that each ward had informal representation on the BPL: when no one from a ward was a regular member of the BPL, an observer was invited to attend meetings, though of course without the vote. The secretary-general of the ward and the other leading political figures largely replaced the ward/village chief as the main political representatives of the ward; indeed, it could even be argued that they were more effective in this task than the chief ever was. In 1965 the political and social importance of the wards was further increased by establishing the consumers' cooperatives on a ward basis. Thus the wards in Kita—and in other Malian towns—play a crucial role in administration and politics, a role which is recognized and utilized by the government.

The extent to which separate ward identities divide the unity of the town is, however, limited by the existence of many other kinds of ties that cut across ward boundaries. As the figures in table 4 show, the wards do not correspond in any way with ethnic affiliation. Only the two smallest wards have more than half their population from a single ethnic group. Nor do the wards correspond to the factions characteristic of Kita politics. There is a certain tendency for nonlocals and civil servants to be concentrated in Gare (railroad workers) and Ségoubougouni (clerks and administrators), but there are many nonlocals and many civil servants in other wards as well. Catholics are only characteristic of one ward. There are a host of other ties, such as school attendance, the home town of nonlocals, playing on the same football team, work, affinal links, and so on, to mitigate the effect of ward loyalties. This loyalty is but one kind of bond that can exist in Kita.

NATIVES AND NEWCOMERS

Cutting across the territorial division of the town into wards is a division based on the relative length of time that individuals and families have been present in Kita. There are three main groups: those present when the French arrived in 1880, those who arrived after 1880 but according to the traditional pattern (usually in the period from 1885 to 1905), and those who entered the community in the last two or three decades, but not according to the traditional pattern. Within each group, there are further differences of status derived from the circumstances of arrival. The distinctions among lineages present in Kita in 1880, for instance, were based on their roles in the myth of the founding of Kita and on other traditional social distinctions, such as castes, slavery, and so on.

The accepted pattern for entering a community is as a *dunan,* a stranger. To be a *dunan,* one must have a *diatigi,* a host. Thus all *dunan* are linked with a citizen of the town, and through him with the political and ritual chiefs. If a stranger stays in town long enough, he may come to have a voice in its councils; he understands local problems and knows who people are. He is then said to have become a *duguren,* someone who knows the country. His children will be *wuluden,* or natives. However, the memory of the original arrival as a stranger will be retained, and in relations between the descendants of the original stranger and those of the original host, the former will still be referred to as *dunan.* Thus a second or third generation Kitan will be considered a *dunan* in some contexts and a *wuluden* in others.

The Muslim merchants who settled in Kita between 1885 and 1905 followed this pattern. They had to find *diatigi,* and a chain of *diatigi-dunan* ties was created that led back to the "original" settlers of Kita. The first wave of merchants are known as *sogomadunan,* "morning strangers," while those who arrived a generation later are known as *wulafedunan,* "afternoon strangers." In the 1960s this distinction was particularly relevant in Moribougou, where the Cissé family were the *sogomadunan* and many of the other merchant families were *wulafedunan* who had the Cissé as *diatigi.* The Cissé liked to remind others that they were Cissé *dunan* and as such owed the Cissé deference; this claim was rejected by the *wulafedunan,* who felt that after three generations in Kita they should no longer be constrained by such customary obligations. This resentment was a major political theme in Kita.

Relations between townspeople and villagers are also channeled through the institution of the *diatigi.* Every villager has his *diatigi* in Kita, with whom he stays whenever he has occasion to visit the town. It is considered good manners to bring the *diatigi* a small present, although *nyamakala* sometimes take advantage of their position to omit this. If one does not have a present, then one should approach one's *diatigi* only through an intermediary. If the villager has business to transact and needs someone's help, he may call on his *diatigi* to act as intermediary and intercessor (see chapter 3). Not all villagers, however, choose their *diatigi* in Kita according to how helpful he may be. Some choose their *diatigi* among matrilateral relatives, affines, or simply friends. Some systematically avoid kinsmen as *diatigi*: others follow kin ties. A prominent Kitan, however, who has many affinal, consanguineous, or commercial ties in the villages, will tend to have many *dunan* from the villages, as people follow up on the links they have with this person.

Townspeople who visit a village, especially if they visit one regularly, also have a *diatigi* there, and normally their *diatigi* in the village is their *dunan* in Kita. Villagers who frequently visit another village have a *diatigi* there, too, unless it is a village where their patrilineal kin are the chiefly lineage, for there they are considered to be at home with no need of *diatigi*. In a looser sense, whomever one stays with or visits in a village is one's *diatigi;* habit transforms this into a more formal relationship.

In recent decades, movement into the town community has often occurred entirely outside traditional patterns. The type case is the civil servant, who comes to Kita because the government assigns him, but the same pattern is sometimes followed by merchants and craftsmen. The civil servants are not considered to have settled in Kita permanently (although some have been in Kita for twenty years or more and have taken local wives) and are not considered to have any stake in the community. They are the real *dunan,* known as *na,* or newcomers.

There are various ways in which newly arrived civil servants can integrate themselves into Kita life. The best way is to marry a local girl (having a wife already, as some do, is no hurdle in a polygynous society). This happens so frequently in Kita that one can almost state as a general rule that any civil servant assigned to Kita for four or five years will have at least one Kita wife. Kitans regard this as a natural and sometimes even a good thing: a civil servant with a local wife seems more subject to local control.[9] One can also participate in local activities such as theater and sports: a town will go to great lengths to retain a good football player or actor. Few officials, however, purchase house sites or build homes. This is felt to be a sign of intention to stay indefinitely, and people like the idea that powerful *na* are only transitory, even if they have been in Kita for twenty years. Out-of-town civil servants are in some ways restricted to the margin of town society. When a powerful *na*

9. In precolonial times a merchant who settled far from home frequently took a local wife. The drama comes when the merchant or the civil servant moves on. The old merchants often left their wives behind; with better communications and a different context for the marriage, the civil servants take them along.

married a local girl, that was taken to be an encouraging sign; but when he started to build a house people began to worry. Whether because of this or not, the wheels were shortly afterwards set in motion and he was reassigned. People pointed out that although the highest non-Kitan in the party hierarchy had lived and worked in Kita for twenty years, he had never built his own house there.

Most civil servants rent houses; here the link between the owner and the renter is commercial rather than ceremonial and strictly speaking the owner is not the *diatigi* of the out-of-town civil servant. But the word is still used in this context, and relations are usually friendly. The *diatigi* and his family may introduce the civil servant and his family into local society. Such a reinterpretation depends on the personalities of the people involved and seems more frequent among women (that is, between the *diatigi*'s wife and the civil servant's wife).

Those families present in the villages of Kita when the French arrived in 1880 can be considered "citizens" of Kita in the sense that their "right" to be in Kita is considered established without the existence of a *diatigi-dunan* tie. The first addition to the Maninka peasant base were the Muslim merchants; after these had been "naturalized," the group of "newcomers" began to grow. These three broad categories do not exhaust all the people living in Kita, but they cover most of them, and they are the main groups important for an understanding of Kita society. In recent politics, the first two groups, now all "citizens" and *wuluden,* have been opposed to the third, the "newcomers," as people complain that "the *na* run things in Kita." The clearest expression of this sentiment was the founding of a short-lived Kita Natives' Association in the late 1950s (see chapter 6). Here the symbolic distinction was between those who were born in Kita (usually extended to include the whole circle) and those born elsewhere. The demands of politics meant that a subtle system, with practically every individual a separate category, was reduced to a polarization between two extremes. This polarization was based on place of birth, itself a radical departure from the older system where it was the social group into which one was born that counted. Despite this polarization, the distinction between local and nonlocal birth was not absolute; the old emphasis on naturalization and the status of *duguren* continued to exist and to allow non-Kitans to participate effectively in Kita's politics.

Occupation

The metamorphosis of Kita from a series of peasant villages to a small Malian town has also involved shifts in the pattern of economic specialities. In precolonial Kita many locally consumed products were manufactured, but only some smiths and weavers were full-time artisans (Tellier 1898:218). Whatever other specialties people had, everyone was more or less a farmer. During Kita's growth in the late nineteenth century, a sizeable community of merchants came into town, and for the first time there were full-time specialists in administration—government clerks, African soldiers and policemen, and so on—and full-time wage laborers such as railroad workers. A number of new crafts sprang up around the new material culture (mechanics, drivers, tailors). Meanwhile, in the urban environment, the old crafts were able to provide a full-time living to their practitioners.

At present in Kita there are three categories of occupation with major social and political implications. First there are farmers; then there are those who make their living in the marketplace, both merchants and artisans; and finally there are those who work for a salary, which means to all intents and purposes those who work for the government in various capacities from the most menial to the most lofty.[10] Table 5 gives the numbers of heads of families in these three categories. Farmers, merchants, craftsmen, and religious figures with no other occupation are included in a single overarching category of the self-employed, in other words those who earn their living irregularly and from day to day. This category of the self-employed is contrasted with the government workers and other salaried workers, who know they will receive a set sum at the beginning of the month, and also with the unemployed, who are mostly elderly widows living alone.

The third column gives comparable figures for Bamako (Meillassoux 1968:25), a much more urban place, as is shown by the smaller percentage of farmers and the larger percentages of merchants and craftsmen on the one hand and salaried workers on the other. The figure for "unknown" under Bamako represents "no

10. Practically the only other employer in Kita is the Catholic church, which hires a few maintenance men and some Malian teachers. They are included as "government employees" because they too live from a regular salary. The few Europeans in town and some Malians had domestic servants, none of whom appear in the table as they were not heads of families.

TABLE 5
Occupation of Heads of Families in Kita (1965)

Occupation	Number in Kita	Percentage in Kita	Percentage in Bamako
Self-employed			
merchants	99	10.7	18.1
craftsmen	145	15.7	18.0
farmers	342	37.1	10.0
religious figures	5	.5	—
Total	591	64.0	46.1
Government employees	202	21.9	42.5
Unemployed	37	4.0	4.1
Unknown/no occupation	93	10.1	6.8
Grand total	923	100	99.5

occupation." The Bamako figures are for a sample of the total population, rather than just for heads of families.

At the apex of the civil service pyramid is the Commandant de Cercle; beneath him the various department heads ("chefs de service"); beneath them technicians, nurses, teachers, clerks, and so on. All these are in some sense white-collar workers who have had from six years of schooling to a year or two of university training. I have also included in the government employees category, however, all the more menial employees: mechanics, drivers, carpenters, foremen, railroad workers, janitors, guards. By and large, these people have little or no education; the mechanics are an exception.

The merchant category also includes people at various levels of prosperity, although by Malian standards there are no really big merchants in Kita. When a law was passed regulating commerce above a certain level in Mali, there was no merchant in Kita large enough to fall under the law's provisions. Many of these merchants conducted most of their business during the peanut trading season; they were severely hurt by the abolition of free trade in peanuts and most staple goods. The category includes small peddlers in the market, who have a table on which a few low-priced items are displayed, kola merchants, merchants with small shops ringing the market, who sell dry goods, kerosene, kitchen ware, and occasionally more imaginative items such as medicine and school supplies. It also includes the larger merchants who deal in peanuts and who by and large do not operate through a shop in the market.

The craftsmen include smiths, tailors, weavers, masons, leather-workers, mechanics, carpenters, barbers, bakers, jewellers, photographers, mattress makers, and so on. These are mostly people who work on their own account directly with their clients, although some of them are formed into associations. The masons formed a cooperative around 1961 in order to comply with a government preference for dealing with cooperatives in handing out work. They were disappointed in their efforts, for the government has given them practically no work to do despite the trouble and expense they went to in forming their cooperative. The weavers are mostly Fula from Diomboko (near Kayes) and are organized under the man among them who has been longest in Kita. He occasionally takes orders from townspeople and distributes them among the other weavers; usually, however, people deal directly with individual weavers. The leatherworkers are mostly Soninké from Nioro; they live in Gare and work in the marketplace. Sometimes they tour the villages looking for work in making amulets and repairing slippers. An old leatherworker from Nioro who has been in Kita for several decades claims to be their titular head. Few of the leatherworkers and weavers are counted among the 145 craftsmen listed in Kita for they have maintained their names on the rolls of their home towns, to which most of them frequently return.

There are a fair number of farmers residing in Kita, for there are fields in every direction within a few kilometers. Some of the names carried on the rolls of Kita actually represent individuals who live in bush hamlets. Other men listed as farmers are too old to farm actively, and would be better listed as "retired farmers," since their families are being supported by a son who is a merchant or a civil servant. There is a certain tendency for "farmer" to be a residual category, and thus to shade into the category of "unknown."

The figures given in the table only include the heads of families, and so there are many economically active men (and women) who are not included in it. There are some indications in the census material on which these figures are based as to the occupation of nonheads of family, but these indications are too fragmentary to be useful. The various suggestions that I gathered during my field work lead me to suspect that the figures underrepresent the total number of merchants, craftsmen, and junior civil servants, and overrepresent the number of farmers.

For political purposes the essential occupational distinction is between the salaried workers and merchants and craftsmen who work independently and depend on market conditions. Those in the latter group are slightly more numerous among heads of families (244 as against 202), but the true size of both groups is underrepresented. During the struggle against the colonial power, both merchants and government workers were largely on the side of the RDA. The merchants expected that they would benefit materially by taking over the commercial position of the French and Lebanese merchants. Most civil servants who supported the RDA were teachers. Clerical workers, especially those working directly under French administrators, tended to favor the PSP, as did some merchants. Thus the colonial period did not see a conflict between the two groups. This came only after independence when the civil servants tried to strengthen their grasp on the economy by putting it under state control and reducing the role of private merchants. The merchants resented this turn of events, recalling how much they had contributed in money and energy to the independence struggle; they pointed out that, without the credit they had extended to hardpressed civil servants during that period, the civil servants would have had a very hard time of things. Thus these two groups came into conflict: the merchants wanted a free, open market which would allow them to continue to make their living through commerce; the civil servants, if not in favor of a socialist state-run economy, were at least not economically threatened by it.

It is worth pointing out that the roles of the merchants and the civil servants in political life vary because of their different commitments to the community. In both cases, a political role is conceived of as coming after a man has already attained some stature in a different field. Thus anyone holding a relatively prominent government position (that is, department head) would expect to be chosen for some political post. The same was true of prosperous merchants. Which post they held depended on how long they had been in Kita, their background, their talents and ambition; but the problem was which, not whether. Both merchants and civil servants gained prestige from political participation.

But there were also differences between them. The civil servants, especially those of department-head status, were typically not native to Kita and furthermore were subject to reassignments and

promotions, so that it was never certain how long they would remain in Kita. In contrast, the merchants formed a relatively stable political field in which rivalries and alliances were frequent tactics. There was no question of a merchant being "parachuted" in to take a prominent political post, and there was no question of having a political situation suddenly upset by the reassignment elsewhere of one of its key figures. It was not surprising therefore that on the whole the merchants were concerned with Kita politics while the civil servants were concerned more with national or even international politics. The merchant was more likely to be committed to the community, for he would spend his whole life in it.

Prestige and status in contemporary Kita were linked to occupation. The hierarchy of government jobs provided a ready scale on which to gauge relative status, but the differences among merchants and artisans were no less clear. Malian parents appreciated that their children would achieve status through success on the occupational ladder, and so they were anxious for their children to be educated. The trend towards the importance of occupation was pronounced, and the high esteem in which the relatively clear-cut civil service careers were held means that young Malians were drifting away from the vaguer and more generalized occupations of merchant, transporter, and so on. This trend is bound to have political consequences in the future, as it changes the nature of the participation of the town's leading citizens in its politics and presumes a different economic basis for political involvement.

This chapter has been devoted to an exploration of the various categories that differentiated and grouped people in Kita. Ethnicity as a differentiating factor gave way to an urban consciousness as a unifying factor in the town; this process was reinforced by the development of Islam into a majority religion, for Islam provided the rituals and the rhetoric for town unity. Ward affiliation was the most important of the differentiating factors, yet the same emphasis on proximity of residence that made ward membership so strong a bond within Kita also served to strengthen Kita's unity in the national context. The community was also both divided and united by the line that was drawn between native-born and immigrant, a development from the old stress on order of arrival. Occupation was the principal means by which differential status was determined. None of these sources of identity and status, however, holds the answer to the kind of politics characteristic of Kita. Kita politics was not ward politics, or a conflict between merchants and civil servants, or an effort by the native-born to exclude immigrants from key political roles, although all these elements were present. Even less was it religious or ethnic politics. The essence of Kita politics lay in the kinds of interpersonal relations, in the procedures for mobilizing and channeling public opinion, in the shifting pattern of alliances and antagonisms, and in the contrast between different cultural interpretations of political reality. It also lay in the social organization of politics, that is, in the organization of the state, the party, and the cooperatives. The next chapter deals with this topic.

5

State
and
Party
in
Kita

The various ways in which Kita has been governed, the economic changes of the colonial period, and the emerging social structure of the town with its emphasis on occupation, residence, and birthplace formed the background against which the Malian government tried to introduce its new institutions. The major concern of the government was to cope with independence and the problems that arose from its socialist option. These problems included not only the day-to-day administration of the country and the attempt to initiate new programs and controls, but also that of coping with the intense political activity that reigned throughout the country. The two main tools that the new government disposed of were the administrative hierarchy which it had inherited from the colonial government and the party organization which it had itself developed during the fifteen years of struggle against the colonial régime. Both these institutions were expanded and adapted at the time of independence, when a pattern of cooperation replaced one of confrontation.

The administration and the party quickly became the warp and woof of Kita politics. The administration became ever more important in the lives of Kitans, both for what it could do or refuse to do, and because of the large number of Kitans who worked for it. If Kitans wanted to marry or divorce, buy or sell property, travel or communicate with friends and relatives elsewhere, they had to deal with some branch of the government. Kitans were passionately interested in the schools and the hospitals, and both were government institutions. At the same time, the party structure shifted rapidly from one oriented toward competition in the political arena to one acting as an effective instrument for local self-government. Everyone was brought into the party, at least in theory, and its meetings functioned like popular assemblies where all views could be heard. The number of offices available expanded considerably: some 211 individuals held 330 different posts (about 80 percent of the total) in the party, the cooperatives, the unions, and the sporting associations. Roughly one individual in forty—men, women, and children—in Kita held an elective post.

The leaders worked through these institutions to organize the application of policies from a higher level in Kita and to make local decisions without appealing to the higher level. As long as the leaders had a fair amount of popular support they were able to govern Kita and to mediate between the town and the higher levels of government. The hierarchies and posts that people competed for were in the institutions of state and party, and whatever the informal pressures might have been, the critical decisions in Kita were made by people who held these offices, in accordance with their by-laws and regulations. The state and the party were the institutions through which the center tried to push reforms, but they also provided the framework for popular government in Kita. This dual role was not without its complications.

The following description of state, party, cooperatives, and unions is of course relative to the period of 1964–65 when field work was carried out. The first substantial changes from the situation described here began in July, 1967, when the national-level party and government launched the Malian "cultural revolution" in response to a threat to the regime. Many individuals were purged, often in favor of younger men, and many institutions were changed or abolished at that time. Following the coup of November, 1968, what was left of the party structure was abolished. The description given here should be taken as a picture of a small Malian town and its institutions at a particular point in time. The point is not the institutions themselves but the uses that people were able to make of them and the ways in which they were viewed—the way, in short, in which a livable system had developed.

CIVIL ADMINISTRATION IN KITA: THE STATE

In 1920 there were twenty-eight civil servants in the circle of Kita, including the fourteen constables (*gardes-cercle*) who represented the military and punitive aspect of the administration. The others included eight involved in general administration (including the commandant), two teachers (both African; one in Kita and the other in Toukoto), a doctor with an African male nurse, and a French sergeant who served as a telegraphist, with an African clerk, for communications (GGAOF 1921:846). By 1965 there were perhaps ten times as many.[1] The big expansion was in technical personnel, from teachers and nurses to agricultural agents and cooperative agents. There were still about a dozen constables, but they had been supplemented by a dozen policemen and a half-dozen gendarmes. The number of people directly concerned with administration in the strict sense had barely risen.

The state, through its bureaucracy, was concerned with providing general administrative services to the population (census rolls, issuance of permits and affidavits of various sorts, tax collection, performance of civil marriages, organization of the peanut-trading season, and so on), with maintaining law and order and justice, with promoting the well-being of the population (schools and hospitals), with favoring economic development (especially with regard to raising peanut production). The personnel manning the bureaucracy at the higher levels tended not to be natives of Kita, while the clerical and subordinate personnel were mostly Kitan. The state was the arm of the central government in Kita; although most of the civil servants' work was done from day to day and was responsive to local conditions, changes in policy and practice were initiated by orders sent down from above. The central government also occasionally expanded the bureaucracy in Kita: a people's pharmacy was created in 1965, as the Somiex had been around 1963 and the municipality itself in 1959.

The state was represented in Kita by the officers of the general administration and by the special services (see figure 2). The symbol of the central government in Kita was the commandant de cercle (the administrator), who supervised all the activities sponsored by

---

1. Actually the 1920 figures include no railroad workers, although some must have been present then. Today they form a large portion of the government workers.

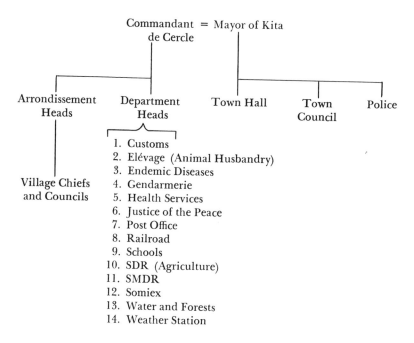

FIGURE 2. ORGANIZATION OF THE STATE IN KITA (1965)

the state in the circle. He was responsible for law and order, for security, for coordinating the efforts of the agencies concerned with economic development. He was simultaneously the mayor of Kita and an ex-officio member of the local political bureau. His office in the circle office building was the scene of many of the important decisions affecting the circle. His symbolic importance was recognized in various ways: when he was asked to lead a Muslim prayer or when he called on the imam at Ramadhan and 'Id el-Adha; when the *dieli* came to "greet" him on feast days; when he was given a prominent seat at a public meeting or sat front row center at a theatrical performance.

The commandant had under him the heads of the territorial subdivisions within the circle—the arrondissements; and the heads of the specialized agencies—the department heads. His deputy doubled as the "chef d'arrondissement" for the rural areas around the town of Kita and was also an ex-officio member of the section's BPL. The chefs d'arrondissement had general administrative responsibilities; they were the replica of the commandant at a lower level.

The department heads were concerned with specialized problems. Their responsibilities in most cases covered the entire circle, but their offices were in Kita town. Some picture of the activities of the state in Kita may be gained from the following list of specialized agencies:

1. Concerned with general administration: the post office; the weather station; the police (for the municipality); the gendarmerie (for the rural areas); and the justice of the peace.

2. Concerned with the welfare of the people: the hospital, with its maternity ward and rural dispensaries; the schools, under the senior headmaster in Kita.

3. Concerned with economic development: The Somiex (Société Malienne pour l'Importation et l'Exportation), concerned with the export of Kita's peanuts and the import of those products over which it had a monopoly at a wholesale level; the SMDR (Société Mutuelle pour le Développement Rural), concerned with financing and supplying rural cooperatives and organizing the marketing of peanuts through the cooperatives; the SDR (Service du Développement Rural), concerned with improving agricultural production and organizing cooperatives; Elévage (the Livestock Service), concerned with improving cattle and preventing bovine diseases; and the Eaux-et-Forêts (Water and Forestry Agency), concerned with protecting reserved forests.

MUNICIPAL ORGANIZATION

The commandant was also ex-officio mayor of Kita since Kita was a "commune de moyen exercice" (partly self-governing commune) [2] and was under the tutelage of the administration. The town was governed by an elected town council of twenty-three members. The people elected to the town council elected two assistant mayors from within their number. The daily business of the municipality was run by the town clerk (secrétaire de mairie) who had a staff of clerical workers under him. The town clerk took most of his orders from the commandant and worked closely with him. The main

---

2. Kita became a fully self-governing commune ("commune de plein exercice") in 1966. The major change was that the commandant de cercle was replaced by an elected mayor at the head of the municipality.

tasks of the municipal government were to keep the census records and collect head taxes from those who owed them, issue legal documents, perform civil marriages, run the market and collect market fees from traders, and oversee the maintenance of streets, bridges, and other public facilities.

The town council in office during my field work was the first one elected, in 1959. It was elected after the fusion of the PSP with the RDA and contained some of the leading PSP members. It was generally speaking a council of notables and contained a high proportion of illiterate merchants in addition to farmers who came from traditionally important families in Kita (see table 6). It seldom met; most of the tasks that it might have done were in fact done by Kita's political bureau (see below) or by specialized commissions, such as the Commission du Lotissement which was concerned with allotting building sites in the town. It was legally required to approve the town budget, however, and met at least once a year for this purpose. Most of the important members of the town council were also members of the political bureau: nine members of the 1959 town council were also on the 1962 political bureau, and nine members of the new 1966 town council were also on the 1965 political bureau. There seemed to be a greater reluctance to elect non-Kitans to the town council than to the political bureau, perhaps because of the more restricted geographical scope of the council's power.

The police were technically concerned with maintaining law and order in the town, but in practice they extended their influence far beyond the town's boundaries. In 1964–65 the police were the major means by which the commandant-mayor controlled many aspects of life in Kita. At one point, before the opening of the consumers' cooperatives, the police had the responsibility of giving people permission to buy scarce foods, such as rice. The police chief was also the man who knew who had a house to rent; he operated an informal labor market; he ran a garage on the open space next to the police station, complete with welding tools to repair the trucks used to bring peanuts in from the bush; he gave permission for the trucks commandeered for the peanut harvest from other parts of Mali to return home from Kita. The police chief also acted as an informal go-between for the two factions at the height of their struggle in 1963 (see chapter 6) —at the same time collecting information for the state on what the leaders were up to. The police had

TABLE 6

ANALYSIS OF THE MEMBERSHIP OF BPL, BEJ, AND TWO TOWN COUNCILS

	1965 BPL	1961 BEJ	1959 TC	1966 TC
Decade of Birth				
1890s	—	—	3	—
1900s	3	—	8	2
1910s	4	—	5	6
1920s	9	8	6	12
1930s	2	9	—	2
??	—	—	1	1
Occupation				
government employed	14	14	8	17
self-employed	4	3	15	6
Local Origin				
local	14	13	19	21
nonlocal	4	4	4	2
Ethnic Affiliation				
Maninka	8	7	12	11
Fula	4	5	4	5
Soninka	—	2	2	2
Bamana	3	—	1	1
other	3	3	3	3
unknown	—	—	1	1
Ward				
Kita-Gare	—	—	—	3
Lenguékoto	1	1	—	3
Makandiambougou	7	2	8	4
Moribougou	5	4	7	8
Saint-Félix	1	2	1	—
Samédougou	—	—	1	—
Segoubougouni	4	8	6	5
Total	18	17	23	23

The 1965 BPL represents the 1962 BPL as reorganized in September 1965 to compensate for those who had left town or been suspended from the party.

The 1961 BEJ was chosen "temporarily" in April, 1961, but has been kept up to strength since then through co-option.

The 1959 town council was the one in office during field work. The 1966 town council was elected in June, 1966, the first with Kita as a "commune de plein exercice."

also become an authority to which people would appeal in their personal quarrels: some people would bring complaints against their neighbors, if they were quarrelling with them, in the hopes of being found right by the police. Many cases were arbitrated by the police chief and never reached the judge (see chapter 8). The police had completely eclipsed the gendarmerie and made numerous forays into the countryside.

The municipality had its own budget. The main sources of income were the market taxes and a share of the head taxes paid by Kita residents. In addition, it got some money from fines levied by the police for not having a bicycle license, for having allowed one's cow to get into someone else's garden, and so on. As money from these sources was insufficient to meet the needs of the municipality, the central government usually offered a subsidy. The town authorities complained that they had fewer sources of income than other municipalities in Mali, largely because there was no through truck or collective-taxi traffic on which fees could be levied. Whatever the cause the municipality was notoriously impecunious. One year they had to do without the state subsidy, and the only way in which the municipality could meet its bills was by being particularly severe on a whole series of minor offenses (like allowing cattle to stray) in order to pay salaries from the fines gathered. This worked until people began to complain of the harassment, but by that time the financial worst was over.

Each ward had a chief, a holdover from the days when the wards were considered to be villages in the administrative hierarchy. The ward chiefs were in a somewhat anomalous position as they were not really recognized by the town government although they were used by it, particularly in the collection of the head tax. The chiefs holding office in Kita in 1965 had all been in office since at least 1959, so the problem of succession under the new regime had not come up. The chiefs had symbolic importance in their wards, especially in life-crisis rites. They were always informed of naming ceremonies, marriages, circumcisions, and funerals, and often attended them. Their chief material reward was a rebate on the head taxes collected in their wards. This was originally a percentage but in later years tended to be a set sum. The chief of one of the smaller wards received 6,000 Malian francs ($24) in 1965, as against 7,500 Malian francs ($30) in 1963. The service they performed to merit this payment was to inform residents of their wards that the time for the annual payment had come. Presumably this enabled the government to reach some people it could not reach through the institution of public meetings, which the less sophisticated, more marginal heads of family might not attend. My impression was that ward chiefs took this aspect of their post quite seriously; it was, after all, one of the rare ways in which their position in society was reinforced. The ward chiefs were originally the same as the village chiefs still present in every village (they are referred to by the same word in Maninka: *dugu tigi*) but they were caught up in the municipality of Kita and had to deal with a population more sophisticated than in the rural areas and frequently more sophisticated than themselves. The municipality officials seemed embarrassed by their presence and would probably have preferred to do without them.

The Party—I: The Section

The party section corresponded to the circle, just as the subsection corresponded to the arrondissement and the committee to the village or the ward (see figures 3 and 4). The Kita section of the RDA covered the 135,000 inhabitants of the circle of Kita. The section's political bureau (usually known as the "Bureau Politique Local" or BPL) had its seat in Kita town, and all its members were normally resident there. The importance of Kita town in the circle was thereby symbolized. The BPL in fact frequently functioned as

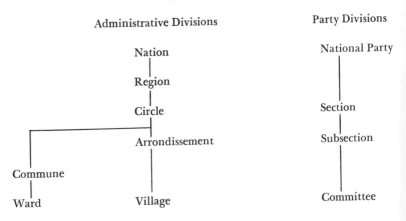

FIGURE 3. PARALLELS BETWEEN THE ORGANIZATION OF STATE AND PARTY IN MALI (1965)

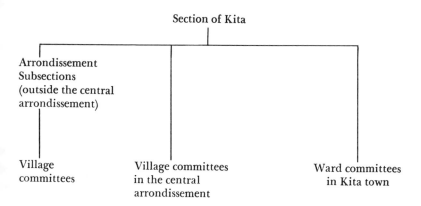

FIGURE 4. THE SECTION OF KITA (1965)

the central political body for the town, as though the BPL were chosen only by the townspeople of Kita through their committees, and as though Kita's preeminence in the circle were a natural consequence of its being the main town of the circle, the seat of the state apparatus. There was also a practical reason for the absence of any delegates from elsewhere in the circle on the BPL: the difficulty in participating in the BPL's work without living in Kita. An attempt was made to remedy this situation at the 1962 Conference by creating a steering committee ("Comité Directeur") including the BPL and two delegates from each of the five subsections plus four from the central arrondissement, which did not have a subsection; but this committee met much less frequently than the BPL, and the bulk of the decisions were still made by the BPL acting alone.

The BPL was responsible for the entire circle and supervised the work of the five subsections outside the central arrondissements, but we shall mainly be concerned with analyzing its role and activity in the town of Kita. The BPL effectively replaced the town council as the chief representative body for the town. This was due to the duplication of responsibility between the two bodies, to the fact that the most important politicians were members of both, and especially to the place of the BPL in the direct line of the party hierarchy. The members of the RPL were the people with the greatest political influence in Kita town, and all the important questions and quarrels affecting the town were usually raised in BPL meetings. The BPL discussed the programs proposed by the national party and state for implementation in Kita and could modify them. It acted as a buffer between the people of Kita and the national government.

Members of the BPL frequently toured the countryside. This brought them into contact with the political leaders who had posts on the political bureaus of the subsections as well as with the peasants. Some members of the BPL "specialized" in certain rural areas, with which they often had some kind of kin tie (that is, they themselves, their mothers or their wives were from the areas in question) : they were always on any delegation to visit that area. This gave the BPL members a chance to appeal for support in rural areas and subsection bureaus as well as in Kita, and this was useful when a new bureau was chosen by a conference. The contact with wide sections of the population also gave them an advantage over people not on the BPL whose jobs kept them in Kita. Thus, while the BPL members were all Kita residents and while they often functioned as though it were Kita town alone that concerned them, they also made decisions affecting the rest of the circle, and their political positions as members of the BPL were reinforced by the support they had from rural areas and subsection bureau members.

The BPL met once a week under normal conditions (rarely less often, occasionally more often) for several hours. Although I was unable to attend any meetings, my impression is that discussion of the problems raised was fairly open and frank and that decisions were reached by consensus. The meetings were chaired by the secretary-general, if he were present, or by the next man in line if he were not. Minutes of the meeting were forwarded to the national party in Bamako. If any question was to be discussed which would require the presence of anyone not on the bureau, that person was invited to attend—for the discussion of that question. The police chief was often invited, and the secretaries-general of the committees in Kita's wards were invited when the BPL was discussing some matter affecting the town especially. Otherwise, the BPL preferred to keep its deliberations secret.[3]

The section had a headquarters, situated in a building near the market in the center of Kita. There was a small permanent staff, consisting of a typist or two and a permanent secretary whose job it

---

3. At least in theory. There were in fact frequently people, including young boys, hanging around outside the meeting room.

was to provide continuity in the application of decisions in the absence of the secretary-general. The permanent secretary had the right to attend BPL meetings. The secretary-general was also usually present in this office, when he was not in Bamako (he was also a deputy) or touring the circle.

The main source of the section's income was from the sale of party membership cards. The money collected from this sale was divided between the various levels of the party according to a fixed schedule, with the higher levels getting a larger share. Party cards were sold through the committees. The usual method in the town of Kita was to make the committee buy the cards, which it could then resell to individuals. In this way, even if all the party cards were not sold, the party maintained its level of income. In the rural areas of the central arrondissement, which were directly under the authority of the BPL since there was no subsection, the people were assessed for their cards at the same time that they paid their taxes. I estimate that the section had a theoretical income on the order of 2.5 million Malian francs ($10,000) from this source.[4]

The main expenditures of the section were to finance travel by its delegations in going to and from Bamako and while touring the bush; to support official visitors, both high-level delegations from Bamako and low-level delegations from the bush; and to organize the conference theoretically held every three years. The section had to purchase stationery and other minor items and pay the salary of the permanent secretary and the typists. A major crisis struck the section's treasury when President Modibo Keita visited Kita in April, 1964; the total cost was established at 600,000 francs ($2,400) and that ran the section's treasury so dry that it had to call on the committees for help. The periodic conferences were another potential drain on the section's resources; real or fictitious lack of funds was often given as a reason for not holding the conference on schedule. Other expenditures included a gift of 100,000 francs ($400) to the victims of a flood in central Mali and support given to Kita's theatrical troupe and to the fair organized in Kita in February, 1965.

4. This assumes that 100,000 people out of a population of 135,000 bought cards; the figure was probably less. Children under eight years were not liable. The card cost fifty francs, which was divided as follows: 20 francs to the national party organization, fifteen to the section, ten to the subsection, and five to the committee. In Kita there was no subsection, and that share was taken by the section, so that the section got twenty-five francs for every card placed.

There were no mass party meetings for the entire section. When the 1962 conference was held, each committee sent a delegate to Kita to participate. On other occasions the BPL expanded itself to include delegates of the subsections and of Kita's committees, thereby becoming more representative. While people might participate directly in the committee, they could only participate in the section through representatives.

Meetings were occasionally held for the people of Kita town, to which all were invited (see chapter 8). These were called "information meetings." Their organization was very similar to the general assemblies in the committees except that they were considered to be ad hoc and so were not qualified to make decisions. Such meetings were called on occasions when the BPL had something to communicate to the population (an analysis of a new law, a visit from a Bamako delegation, an announcement that new men had been coopted into the BPL, and the like) and preferred to do so directly rather than through the committee general assemblies. These meetings were in fact treated as general assemblies for the town, and one of their main functions was to allow people to raise new issues or to express their sentiments in public once the main issues on the agenda had been dealt with. Five such meetings were held between April and October, 1965, and they seemed to fill a real gap in the town's political organization.

The BPL in office in 1964–65 was chosen at a conference held in the summer of 1962 (see chapter 6). The conference had three parts. First, the outgoing officers reported to the conference on their activities. Then there were questions and discussions from the floor, led mainly by people who hoped to remove the outgoing secretary-general from office. Finally, eagerly awaited, was the choice of the new BPL members. This was not done by the conference as a whole, but by a selected group consisting of members of the Bamako delegation, the members of the outgoing BPL, and delegates chosen from among others on a regional basis (one for each arrondissement, and weighted representation for the town of Kita). Retiring to the Kita equivalent of the smoke-filled room, this group chose a single slate of nominees. This slate was presented to the conference, which approved it by acclamation.

By the summer of 1965, attrition due to reassignments elsewhere and suspensions from the party had reduced the number of

BPL members to the point where a quorum was almost impossible to obtain, and so five old members were dropped while six new ones were coopted into the BPL. The members of both the old and the new BPL represented a wide cross-section of the population. There were more local-born than foreigners, more civil servants than self-employed, and more affiliated with the Maninka ethnic group than with others, though the proportion was roughly equal to the proportion in the general population (see tables 3 and 6). The average age of the bureau members chosen in 1962 was 43.8 years at that time; in 1965, after the new replacements, the average age was 44.4 years. The number of civil servants was striking, particularly if we consider that six persons had posts at the department-head level. The high degree of interlocking between the top level of the party and the top level of the adminstration was reinforced by the ex officio status on the BPL of the commandant and his deputy.

THE PARTY—II: THE YOUTH

The affairs of the young people in the section of Kita were handled by a separate bureau, the Bureau Exécutif de la Jeunesse (BEJ). Just as all people in the section were presumed to be party members, so all young people in the section were presumed to be youth members. The levels of the youth organization and its bureaus paralleled exactly the levels of the senior party organization. The section BEJ was subordinated to the section BPL on the one hand and to the national BEJ on the other. Until 1962 the youth movement functioned as an entirely autonomous organization, which is to say that in Kita the BEJ was independent of any formal supervision by the BPL. In 1962 a national party congress decided to establish formal institutional links between the two. The BPL was to include a member whose job was liaison with the youth, and who was thus ex officio entitled to attend BEJ meetings (in fact, he held another post on the BEJ and would have attended the meetings anyway). There were four others who held posts on both bureaus, most notably the secretary-general of the youth, who was the organization secretary (third in rank) of the BPL.

The BEJ ran programs of concern to the young people. These included the militia, which was a supplement to the military in time of war, the Brigade de Vigilance which acted as a supplement to the police force at night, the Pioneer movement for schoolchildren, and the theatrical troupe. The BEJ also had an interest in sports, although football, the main sport in question, was the concern of a special body, the Kita district of the football league (see below).

The militia was originally formed in 1960 when it was thought that Mali might be invaded after the break with Senegal. There were at that time both a men's and a women's militia; training consisted of physical training and drill, led by veterans of the French army. The chief function of the militia in 1964–65 was to march in parades.

The Brigade de Vigilance (BV) was an organization of the young men which patrolled the streets of the town from midnight to five A.M. every night to prevent crime, immorality, and subversion. The members were organized on a ward basis and patrolled mostly in their own wards. In the beginning all the young men took part, and there was a certain rivalry between the wards concerning their efficiency. But gradually the more sophisticated of the young men got tired of it, and so most of the participants were men marginal to Kita society who felt they could attain a certain status in society by being in the Brigade de Vigilance. In one of the larger wards of Kita there were supposed to be a total of 49 BV members, divided into seven teams of seven men each, one team for each night of the week. Each night the duty team would split into three pairs to patrol the streets, and the seventh man was a supervisor. They also marched in parades. When the Brigade was reorganized in 1965 the ward basis was temporarily put aside and the group was organized on a Kita-wide basis. At this time also, the BV members were made especially eligble for any new jobs that would become available in Kita (see chapter 8).

A brigadier's life was not a happy one, however, and they were constantly being criticized in their committee youth meetings for leaving their posts, going to sleep, and being rude to people. Special procedures had to be established to guide BV members who found someone abroad after midnight; they must greet him, for example, before asking for his papers.

In the early days people felt that the BV served a useful purpose in reducing nighttime crime, but gradually a certain amount of popular irritation developed since the aspect of its activities which affected most people was the puritanical, anti-immorality effect it had, rather than the prevention of crime or subversion.[5] The BV members themselves felt that their sacrifice of time and sleep was only worthwhile if there were tangible results, which meant people arrested and fined or jailed, and consequently would have liked to be a lot stricter than the political leaders would allow them to be. For instance, in a burst of enthusiasm they examined the baggage and papers of the passengers taking the early morning train to Bamako, inconveniencing the passengers and provoking some political reaction from them. The BPL put a stop to this practice. In another case, some BV members stopped a man late at night. An altercation developed when he would not show his papers right away, and he eventually hit one of the patrol. The BV members insisted that he be punished, but the BPL refused to allow it. As far as the BV members were concerned this was adding insult to injury, for it implied that their version was not believed, and they refused to continue their patrolling until the BPL settled the matter to their satisfaction (see chapter 8).

The Pioneers formed the children's branch of the youth organization. Both sexes belonged and the children between eight and sixteen were organized into three classes according to age. They were usually organized from the base provided by the schools, where the children were already grouped together. Their leaders were mostly young men between sixteen and twenty-five years old and were mainly teachers and older pupils. The Pioneers were plagued by the lack of any concrete set of activities. They were most successful when operating within a competitive framework, setting children of one ward against those of another, or those of Kita against those from other towns. Both football and theater, organized in this way, were successful. Ideally the leaders would have liked to include scout-type activities such as hikes and crafts in their program, but they were hampered by lack of transportation, lack of materials for crafts, uncertainty as to procedure, bad leadership, but above all by the reluctance of many parents to allow their children to participate in the Pioneers. Parents argued that Pioneer activities interfered with studies, and caused their children to fail their courses. They also objected to purchasing the uniforms that Pioneers were supposed to have. Parents of girls were anxious, not

---

5. The subversion in question was against the nation. No one tried to use the BV members for quarrels internal to Kita, for the balance was too delicate.

without some justification, about the integrity of male Pioneer leaders.

The theatrical troupe of Kita presented plays, skits, songs and dances, usually in competition with a troupe representing a different section (cf. Hopkins 1965). Yearly competitions were organized on a nationwide basis. The actors and dancers were chosen from the entire circle, but most were from Kita town as it was difficult to find people from elsewhere willing to leave home for such long periods of time; when they were able to, they presented special problems to the BEJ authorities in Kita. The actors and dancers spent a great deal of time rehearsing, often until midnight five nights a week. When the theatrical troupe performed against other sections' troupes, Kitans took a great and emotional interest in its success: the troupe symbolized Kita's identity as against other towns, and victory was important to Kita's self-esteem.

The Kita football district was formed of representatives of all the football clubs in the circle, including the two in Kita. As with the political bureaus, all the football bureau members except the club delegates were resident in Kita. The president of the football district was also the BEJ secretary-general, and three other persons had posts on both the district bureau and the BEJ bureau.

Like the theatrical troupe, Kita's football teams symbolized the town when competing against outside teams. The greater part of the Establishment turned out for major football games; and popular feeling often ran so high that a visiting team might count itself lucky to leave town in one piece. The more important of the two football teams in Kita, the Union Sportive de Kita (USK), was founded in 1952 by a group of young men, mostly associated with the RDA. The leader of this group was the BEJ secretary-general and district president in 1965. The other team, Amicale, was actually older but had had a more checkered career. It recruited most of its players from among civil servants, who were liable to transfer, while the USK as a matter of policy tried to form the nucleus of its team from tailors, craftsmen, mechanics, and others in order to ensure continuity. Periodically people suggested that the two be fused, but the idea was always rejected on the grounds that having competition between the two was beneficial to Kita football. This did not prevent all-Kita teams from playing against special visitors. Both USK and Amicale operated as sporting clubs, with as much emphasis on the club as on the sport. They sponsored dances to raise money to cover their football expenses (uniforms, balls, boots, travel, hospitality for visiting teams). They also on occasion lent money to their members, particularly if the reason for which the latter needed money was to pay bride wealth.[6] Their members had their favorite meeting places: for USK, a tailor shop just off Kita's market. Thus they functioned like some of the voluntary associations mentioned by Little (1965) and Meillassoux (1968).

Apart from football, the other recently introduced sports of basketball, handball, and track and field were the concern of the BEJ. These sports were the subject of interest to the National Youth Commission, which was trying to develop them; and the BEJ appointed people to develop teams in these sports.

In all these special activities, the BEJ was concerned first of all with Kita town. These activities were carried on to some extent in the arrondissements where the subsection youth bureaus supervised them, but were hardly present in the rural villages of the central arrondissement. The teams and troupes which Kita's BEJ developed in the town were taken to represent the section as a whole.

The BEJ did not serve as a political forum to anything like the extent that the BPL did. Its decisions only affected the internal organization of the youth or settled quarrels that arose while carrying out youth activities. Many of the activities described above (militia, BV) were actually carried out on behalf of the BPL, and in times of crisis the BPL dealt with them directly. This happened in 1965 when the BPL negotiated directly with the BV for a resumption of its activity after the interruption referred to. The BEJ maintained the same kind of communication system with the subsections and committees under its jurisdiction that the BPL did, but it used it a great deal less. Partly this was because it was less active as a bureau, not dealing so much with substantive issues, and partly, especially inside the town, because the BEJ tended to deal with youth affairs for Kita town itself, without calling on the youth committees in the wards. The BEJ met weekly in the Centre d'Education Populaire, but had trouble making a quorum because of the many absent members. The youth held no general assemblies,

6. On one occasion, just as a young member of one of the clubs was about to be married in the Town Hall, another man telephoned from Bamako to say that he had paid bride wealth for the girl and he would only relinquish his claim if he were reimbursed. Fellow club members came to the would-be groom's aid, and the money was raised in less than a day.

though many nonmembers attended the BEJ meetings which were the chief institution through which youth affairs were run. The relative inactivity of the youth was due partly to some factors inherent in the situation, such as the plethora of other organized activity and its lack of any political influence in Kita, and partly to the personality of the leaders.

The main sources of revenue for the BEJ were more varied than for the BPL. No membership cards for the youth were sold; the feeling was that the general party membership card was enough. Nor were dues collected, although the monthly rate was officially reduced from fifty to twenty-five francs (twenty to ten cents). But the youth had other sources of income. They were given the management of the Centre d'Education Populaire, a hall used for dances, meetings, and plays, and derived some money from the occasions when the hall was used for events for which admission was charged. If there were a dance, the BEJ paid the orchestra an agreed sum and kept the balance of the admission money. Money paid for admission to theater performances was also divided between the theater troupe (which needed it for costumes, travel, stage sets, and the like) and the BEJ. The BEJ also sponsored football games, and derived some money from that, although they were not the only ones to do so. The BEJ also derived some income from renting the chairs belonging to the Centre d'Education Populaire at twenty-five francs each to private persons who wanted them to seat guests at naming ceremonies, marriages, and so on, but this was often short-circuited by the practice of "lending" them to people connected with BEJ members.

The expenditures of the BEJ were the usual ones for upkeep (stationery, travel, hospitality offered to guests), plus the support granted to the theatrical troupe (which evidently required a great deal of money) and the occasional use of BEJ money to buy uniforms for Pioneers, BV members, and so on. The uniforms were bought because the leaders were anxious to have marchers appear well-dressed at parades on Independence Day and other occasions; they used party money to buy uniforms for people who could not or had not bought them for themselves. The resulting lack of money in the treasury to pay the expenses of a section youth conference was given as the reason for the delay in renewing the BEJ.

The BEJ in office during my field work was chosen provisionally in April, 1961; in other words, it was named from above. It consisted of seventeen members, each occupying a ranked post with a specific job attached to it, just as in all the bureaus. After the BEJ's original formation, many vacancies opened up, caused by the departure of its members for new posts, and the BEJ typically filled these vacancies by cooptation, using the procedure more extensively than the BPL. I do not know what proportion of the 1965 Youth Bureau were original members, but, of the list given to me in 1965, four had arrived in Kita since 1962 and three others were permanently absent from Kita (including one who had himself been coopted into the bureau after 1962). The turnover was high. Kita's youth criticized the BEJ because it had been temporary for so long—it had never been properly elected—and because so many of its members had been coopted.[7] The exact membership of the BEJ seemed to be somewhat fluid; young men new in Kita were incorporated into the bureau if they struck the fancy of the secretary-general and if there were a need to involve more people in the BEJ's work.

The breakdown of the BEJ by age (see table 6) shows that almost half its members were over thirty-five, and all were over twenty-five. The average age was 33.9 years. The secretary-general himself was forty-one in 1965. There was also a concentration of BEJ members (eight out of seventeen) in Ségoubougouni, which was the home ward of the BEJ's secretary-general and where many of the younger civil servants lived. Otherwise, the BEJ had the same importance of government workers and locally born that the other bureaus did, and the ethnic distribution followed that of the general population.

The age question was part of the reason why there was so much delay in electing a new BEJ. The secretary-general, being over age, should have retired. As he had reasons for not wanting to, he used all the influence of his position to prevent renewal. In theory, after the 1962 national reorganization the youth had a maximum age limit of twenty-five years. All the members of the BEJ were overage by that standard (and so, for that matter, were the secretaries-general of the youth committees in the wards). This discrepancy did not indicate any perversity on the part of the Kitans, but the fact that the age limit of twenty-five was unrealistic. The ages

7. These were among the causes of the outburst against the youth leadership in front of a BPN delegation; see chapter 8.

that were regarded as appropriate for youth group membership were roughly the same as those considered appropriate in the youth associations prevalent in villages throughout the Western Sudan (cf. Leynaud 1966: 52). Until one is a *tiekoroba* (a fully mature man) one is a *demisenu* (a youth, post-circumcision), and the transition from one to the other occurs normally at around thirty-five or forty years of age. The transition is also voluntary: no one can be obliged to stop considering himself a *demisenu*. Considering the number of young men in their late twenties and early thirties who considered themselves to be *demisenu*, it was inconceivable that someone under the age of twenty-five could become their leader. Once in scanning the town with an informant for possible candidates under the age of twenty-five, it proved impossible even to name a reasonably well known and well thought-of man under twenty-five who might become BEJ secretary-general.

In conclusion, the youth acted less as a political pressure group, or as a forum for making political decisions, than as an association of young men concerned with organizing their leisure-time activities: theater, sports, dancing. The bulk of the activity of the youth was with the special projects listed above, especially the theater and football. There was some attempt to use the youth as a police or militia force (a role the traditional youth often played and still does play in the villages), but this ran into the problem that the political leaders refused to accept the popular discontent arising from what the young men did when acting in this role. A young man interested in politics and with the qualifications to make him a possibility would get involved not in the youth movement, but in the regular party movement, where many of the participants and leaders were no older than the youth leaders. (When there was a short-lived subsection for the central arrondissement in 1963, the youth secretary-general was older than the political bureau's secretary-general!)

The Party—III: The Committee

The residents of each of Kita's wards formed a committee in the party organization, except for the two smallest which were fused into a single committee. The committees of Kita town were directly under the authority of the section BPL. All residents of a ward were members of its committee. The committee organization consisted of a political bureau for the entire committee, a youth bureau, and a women's bureau. The political bureau acted as the executive for the committee, which met frequently in the form of a general assembly which all members could attend. The political bureau and the general assembly were the chief institutions through which ward residents participated in the government of their ward.

The general assembly *(laje)* was a meeting which any ward resident was eligible to attend, and which therefore, in the eyes of the people, could make decisions binding on the ward as a whole. The political bureau, and especially the secretary-general, applied these decisions, acting on behalf of the committee. The secretary-general and the political bureau were also the link connecting the mass of people in the ward with the higher political leadership as represented by the BPL. Communication along this chain tended to be mostly in a downward direction. Decisions made in the BPL's weekly meeting were passed to the committee bureau for application. The committee bureau received the instructions; if they required communal action the matter was brought up in a general assembly. The general assembly knew it could not reverse the decision, at least not directly, but it could and did discuss the mode of application. Then the secretary-general was able to take the necessary steps to apply the decision.

In two of the committees, meetings followed a regular schedule—every week or every other week depending on how much work needed to be done. In those committees where a regular schedule was not followed, meetings of the political bureau and general assemblies were called by the secretary-general when there was a matter to discuss (usually a matter sent to them by the BPL). Meetings of the political bureau were followed in most cases by a general assembly where the secretary-general of the bureau and the other members presented to the people of the ward (the committee members) the questions under discussion. I estimate that in wards not following a regular schedule, the political bureau and the general assembly met at least once a month, more frequently when there was a major problem such as the organization of the consumers' cooperatives to discuss and less frequently during quiet periods. Each ward had a regular place where it held its bureau meetings and one where the general assembly met.

There was some variation among the wards in the matter of attendance. One informant estimated that in his ward one person in twenty attended the general assembly. In another ward those who attended the general assembly were mostly the heads of families plus any others who were interested (the "militants"). A third committee made a special effort to have women attend the general assembly—in fact, its leaders boasted of this—while in other wards only one or two women attended regularly and acted in effect as liaison between the general assembly of men on the one hand and the ward's women on the other.

Committee general assemblies were usually announced during the day by a town crier who circulated in the ward, attracting attention by beating a drum and then making the announcement. People came after they had finished their evening meal and relaxed a little. Formally the meeting was set for 9 P.M.; in fact, people's tardiness often caused it to start later, and leaders (who often had several meetings of different bureaus every week) complained about the waste of time. Political bureau meetings also started at 9 P.M. and were announced by word of mouth or by means of a typed or written circular which members were required to initial to show that it had reached them.

The general assemblies were a forum where new projects were put to the people by members of the political bureau. The people then discussed these projects and decided how they should organize themselves. Here is an example. One of the committees was supposed to build an isolation ward for people with contagious diseases. The BPL instructed the committee political bureau to arrange to have it built using *fasobara* (human investment). After discussing the project, the political bureau then brought the matter up in a general assembly. Several courses of action were suggested in the general assembly. Some suggested that the profits from the ward's consumers' cooperative be used to hire masons; others wanted each person to contribute a certain sum to hire masons; and others felt that the isolation ward should be built by *fasobara* so that no money need be expended. The general assembly eventually developed a consensus in favor of the second alternative.

The general assemblies also served as a forum where people could raise new issues. Most of these were complaints about circumstances in the ward. Such complaints were usually directed to the secretary-general, who thus found himself thrust into the role of intermediary between the people and the BPL. One way in which the secretary-general could avoid answering the complaints was by denying that they fell within the committee's competence. Once the administrative councils of the consumers' cooperatives had been set up (see below), one secretary-general refused to entertain any more questions on the cooperative (then a source of many questions and complaints) on the grounds that that was no longer committee business.

Some of the communications which the BPL made to the bureau for discussion in the general assemblies did not call for decisions or action. For instance, at one point there was a circular advocating a reduction of the amount of ceremony and festivity connected with marriage and other life-crisis rites. This circular (which had originated with the Bamako Women's Social Commission) was read in general assemblies and the secretaries-general explained it. Though compliance was suggested, it was not up to the committee to take any action. The secretary-general could also bring up points concerning his activities, for instance the way in which party dues would be collected, or what people should do if they wanted their names on a list of people looking for work.

The most important person in the committee was the secretary-general. He functioned in many ways as the representative of the ward community to the outside world. In this capacity he was often invited to attend the weekly meeting of the BPL (if he were not already a member). He was frequently called on to act as a broker with the higher-ups both by individuals in his ward and by the community. He had to organize the political activities of the ward (call meetings, get people out for *fasobara* projects). He was also regarded by the BPL as the man most responsible for the success or failure of enterprises undertaken by the ward. He was called on to do many other things on behalf of the committee—and the ward. The secretary-general compiled a list of those looking for work, received complaints on a personal basis outside meetings, was requested to arrange many personal favors, found volunteers to attend the Ecole Fondamentale du Parti held in Kita, collected as much of the money owed in dues as possible, and in general took an interest in all that went on in the ward. He found himself attending more life-crisis rites (especially naming ceremonies and funerals) than he otherwise would. Most interesting of all, he was called on to defend the traditional interests of the ward against the administration. Two of the wards of Kita have daughter-hamlets in the bush; in both of them the same problem arose. The administration wanted to separate the daughter-hamlets from the mother-village, in this case a ward of Kita; but the people protested on the grounds that this would separate members of the same family into two different villages. In both cases, the ward secretary-general was called on by the traditional leaders of the ward (the heads of the traditional families, branches of which were in the daughter-hamlets) to intercede with the administration. In both cases the secretary-general did so and was successful. Thus the role of the secretary-general came to be interpreted in ways that went far beyond the formal role. He became a representative of the ward as much as an official of the party.

The secretary-general was the formal political leader of his ward. But he was not always its most important politician. This was especially the case for the two largest wards in Kita. In such cases the secretary-general had the added complication of satisfying the wishes of the more powerful politicians in his own ward as well as those on the BPL—and all without losing popular support.

The secretaries-general tended to come from established families if they were local-born, or to be particularly high-ranking civil servants if they were not. Most combined these two traits. Ten of thirteen people who held this post at various times from 1959 to 1965 were local-born; the three others were all department heads. Two of the nonlocals were secretaries-general in wards (Ségoubougouni and Kita-Gare) where nonlocals were always more numerous both in the population and on the bureaus. Twelve of the thirteen were civil servants, including six who were department heads. Eight were simultaneously members of the BPL, although only three (included in the eight) were town council members. After the 1965 partial renewal of the BPL, which brought politics up to date, so to speak, four of the six committees had secretaries-general who were also BPL members. The secretaries-general ranged in age from thirty to forty-five. They were not typical of their bureaus; they were more likely to be local-born and civil servants than the other members were, and they were less likely to be very old or very young.

The typical committee bureau member was a middle-aged civil servant of local origin, but, as table 7 shows, there were many other kinds of people in the bureaus. The middle- and high-level civil servants occupied the main executive posts; the older men, many of them with less formal education but more experience and perhaps more influence in the ward, many of them merchants, had posts

TABLE 7

MEMBERS OF COMMITTEE BUREAUS (1965)

Age	Number	Ethnic Affiliation	Number
20–29	13	Maninka	36
30–39	28	Fula	22
40–49	29	Bamana	12
50–59	11	Soninké	12
60–69	8	Wolof	3
70–79	2	Moor	3
Unknown	9	Kasonka	2
	100	Dioula	2
		Dogon	2
Occupation	*Number*	Sonrai	1
Government-employed	60	Kagoro	1
Self-employed	34	Unknown	4
Unemployed	6		100
	100	*Local Origin*	*Number*
		Local	70
		Nonlocal	30
			100

N = 100 (five bureaus of 17 members, one of 15)

where they dealt with money and dispute settlement; the young men, often civil servants at a lower level, occupied such posts as youth commissioner, commissioner for union affairs, or press secretary; and the women were represented by their president or their secretary-general. Nonlocal people were in the posts where they dealt with technical matters, in which many of them were specialized (for example, agricultural agents were made secretaries for economic and social affairs). The distribution of bureau members among the different ethnic groups was roughly the same as in the general population. Thus all segments of the community that was the ward were represented in the political bureau.

The committee, like the section, drew its main income from the sale of party cards once a year. The committee was entitled to five francs (two cents) for every card sold. The amount of money thus gained was not great; a committee selling two thousand cards (the maximum for Kita) would receive ten thousand francs (forty dollars) for its treasury. Dues of fifty francs (twenty cents) per person per month were rarely collected. The committee also had very few expenses. The main ones were a tip for the town crier for announcing the meeting and the expense of the kerosene used in the Coleman lantern: roughly two hundred francs (eighty cents) per meeting.

The bureau, and particularly the secretary-general, had to devote a great deal of energy to collecting the money for the party cards. The bureau used the census rolls established by the municipality to calculate how much each family owed. One year the secretary-general of one ward divided up the responsibility for collecting the membership fee among the bureau members, but found that this led to confusion, and so the following year resolved to do it all by himself, although that would take longer. The secretary-general had to be careful, in collecting the money, not to offend people by insisting too much; he had to persuade.

The committee served as a channel for a number of other transactions. If the committee decided to collect money to pay workers on its *fasobara* projects, the money was also collected through the same channels. The committee might also be instructed to collect money for certain special projects of section-wide or national interest. Money was collected in this way to repatriate Malian workers from Senegal after the 1960 break, to help purchase a powerful transmitter for Radio Mali, and to help defray the costs of a presidential visit to Kita. One secretary-general commented that politics consisted chiefly in working with his organization secretary to collect money.

Here is an example that shows both how the chain of communications worked and the kinds of demands that were made on the committee's treasury. A fair was organized in Kita, and the BPL wanted to impress the delegation sent from the capital. So each committee was instructed to ask its *dieli* to show up for a "tamtam" in front of the town hall. The secretary-general of the ward where the representative of the chief of Kita's *dieli* (who himself lived in a village) lived contacted him to arrange for this. He refused to ask any *dieli* to come on this occasion, however, unless the secretary-general agreed to pay them from the committee treasury, as he did not trust the BPL to pay.[8] The secretary-general agreed to this. After the fair, the *dieli* chief's agent presented him with a bill for 3,500 francs

---

8. It is customary to give *dieli* a gift when they perform for you, or when they come to greet you. Here the gift has been transformed into a payment.

($14). The secretary-general postponed payment of this amount temporarily, saying that he could not pay such a large sum without first consulting the full political bureau. He also wanted to ask the BPL secretary-general to pay the sum from the section's treasury, especially as these were the only *dieli* who turned out.

One of the major activities which the committee bureau organized was the *fasobara* program. *Fasobara* consisted of mobilizing the maximum number of people to accomplish a particular project in the minimum time possible. It was labor intensive investment, and was supposed to save the state using scarce money to hire labor. In Kita the timing and nature of the projects were decided by the BPL, but the mobilization of the people was left to the committees. *Fasobara* was used in Kita to build schools and other buildings, to farm collective fields, to repair roads, and to clear grass from public places after the rainy season. In these projects each committee was assigned a share of the work, and it was the responsibility of the secretary-general to get his committee's share done. The accepted method was to get everyone in the committee out to the work site where they worked in an atmosphere of enthusiasm and gaiety; this was not appropriate to all projects, and the committee might decide to organize the work differently. One committee, the largest in Kita, decided to divide itself into four parts, each part to work on the project one Sunday in rotation. This was somewhat more successful as it reduced the number of people who stood around because there was no work for them to do. Later on, this committee and another one decided to assess everyone a small sum of money to pay workmen a wage, rather than mobilize everyone for a project unsuited for mass labor (in this instance, building a school). These rearrangements were made when, after both persuasion and force failed to get everyone out, it became apparent that mass labor was not the best way to build a school. The work load fell on the masons and a few others, and they resented the fact that no one else was working.

Neither the committee youth bureau nor the committee women's bureau was as active as the political bureau in the wards. The youth organization in Kita was concerned primarily with recreation, and most of this recreation was handled by the section's youth bureau. The BV and the Pioneers sometimes functioned in the wards. At one point it was the responsibility of the committee's youth bureau to organize its own BV; the committee youth bureaus organized football teams of Pioneers to play against one another. But the youth bureau did not have the continuing concern with the ward's affairs that the political bureau did; any young man interested in participating in those affairs would try to be a member of the political bureau in addition to or instead of the youth bureau. On the average there were four people in each ward who held posts on both the political and the youth bureaus, out of a total membership in each case of seventeen.

The women's committee grouped all the women in the ward. It did not have many activities associated with it: one disillusioned former secretary-general of a woman's committee told me that the two activities of women in politics were to take care of guests and pay dues. In another ward, the women sporadically tried to organize themselves to prepare a theatrical evening or to have a dance, but the enthusiasm never lasted long. Most women regarded politics as men's business, and considered the idea that a woman could have a higher political position than a man, and thus "command" him, as ridiculous.

The women were usually represented on the political bureau of their committee by an older woman who was the effective head of all the women of the ward, and who was known as their "Présidente." Because she was usually illiterate and thus unable to handle the paperwork of the committee, there was also a secretary-general, a younger woman who was usually a civil servant (midwife, teacher, or nurse). In one ward the secretary-general was on the committee political bureau, perhaps because that ward's "Présidente" represented all the women of Kita on the BPL. Since the women rarely met, the political bureau, if it wanted to communicate with them, worked through the women's delegate on the bureau. Another alternative was to announce through the town crier that women as well as men should attend the next general assembly. When the consumers' cooperatives were being organized, one of the committee secretaries-general called a special meeting of the women, apart from the men, to explain the new organization to them.

My discussion of the committee has focused on the ways in which it functioned as a "government" for the community, in this case the ward. The general assembly was a forum in which the heads of families and other interested parties discussed the affairs of the ward and complained about arrangements they disliked. It made decisions concerning the ward and chose a bureau to represent it, sometimes going to great lengths to preserve free choice in the face of possible BPL interference. In order to settle on their choices, one ward met "secretly" before the meeting at which they were to elect a new bureau. At the actual election, when delegates from the BPL were present, they feigned a debate over the relative merits of various candidates, but somehow those who had been agreed on at the "secret" meeting were elected. The bureau acted as the executive, organizing *fasobara* and collecting money for various purposes. The key man was the secretary-general, whose position involved him in many jobs, some of which went beyond the sphere of party activity and government.

THE CONSUMERS' COOPERATIVES

The consumers' cooperatives (Coopératives de Consommation or CC) were introduced to Kita in 1965, sometime after they had begun in other Malian towns. The purpose of the cooperatives was to replace the small private retail outlets and the unofficial Somiex retail outlet in the distribution to consumers of certain essential goods, such as grains, cloth, kerosene, cigarettes, sugar, salt, and so on. This procedure was to represent a saving to the consumer, for the prices would be lower. It would also provide a structure for distributing scarce goods equitably among the population.

Four consumers' cooperatives were established in Kita, one for Kita-Gare, one for Moribougou, one for Ségoubougouni and Saint-Félix, and one for Makandiambougou, Lenguékoto, and Samédougou. The original organization of the cooperatives was done in the bureau and general assembly meetings of the committee. The local party officials had heard of the difficulties that the cooperatives had encountered elsewhere in Mali (mostly due to bad management), and they were determined that the cooperatives should succeed in Kita. They tried to take all precautions to ensure that the cooperatives got off to a good start. The new institutions were explained to the people in numerous meetings, including the special one for women mentioned above. Care was taken to choose responsible people to run the cooperatives. People put special emphasis on the overseers' committee (Comité de Surveillance) which was supposed to keep an eye on the manner in which the cooperative was run and also to prevent the development of a black market by making sure that no one resold what he received from the cooperative at a higher price. People felt that between the overseers' committee and the Kita price commission there would be little chance of a black market, even when goods were scarce. Special measures were taken to ensure that accounts were properly kept. In one cooperative the storekeeper had to give daily accountings to the treasurer of the administrative council (Counseil d'Administration), who then reported the results to the council's president.

Despite all the good will shown by the political leaders, people were skeptical about the cooperatives when discussions began in early 1965. They felt that the cost of belonging was too high, since there was so little money in Kita; they were not sure how long the membership card they were buying would be good; they were not convinced that the goods on sale would be cheaper, or that they would not still be available elsewhere; and they feared that the establishment of the cooperatives was a prelude to general rationing of food and other items. Many people were fatalistic about the cooperatives, feeling that as they probably would materialize as planned, whether or not they acquiesced, they had no option but to join. The leadership had to allay these fears so that two hundred people in each cooperative would buy membership cards and thus the minimum social capital would be obtained. Once this amount had been collected, the cooperative could be organized and put into operation; then the people would see for themselves what it was. In fact, by the time the cooperatives had been in operation for several months, such skepticism had largely disappeared. Within two months after its opening, one of the cooperatives had increased its membership by 30 percent—in part because of a food shortage and in part because people had compared prices with the Somiex and realized that the cooperative's prices were not higher. They had gained confidence in the management of the cooperatives.

The organization of the cooperatives in Kita was carried on mainly in the general assemblies of the committees, which were simultaneously the general assemblies of the cooperatives since both defined the general assembly as consisting of all the people in the ward. Where two committees were associated in a single cooperative, they met jointly. When the broad outlines of the project had been established and approved by the general assembly (the state made available model documents and a model organization to follow), the officers of the cooperative were chosen, and they were then responsible for most of the detailed organization. Each cooperative had an administrative council of ten members in charge of organization and operation. The ten members included a president, a vice-president and various officers in charge of specific duties (treasurer, in charge of supplies, and so on). An overseers' committee of five members, with no individual tasks, was also chosen at this time.

I analyzed the membership of the administrative council and the overseers' committee of two of the cooperatives, a total of twenty-nine individuals. Three-fourths of the members were between twenty-five and forty-five years of age. Of the twenty-nine, twenty-seven (93.1 percent) were locally born, and twenty (69 percent) were government employees. All nine of the overseers' committee members in this group were government employees; the administrative council members were divided between eleven government employees and nine self-employed (mostly merchants). Of the twenty-nine, twenty-four (82.8 percent) had other committee posts (twenty-two on the political bureau, only two on the youth bureau), and of these twenty-four, five were also on the BPL and two on the town council. One of the five with no other office at the time of his election to a cooperative post was subsequently (in 1966) elected to the town council; along with another of the five he had been absent from Kita at the time of the election of the committee bureau members. So the people who ran the committee also ran the cooperative.

The president of one of the cooperatives was the former canton chief, now a respected elder member of the BPL, while the other was an experienced clerk and administrator in the local services of the Ministry of Development. The president of one of the other two cooperatives, on which I was unable to gather detailed information, was the head of the SMDR; the president of the other was a former stationmaster who was the wealthiest man in his ward. The former canton chief had run a cooperative for peanut producers during the 1950s (see chapter 3); and the development ministry clerk had had wide experience with cooperative affairs in his job. Each president had a respected merchant as vice-president. In each case the less literate people were put in charge of organization, which implied calling people to meetings rather than any paper work; people working for the two major supply sources (Somiex and the SMDR) were put in charge of supply along with, in each case, an experienced merchant.

People wishing to join the cooperative had to pay 1,250 francs ($5) for each card, of which 250 francs was an initiation fee and 1,000 francs was a subscription to the cooperative's social capital and could in theory be returned on the demand of the member if he, for instance, left town. The cooperative used this money as working capital, to cover initial purchases of goods and a certain number of overhead expenses, such as the expense of printing the proper forms (which had to be done at the National Press in Bamako and paid for in advance).

One of the main problems that arose in the organization of the cooperatives concerned the policy on the number of cards a family should have. People from Ségoubougouni, where most of the civil servants lived, favored a policy allowing each family to buy as many cards as it wanted, arguing that this would raise the necessary minimum of social capital rapidly. People from Moribougou, the largest ward, argued that each family should only be required to have a single card, on which would be marked the number of people in the family, arguing that this would ensure a more equitable distribution of goods. Under the Ségoubougouni system, each card would entitle the bearer to a share, and the amount given their cooperative would reflect the number of cards sold. Under the Moribougou system, each card would entitle its holder to a share commensurate with the number of people noted on it, and the amount given their cooperative would reflect the number of people represented by cards holders.

The concrete difference between the two systems can be illustrated by the following incident. When scarce rice was divided up among the cooperatives according to the Ségoubougouni system, the Ségoubougouni-Saint Félix cooperative was able to distribute 1.5 kilos per person, while the Moribougou cooperative was able to distribute only .8 kilos per person. Had the Moribougou system been followed, the amounts ought to have been equal. People from Moribougou argued that the Ségoubougouni system was detrimental to the poorer people, some of whom had trouble purchasing a single card for a very large family. They feared that families with many cards (the richer ones who could afford to buy many cards) would get more of the scarce goods than they could use and would sell the rest on a black market for higher prices. The people from Ségoubougouni argued in return that the cooperatives were for people on a salary (civil servants), and that everyone else was at least a part-time farmer anyway and so had other sources of food. (There had been many full-time merchants and craftsmen in Kita, though certainly events were pushing them to start their own fields outside town.)

This was an on-going quarrel that had gone through several major debates by the time I left Kita in November, 1965. The upper hand always seemed to go to the civil servants of Ségoubougouni. The matter had been discussed in the BPL and in a special meeting bringing together all those connected with cooperatives. A few days before I left, one of the leading figures in Moribougou brought up the issue in one of the information meetings for the whole town (see chapter 8). It looked as though the greater number of top civil servants who stood to benefit from the Ségoubougouni system would result in that system's becoming the standard way of calculating the division of goods among the cooperatives, if not among the card holders in a cooperative.

Problems of organization also accompanied the foundation of the cooperatives. The original plans for the cooperatives in Kita foresaw three of them, not four. The difference was that Gare was to be included in the same cooperative as Ségoubougouni and Saint-Félix, which would have meant that each of the three would have covered roughly the same size population. But the people of Gare objected to this on the grounds that they were too far from Ségoubougouni and Saint-Félix and it would be a hardship to have to go to Ségoubougouni every time they wanted something from the cooperative store. The question was brought up in the BPL, and, although it did not believe that Gare had a large enough population to support a cooperative, the BPL allowed the people to go ahead. Gare managed to get a store opened, although they were having a hard time collecting the necessary minimum social capital.

Another difficulty that arose concerned Ségoubougouni and Saint-Félix, which were to form a single cooperative. The two wards approached each other very gingerly, as Saint-Félix was afraid of being dominated by the larger Ségoubougouni and also suspected it of being anti-Christian. The two issues that Saint-Félix was anxious about were the location of the store and the membership of the governing and overseeing bodies. The Saint-Félix committee organized general assemblies to instruct the bureau members how to deal with Ségoubougouni. The first joint meeting between the two wards was to discuss how and where to hold the other meetings.

But these suspicions were overcome, and after a series of joint meetings the members of the administrative council and the overseers' committee were chosen and the site for the shop selected. Once the cooperative was in operation, doubts disappeared.

Each of the cooperatives made its own decisions and arrangements independently of the others, and this led to different policies in each. The result was recriminations by people in less-favored cooperatives. The leaders felt that the best way to avoid ill-feeling and disappointment was to apply a uniform policy to all four cooperatives. If everyone was not equal in this sense, cooperative members would see more advantageous arrangements elsewhere and criticize their own management; the confidence and concord necessary for the cooperative would be lost. Jealousy played a role in enforcing equality.

Here is an example of how this worked. After the cooperatives had been in operation for two months, a meeting was held of all those responsible for the various aspects of the cooperatives. At this meeting everyone was free to bring up problems. Two of the problems that were raised concerned pricing. People complained that the Moribougou cooperative was selling cloth by the yard at the price fixed for the meter,[9] and was thus defrauding people. There was also a difference in the price of millet, which Makandiambougou was selling at a half-franc a kilo more than Moribougou and Ségoubougouni. It turned out that there were two reasons for this. Moribougou's and Ségoubougouni's cooperatives, whose presidents were the two top officials in the SMDR, were getting free use of the SMDR's carts for transporting the grain from the warehouse to the store; and Makandiambougou was calculating more "profit" per kilo than the other two were. Everyone defended themselves against the accusations made, and nothing could be done in the face of the denials. But guidelines were laid down for the future. It was decided, for instance, that everyone would have to pay for transporting grain, and everyone should charge a half-franc per kilo gross profit on millet, to cover the cost of transport and wastage.

The goods sold in the cooperatives came from two sources. Grains (millet and rice) came from the SMDR and had to be paid

---

9. The use of the yard as a measure for cloth is a heritage of the greater English involvement in trade before the scramble for Africa established European boundaries everywhere. There were never any English traders in Kita, however.

for in advance. Other items (tea, sugar, cloth, cigarettes, matches) came from Somiex which granted thirty days' credit. The success of the cooperatives depended to a great extent on their ability to maintain a fast turnover of goods. In one case, a cooperative was able to receive Somiex goods on thirty-day credit, sell them, use the money to buy grain, sell that, and repay the original debt, all within the thirty-day period. The cooperatives were allowed to make a small profit: one made 165,000 francs gross profit and 100,000 net (respectively, $650 and $400) in the first two months of operation, on a turnover of several million francs; another made a net profit of 125,000 francs ($500) after two months. Cooperative expenses included the transport of goods from warehouse to store, the salary of the storekeeper and of the workmen, and the rental of the building used as a store.

Each cooperative was opened with a small ceremony, at which delegates of the administration, the party, and the ward spoke. There were also dances and drumming. Then the ribbon was cut and the important people were allowed to enter the store, where they made symbolic purchases. After they were finished, the common people were allowed to enter, which they did in a great rush. The leaders of one of the cooperatives reported proudly that they had done over 50,000 francs ($200) worth of business the first day, which they felt was excellent considering that the store was not yet fully stocked.

The cooperatives quickly came to have a central part in the life of Kita. They became interesting places for men to hang around for news and gossip: two were located in the market, and the other two on the path that most residents of the wards concerned followed to get to market. The cooperatives were also able to serve as the centers for the distribution of grains during the worst grain shortage in Kita for many years.

In short, the cooperatives illustrated the manner in which the people in Kita, through their committees at first and then through the cooperatives' boards, were able to organize and operate an entirely new structure. Some problems arose but none disrupted the process. The leaders were concerned to make the cooperatives work. A conscientious attempt was made to find responsible people to run them and to organize them in such a way as to eliminate queues, shortages, and corruption. During their first year of operation in Kita, the cooperatives were quietly becoming naturalized.

The Unions

There was a single union in Mali, the Union Nationale des Travailleurs Maliens (UNTM). Its organization, while not parallel to the party, followed the same principles. It was divided both locally and professionally. Locally there was the "Union locale" for each circle; professionally there was a series of "Syndicats nationaux," one for each profession or related group of professions. Most of the "syndicats nationaux" had a "division" for each circle. The divisions were simultaneously subordinated to their "union locale" for matters concerning joint union activity at the local level, and to their "syndicat national" for professional matters (see figure 5). The divisions could be subdivided into sections for their professional subcategories, and the sections into a "Comité d'Entreprise" for each work place, but these distinctions were not operative in Kita due to the small number of people involved. Only the hospital had a Comité d'Entreprise; one of its functions was to decide collectively who would do the least pleasant tasks so that the onus of decision would be removed from the doctor who, as one of Kita's deputies, was very much involved in the political game.

Each of the divisions in Kita had a bureau, containing from nine to seventeen members and having much the same titles as the other bureaus. The Union Locale also had a seventeen-member bureau headed by a secretary-general and including representatives of each of the divisions organized in Kita:

1. Transport (including workers for the Chemin de Fer du Mali and the weather station);
2. Education and culture (teachers);
3. Telecommunications (post office workers);
4. Health (doctors, nurses, midwives, maintenance personnel);
5. Administration (clerks, administrators, maintenance per-

FIGURE 5. UNION ORGANIZATION

sonnel such as mechanics, carpenters, masons, drivers, and so on who worked for the circle and for the municipality) ;
6. Rural economy (clerical and technical workers in the SDR, the SMDR, Eaux-et-Forêts, and Elévage services).

The Union Locale leaders had tried unsuccessfully to organize two more divisions: food and clothing industries (butchers and tailors), and commerce and banks (Somiex workers and private merchants). Perhaps the high ratio of self-employed in these two categories explains their lack of success.

In Kita to be a union member was to be a civil servant. Despite the fact that the union was to all practical purposes an organism of the party-government establishment, the local divisions of the union saw their role as fighting for better working conditions and higher pay for their members as a whole, and as taking the part of a worker who felt he was being mistreated by the government, his employer. The division of administration workers took an active interest in seeing that a number of its members were raised to higher pay categories. A teacher wanting reassignment appealed to his union to intercede with the Ministry of Education. The prevalence of this technique is shown by the fact that one teacher boasted that he had been assigned to his home town without calling on the union for help. The union was also prepared to defend one of its members whom the state tried to discipline as an unsatisfactory worker. When all the teachers in the circle of Kita came to Kita for a pedagogical conference, one of the sessions was organized by the teachers' union to allow the teachers to express their grievances to the inspector.

The union was mainly of importance to the civil servants, for whom it represented an alternative hierarchy that gave them more influence over their careers and working conditions. Within the vertical divisions for each governmental branch, the main union posts were held by the clerical and administrative workers rather than the maintenance and technical personnel, so that the situation of the lower-ranking personnel was dependent on the same group of individuals in both hierarchies. The union's more egalitarian framework did, however, permit people to relate to one another in a more congenial way than in the bureaucratic hierarchy.

The major public manifestation of the union was on May Day, when it sponsored a parade through the streets of Kita with banners and school children singing the "Internationale" in French and Maninka. The union also sponsored a dance in the evening, the proceeds from which went to their treasury (a special effort was made to pay the workers beforehand so they could buy dance tickets).

RELATIONS BETWEEN THE STATE AND THE PARTY

The above analysis raises the question of the relationship between these various hierarchies, particularly between the state and the party. I have touched on some of the details of these relationships in the course of my discussion; the present summary will focus generally on two problems. What was the pattern of relations between the two sets of institutions, the party and the state? Given the fact that many people held posts in both sets, what effect did this have on the institutional relationships?

The formal stated relationship between the state and the party at the national level was that the party should develop an elaborate policy which it was then up to the state to implement. The party then had the further role of mobilizing the people to support the state in its efforts. At the local level it was made explicit that the local party section was not supposed to provide a policy for the local representatives of the state; if the party had suggestions or ideas they were to be transmitted to the national level where, if accepted, they would be formulated as policy and retransmitted to the local level. On the other hand, the local party section was supposed to keep an eye on the local state representatives to ensure that their actions were really in keeping with the principles laid down by the national party (cf. Sy 1965:186ff).

This relationship was alive in the thoughts of the leaders of the different branches of the state and the party. People constantly repeated, "la politique prime l'administrative" ("politics guides administration"). On the behavioral level this principle was reflected by the preeminence of the BPL as the major political institution of the town and by the importance Kitans gave to the party institutions on both the section and the committee levels. Much more interest was focused on the relationships between individuals in the political sphere than in the state sphere; where there were interesting confrontations between individuals in the state sphere, they tended to be interpreted in terms of politics. An example of this was furnished when two of the most prominent civil servants in the town were assigned elsewhere. Local gossip was sure that their reassignment was really a banishment from Kita because of their political differences with one of Kita's most prominent political leaders.

Normally, however, relations between party and state in Kita were characterized much more by cooperation and interpenetration than by relationships of the type implied by the formal pronouncements. Both the commandant de cercle and his assistant were ex officio members of the BPL and participated in all discussions. There was a monthly meeting (conférence des cadres) to which all top officials of party and state came to discuss organizational and administrative matters.[10] When information meetings were held for the town of Kita, the top administrators were there to play their part. Similarly, at the meetings held in Kita to which representatives of all the villages of the central arrondissement came, both party and state representatives were present, and the BPL's secretary-general and the chef d'arrondissement were usually the main speakers. When delegations from Kita circulated in the bush, they invariably included representatives of both the party and the state: a delegation to attend the end of the year ceremonies at an agricultural training school (Ecole Saisonnière) included, for instance, the chef d'arrondissement, the chief of the SDR, a representative of the BPL who was the secretary-general of one of Kita's committees, and the Kita correspondent of the national party newspaper. With so much personal contact in a small society it is not surprising that, if the party could not tell the state what to do in Kita, key party leaders could bend and influence leading administrators, when these leaders themselves were not state officials as well.

Given the fact that many people held both state and party posts, was there any role conflict? There were some examples of this. The president of a cooperative was torn between loyalty to the people of his ward and loyalty to his superior in the state hierarchy. The teachers' unity and sense of professional integrity was sometimes affected by the relations between them in the political sphere. On the whole, however, role conflict was not a serious problem. The reason for this seemed to be that the major orientation was towards governing Kita rather than playing one national hierarchy against another.

10. Zolberg (1965:154) stresses the importance of the "Conférence des Cadres."

The elite formed a face-to-face group in which interpersonal relations were personalistic. The members of the elite all knew each other and habitually worked together in personal contact situations. Relations between individuals in face-to-face situations in Kita were not formal and the formal distinctions between the relevant roles in the various hierarchies were usually considered secondary to the interpersonal relations existing between the persons concerned. Where a need was felt for one individual to separate himself out from the group into a superordinate role, he was likely to go outside the formal roles altogether and to justify his actions on more universalistic grounds, typically with a basis in the traditional value system. Someone might say, "I am talking because I am the oldest." Apart from such justifications, people were unwilling to formalize any superordinate role they held. The most important political relations between individuals were the relations of friendship, of enmity, of patronage and clientage, and of long association through the years in a common involvement in a process which had become legendary (the struggle of the RDA in "double opposition"). It was this emphasis on the informal relations between officeholders that enabled the structures of state and party to serve so effectively as the town's government. The next chapters stress the patterns of informal political relations and the processes whereby Kita was governed.

6

Kita Politics: A Case History

The institutions of the state and the party are the formal political structure of Kita; to understand how the ward committee, local political bureau, and cooperative work and interrelate is one way in which to grasp the workings of Kita's sociopolitical system. But there is another way, and it is perhaps a more fundamental one for elucidating the underlying drives and motive forces of that system. This way requires understanding of the rivalry between individuals for preeminence. Based on the notion that the best thing a man could do with his life was to become a respected citizen whose advice was sought and heeded in community affairs, this competition for prestige gave a particular flavor to the formation of political alliances between individuals and to the tenor of political discourse in the town. In this competition, the party and the state institutions provided the posts that gave or confirmed prestige and offered a wonderfully nuanced hierarchy in which everyone could find a place.

With its distinctive social organization, its active party organization, and its concentration of population, Kita's social system was an arena with relatively firm boundaries within which political careers and events could occur. In a sense, the system of competitive political relations defined the limits of Kita's social system, which for all practical purposes corresponded on the ground to the town of Kita. Neither the nearby villages nor the outlying parts of the circle were included, and citizenship in the town was tantamount to participation in the competition for prestige in the arena. People within the system measured their prestige against one another, and those outside the system, whether they were from rural areas or from the capital, were essentially personal allies of the faction leaders in Kita; prestige in their own political arena depended on the competition there rather than on events within Kita's political system.

While underlining the relative autonomy of each arena, I do not mean to deny that there was mutual influence. Despite trying to keep their quarrels to themselves, Kitans occasionally appealed to their patrons at the national level to intervene on their behalf; even more frequently, national level personalities intervened in Kita affairs in order to make Kita conform to their idea of how Mali should be run. From time to time, too, villagers and people from the smaller towns of the circle were able to exercise some leverage over Kita affairs through offering their support to one or another of the leading figures within the Kita arena.

Within this arena, personal political rivalry led to the formation of cliques and factions and ultimately to what was essentially a local two-party system which maintained itself intact for at least a generation prior to the time this study was carried out. In Kita, far from being a device to limit popular participation in government, factions and their dynamics encouraged the participation of all in a way that assumed that all were equal and that primordial ties were largely irrelevant. The relative independence of the leading political figures from any primordial attachments and their dependence on broadly based popular support for their success also gave a special tone to political discourse in the town. It meant that there was at least as much jockeying for position, preferably in public, as there was serious discussion of the issues, and it meant that those involved in trying to come to a decision or to settle a dispute had to put their personal status on the line; consequently, all such dialogue became essentially political. If a lot of political maneuvering inevitably took place away from the public eye, including the eye of the anthropologist, Kita was remarkable for the number of public occasions on which political relations were demonstrated. Assemblies, which are a constant theme in Maninka social organization (see chapter 3), took place here largely within the framework of the party, and so are another link between the network of formal institutions and the pattern of alliances and personal rivalries.

The present chapter presents a case history of Kita politics over the period of a generation. It describes the kind of people involved in local politics in a backwater Malian town, the kind of issues involved, and the changing ways in which politics was carried on during this period. Besides conveying a sense of the rhythm of competition and the rise and fall of individuals within Kita's arena, this summary provides the basic temporal framework for the following two chapters, illustrating what the specific events were that led up to the situation as it existed at the time of field work. It also raises the question of the relationship between events and structures, for the structures here are simply the observer's abstraction from the rush of events, unlike the more formal institutional structures of party and state discussed in the previous chapter.

The two decades covered here saw a great shift in the manners and goals of politics, despite the common themes that run through the period. At the beginning of the period most politics swirled around the figure of the canton chief and his post. The canton chief and his rivals in the early stages participated in two-party politics, but gradually other people, unconnected with the chiefship, began to come to the fore. Kita politics was affected by outside circumstances, such as the granting of internal autonomy to the French Sudan in 1957, the abolition of the chiefship in 1958, and the disbanding of one of the two parties in 1959, leading up to Malian independence as a one-party state in 1960. The coming of independence did not stop competitive politics in Kita. During the early years of independence a pattern of rivalry within a one-party framework, marked by the importance of public opinion and public discussion, began to emerge.

The story itself has been pieced together from a variety of sources, some of whom were obviously giving versions of events that reflected their participation or their attitudes. Sometimes my conclusion as to what happened is based on inference, sometimes on a direct statement, sometimes on a corroborated statement.[1] There is

1. I was especially fortunate in that I was present in Kita from October, 1961, to July, 1962, including the time of the party conference of June 30–July 1, 1962, as well as from September, 1964, to November, 1965, the time of my field work. My observations of the earlier period helped immeasurably in reconstructing the political history and in getting a sense of the fluidity of the relationship between person and position. Unfortunately I did not have the election figures until after I had left Kita, so I was unable to inquire further into their meaning.

a sense in which what is presented here is only "true" insofar as it relates to the realities of 1965 (this is what made getting an "accurate" version so problematic) and insofar as it presents material which elucidates the social organization of that time. Using arguments about the nature of the past as a way of commenting on the real or desired situation in the present has always been a favorite political idiom in Mali. I can therefore offer no hard guarantee that the version of Kita's political history presented here is historically true in every detail, although I am confident that the broad pattern of events and the major stages are accurate. I feel that whatever cogency the analytical statements derived from this story might have is not dependent on strict historical accuracy. For present purposes the important thing about these stories is not whether they are true or false, but that people saw them as reasonable versions of human activity.

COMPETITION FOR THE CHIEFSHIP: THE EARLY RDA

The pattern of conflict begins with the competition for the post of canton chief of Kita. The last time a canton chief was chosen was in 1942 at the death of Garan Keita, a particularly powerful chief and son of the Tokontan Keita who dominated Kita when the French arrived (see chapter 3). The sons and nephews of Garan all withdrew because they were too young, while his younger brother Demba did not present his candidacy (according to stories) either because he was a devout Muslim who did not want to incur the penalties for the sins any secular chief must commit, or because he was a drunkard. The successful candidate was Fatogoma Keita, of the same generation as Garan's sons (see figure 1), and thus the classificatory son of Demba. This was the first time that someone not from the oldest living generation was chosen. Fatogoma was a schoolteacher, and his education compensated for his being in the wrong generation. He also had the support of some of the influential African merchants of Moribougou, notably Moriké Sissoko, at that time an employee of a leading French trading company. Fatogoma had shown interest in the chiefship in 1939 when Garan succeeded, but had not pushed his candidacy. His candidacy in 1942 was facilitated by the withdrawal of all Garan's immediate family; so his only rival was an ex-army lieutenant of nonchiefly lineage. He was elected by a sizable majority of the village chiefs, the only electors.

BRIEF CHRONOLOGY OF POLITICAL EVENTS IN KITA (1939–66)

1939	Garan Keita chosen canton chief of Kita canton.
1942	Fatogoma Keita chosen canton chief of Kita canton.
1944	Makan Diallo chosen canton chief of Birgo canton.
1946–47	Founding of the RDA and the PSP in the Sudan and in Kita. Elections for the first and second constituent assemblies. Makan Diallo (PSP) elected to the territorial council for the circle of Kita.
1952	Fakourou Sidibé (RDA) elected to the territorial council for the circle of Kita.
1957	Dramane Diawara and Fili Ba (both RDA) elected to the territorial council for the circle of Kita. Internal autonomy for the Sudan; formation of the first African government.
1958	Post of canton chief abolished.
1959	Dramane Diawara and Makan Kouyaté elected to the national assembly (ex-territorial council) from the circle of Kita. Dissolution of the PSP. Formation and dissolution of the Kita Natives' Association. The Sudan and Senegal joined in the Federation of Mali.
1960	Formation of committees in each of Kita's wards. Formation of a provisional BPL under Moussa Sylla. The Republic of Mali becomes independent after the breakup of the Federation of Mali.
1961	Formation of a provisional BEJ under Mamadou Kamara.
1962	Election of a new, permanent BPL under Dramane Diawara.
1963	Exile of the two deputies (Diawara and Kouyaté); futile attempt to form a subsection for the central arrondissement; return of the two deputies from exile; assignment of Sylla away from Kita.
1964	Reelection of Diawara and Kouyaté to the national assembly.
1966	Election of Makan Kouyaté as mayor of Kita.

When the RDA and the PSP were founded in Kita in 1946, the major initial choices were a development of the 1942 situation. Fatogoma Keita, because of his position and because he was a friend of the territorial leader of the PSP (also a teacher turned canton chief) favored the PSP and became its leader locally. The Tokontana (descendants of Tokontan) had decided that it had been a mistake not to have contested the chiefship in 1942, and had been opposed to Fatogoma, especially after Demba's son, Moussa, returned to Kita. Moussa and two of Garan's sons, Seydou and Aliou, became the nucleus of the RDA. Sissoko, who had supported Fatogoma in 1942 in the interests of progress and freedom, at this time

119

KITA POLITICS: A CASE HISTORY

Ba, Fili. Merchant from Toukoto, RDA deputy 1957–59, chef d'arrondissement of Toukoto.

Diallo, Makan. Schoolteacher from the Birgo, canton chief of Birgo (1944–58), PSP deputy from Kita (1947–52).

Diarra, Tiémoko. Schoolteacher from Ségou, served in Kita for about twenty years until 1960, active in RDA.

Diawara, Dramane. Born in Kita canton in 1924, clerk for railroad in Senegal and Kita, secretary-general of the RDA in Kita (1947–57, 1962–this study), RDA deputy from Kita (1957–this study). BPL member in 1965.

Kamara, Mamadou. Born near Kayes in 1924, schoolteacher, served in Kita from ca. 1949 on, active in RDA, football, youth affairs, secretary-general of the BEJ from 1961. BPL member in 1965.

Keita, Abraham. Born in Kita around 1915, administration clerk, active in Kita Natives' Association.

Keita, Aliou. Born in Kita in 1913, to the Tokontana Keita. Stationmaster, RDA candidate for territorial councillor from Kita in 1947, secretary-general of the BPL (1957–58), deputy mayor. BPL member in 1965.

Keita, Fatogoma. Born in Kita in 1900, to the Djita Makadougoula Keita. Schoolteacher, canton chief (1942–58), PSP candidate for deputy in 1948 and 1952. BPL member in 1965.

Keita, Garan. Born in Kita about 1865, died 1942. Son of Tokontan Keita, canton chief (1939–42).

Keita, Moussa. Born in Kita in 1905, to the Tokontana Keita. Merchant, active in RDA from 1946, his relative lack of education may have prevented him from occupying the more prominent roles.

Kouyaté, Makan. Born in Kita about 1917 to an old Kita *dieli* family. Spent many years in Guinea as a doctor where he was RDA. Deputy from Kita (1959–this study). BPL member in 1965. First elected mayor of Kita (1966).

Sidibé, Fakourou. Born in the Birgo in 1891. Schoolteacher, RDA deputy from Kita (1952–57).

Sissoko, Moriké. Born in Kita in 1906. Merchant, active in RDA from 1946, his relative lack of education may have prevented him from occupying the more prominent roles. BPL member in 1965.

Sylla, Moussa. Born in Nioro around 1920. *Dieli,* assigned to Kita's health services (ca. 1955–64). Secretary-general of the BPL (1958–62).

Tall, Mamadou. Born in Mopti around 1933. Schoolteacher.

Tounkara, Douga. Born in Kita in 1936. Clerk in the hospital. Secretary-general of the central arrondissement's subsection (1963).

Traoré, Paul. Born in Kita. Schoolteacher. Active in the Kita Natives' Association.

decided that the same interests required him to support the RDA.[2] So the Kita RDA was founded as a coalition of the Tokontana branch of the Keita and Sissoko with his allies in Moribougou. Chief among these allies were the head of the butchers and one of the most prominent kola merchants. There was some early civil service support for the RDA, notably a schoolteacher named Tiemoko Diarra from Ségou. The basic division was between those who supported the chief and those who opposed him for various reasons, one of which was dynastic.

At the same time, in the canton of the Birgo, neighboring Kita to the south, an analogous situation had arisen. In 1944 a schoolteacher named Makan Diallo was chosen canton chief, on the basis of his education and personality, although his family had no traditional claim on the post. When parties were organized two years later, the Diallo clan became PSP and the chiefly clan, the Sidibé, became RDA. As the Sidibé clan was more numerous than the Diallo, the initial advantage of the PSP disappeared as the electorate was extended.

Makan Diallo was chosen as the territorial councillor for Kita in 1946 as a PSP member. His RDA opponent was Aliou Keita. The election was apparently extremely close, but the results are hard to interpret as Kita was in a single constituency with Bamako. Each list had four names, one man from Kita and three from Bamako, and election was on a group basis. It is hard to say whether Diallo was carried to victory by the PSP strength in Bamako, or whether he won narrowly in Kita.

The next election for territorial councillor was in 1952, and it was an interesting one. It was the last election where it was apparent that some people felt that modern politics was simply a way of playing out traditional rivalries. Four of the five candidates represented chiefly lineages, two in Kita and two in the Birgo. Fatogoma Keita was a regular PSP candidate. Makan Diallo, the incumbent, ran as a "progressive," a splinter group.[3] Daba Keita of Kita (b. 1895, the son of a man who had tried unsuccessfully to become canton chief of Kita in 1925) ran as a "progressive independent," another PSP splinter. Fakourou Sidibé (another schoolteacher) of

2. This is his own interpretation.

3. The split thus indicated between Fatogoma Keita and Makan Diallo may be related to the breakup of the cooperative they had formed (see chapter 3).

the Birgo Sidibé was the RDA candidate. Finally, there was a fifth candidate who ran as an "independent." The results of this election are given in table 8. Approximately one-fifth of the registered voters

TABLE 8

Candidate	Votes	Percentage
Fakourou Sidibé (RDA)	1,969	40
Makan Diallo (Progressive)	1,592	32
Fatogoma Keita (PSP)	1,006	20
Daba Keita (Independent-progressive)	233	5
Mamadou Sy (Independent)	131	3
Total	4,931	

voted. The winner was the RDA candidate, with 40 percent of the vote. As *L'Essor,* the RDA newspaper, commented, "Whose fault is it if in Kita, ambition, the desire for gain pushed the progressives to present five candidates against the single RDA candidate?"[4] The strength of the RDA was that they were able to prevent a split between their Kita and Birgo branches; the Tokontana deferred to the Sidibé, who had a better candidate in Fakourou Sidibé, one of the first Sudanese schoolteachers.

During all this period it seems that the RDA was able to remain united within the circle and town of Kita. The grand alliance between Moussa Keita and Moriké Sissoko represented an alliance between the traditional chiefly family and the new merchants, and at the same time an alliance between Kita's two largest wards. Meetings were held at the houses of the two leaders and both men later looked proudly back to the days when Mamadou Konaté, Modibo Keita, and the other territorial leaders of the RDA used to be their guests. Tiemoko Diarra was the effective leader of the RDA civil servants because of his long service in Kita. Other energetic and powerful RDA supporters among the civil servants served in Kita, but they did not remain long enough to have a lasting influence on

---

4. April 11, 1952. The records show only four non-RDA candidates, but, without agreeing that the desire for gain was the only possible motive, the point remains valid.

the local situation. Diarra spent almost twenty years in Kita, finally leaving in 1960. Moussa Keita and Sissoko were known as the "presidents" of the RDA; there was also a secretary-general during most of this period, but his job was conceived of as more clerical than as a position of executive power and authority. The first secretary-general was Aliou Keita. He was assigned away from Kita to be stationmaster in a village along the railroad in 1947 and was replaced by a young railroad clerk, Dramane Diawara, originally from one of the villages that had branched out from the villages at the foot of Kita mountain. Diawara held the post for about ten years, and then Aliou Keita took it again and held it for a short period around 1957-58.

THE KITA NATIVES' ASSOCIATION

By 1957 the political situation had changed considerably. In March, 1957, the RDA scored its first sizable victory in the territory as a whole, winning sixty-four of the seventy seats in the territorial council. As a consequence, they formed the first African government of the Sudan. In Kita, the RDA received two-thirds of the votes, and elected two RDA councillors: Diawara and Fili Ba of Toukoto (the second largest town in the circle). The dominance of the RDA apparently led to some difficulties for the prominent PSP leaders, such as Fatogama Keita and Makan Diallo. Many of the RDA leaders of this time were civil servants and not native to the circle. By contrast with the period only a few years earlier, power based on position in the traditional system was of negligible importance (Barlet 1966).

The kind of incident that happened in 1958 when the post of canton chief was abolished, or in 1959 after the final electoral victory of the RDA, may be taken as illustrative of the reaction of RDA members to this situation. When the post of canton chief was abolished in 1958, Moussa Keita held a celebration—in front of the door of Fatogoma Keita! For some time after this, Fatogoma was cautious about leaving his house for shame; his children were teased in school; and the young men of the town, if they had some reason to think they were RDA, used to come at night and throw rocks onto the tin roof of his house, hoping he would react by coming out so they could taunt him. Following the election of March, 1959 (when the RDA won 74 percent of the vote in the circle) there were gangs of young RDA members prepared to attack the young men who had supported the PSP. The PSP supporters were dared to come to the market.

At this point, when it was clear that the RDA was overwhelmingly the majority party in the Sudan, a split occurred in the RDA. The form the split took was the creation of a Kita Natives' Association (known as the *kita wulu den ton* in Maninka and as the *Fraternelle de Kita* in French). The association as founded was open only to those whose umbilical cords were buried in Kita, and the main purpose of it was to counteract the influence of those leaders of the RDA who were not native to Kita.[5] As such it represented a xenophobic tendency in Kita politics which remained important for several years afterward, and was perhaps only dormant in 1965. Nevertheless, as the story of the association shows, the issue of alien rule was only one factor involved. Many personal rivalries and animosities also entered in.

There are two stories of the founding of the association. One story was told to me by two young teachers who had been active in it. According to this story, some young men were playing cards together and talking. They began discussing how dissatisfied they were with the way in which the leaders of the party (Moussa Keita, Moussa Sylla, and Tiémoko Diarra) were running it. One of their specific grievances was that when ex-PSP members in the villages wanted to switch their allegiance to the RDA, the leadership charged them fees up to twenty times the normal ones. So they decided to form an organization dedicated to removing these men from office; the idea caught hold, and the association came to crystallize popular sentiment in Kita for a time.

According to the other story, told to me by a younger member of the Tokontana lineage who had not been a *wulu den ton* member, the association was started by an ambitious local politician who hoped to use it as a springboard to power. This man, Abraham Keita, was at the time the paymaster ("agent spécial") in the

5. I do not know how the leaders of the association dealt with marginal cases, such as those born elsewhere but raised in Kita, those born elsewhere of Kita families, and so on. The category of *wulu den* (native) is clear, but the category of *duguren* (one familiar with local life and customs) is more ambiguous (see chapter 4). Given the short period during which the association functioned, marginal cases such as these were probably not an issue; in any case, the essential confrontation was quite clear to all those concerned.

Circle; he came from a small Keita lineage which considered that it had some claim to the canton chiefship; and he felt resentful of the Tokontana because they had treated his mother badly many years before. He was reputed to feel that the post of Commandant de Cercle in an independent Sudan was equivalent to that of a canton chief, and thus he was ambitious to occupy that post. He tried to foster his ambition at this time by making very generous gifts to the *dieli*, in order to establish a reputation for generosity. At the time of the association, he also reportedly offered to "lend" Moussa Keita a large sum of money with the understanding that if Abraham were successful in his ambitions, Moussa would not have to repay the money. As he had not solicited such a loan, Moussa refused. Whether or not this man was instrumental in starting the association, as a high-ranking locally born clerk he stood to benefit from a movement that aimed at putting local people in responsible positions.

Another important supporter of the association was Paul Traoré, a schoolteacher of considerable experience who would have liked to be head teacher in Kita. He had been active in the RDA from the earliest days, but not in Kita. When he wanted to return to Kita, it was made clear to him that he could not be headmaster of the Kita school, despite his qualifications, because Tiémoko Diarra already held that post. He chose to come anyway, saying that his parents were aged, and he wanted to build himself a house.[6] Once in Kita, however, he began to complain that he ought to be made headmaster as he was more qualified than Diarra. He claimed that Diarra only held the post because of his political machinations. Thus Traoré had an interest in participating in an organization dedicated to removing aliens from positions of influence in Kita.

Moriké Sissoko, one of the two founders of the Kita RDA, also supported the association. At this time he had split with his longtime ally, Moussa Keita, and had again moved closer to Fatogoma Keita (whom he had supported for the canton chiefship in 1942). When Sissoko changed sides, he took with him a number of merchants and others from Moribougou, where he was especially influential. Some people from Moribougou, however, remained faithful

6. Wanting to build a house in one's home town was frequently cited as an excuse for wanting to return there. But in Malian terms, any civil servant trying to be assigned to his home town is suspected of having political ambitions there.

to Moussa Keita. One of these was a man who had been opposed to Fatogoma Keita ever since Fatogoma had deposed his mother's brother as village chief of Moribougou. For him, the alliance with his enemy's enemy was more important than his loyalty to his neighbor and fellow merchant, Sissoko.

Those who opposed the association were, naturally enough, the "aliens" against whom it was directed. The two leading individuals were Tiémoko Diarra of Ségou, the school director, and Moussa Sylla of Nioro, in charge of the Epidemic Diseases Service. In addition, there were some young teachers, including Mamadou Kamara from Kayes. The aliens had as their principal Kitan ally Moussa Keita, one of the founders of the local RDA and the leading figure in the Tokontana lineage of the Keita clan.

The organizational and mobilization effort of the new association was carried on largely in public meetings, which were held in people's homes. One was held in the house of Kita's imam, whose brother was one of the leading figures in the association. Another was held in Sissoko's house, and the third was held in the courtyard of a house where many of the RDA meetings had been held. At the third meeting, all those who were willing to join openly were asked to sign up, and many did so. The association elected a regular bureau, and began sending delegations to Bamako to plead its case.

The local figures opposed to the association began growing uneasy when they saw the success it was beginning to have. They too held meetings, particularly one in Moussa Keita's house. The meeting, supposedly secret, was ostensibly of the political bureau, which this faction dominated, although there were some nonbureau-members present. At this meeting it was decided to take action against the association. A great deal of the responsibility for doing so was laid on Tiémoko Diarra; it was said that as school director he should be able to deal effectively with those among the association supporters who had recently been his pupils.

A story which indicates some of the quality of political conflict in those days, as well as the joys of political reminiscing, is that of the infiltration of this meeting by association supporters. Two teachers, one a supporter and the other an opponent of the association, were playing cards when a messenger appeared with a message for the opponent of the association to appear at this meeting. The supporter of the association managed to see the note—not by stealth, but by simply taking it from him, with a joke. The supporters of the association then decided to infiltrate the meeting. They found a younger brother of one of their number and sent him to "play" with Moussa's children in the evening at the time of the meeting. Meanwhile they sat in a house and played cards, waiting for the boy to return. The meeting lasted until 2 A.M., and then their spy appeared with information on what had been decided and discussed at the "secret" meeting.

Eventually, however, the coup de grace to the association came from the national direction of the party. They dispatched an emissary to Kita to tell the association leaders that it was too regional in scope and would therefore have to disband itself. It had twenty-four hours to do so. The association had existed for about three months, during a summer vacation. Following this incident, many of the civil servants who had supported the association were assigned to distant places.

Thus people with diverse reasons for being xenophobic joined together in an attempt to gain control of the political apparatus of the town. On the opposing faction were not only the "aliens" but also local people who had some advantage in supporting them. On an ideological level, the quarrel was between those who felt that Kita ought to be governed by Kitans and those who felt that ability was the only acceptable criterion. The national level of the party supported the latter view.

THE WARD COMMITTEES

A year or so after the incident of the Association of Kita Natives, there was another political confrontation involving roughly the same individuals on both sides. At this time Moussa Sylla was secretary-general of the BPL, and he and Moussa Keita were the most important people in the Kita political scene. The PSP had disbanded itself and its members had been absorbed into the RDA. The new confrontation developed from an attempt by the same people who had been active in the association (some young teachers on summer vacation, Sissoko, Fatogoma Keita, and others) to gain control of the political bureau by outflanking the group in power. The technique was to petition the national party to permit the formation of committees in each of Kita's wards. Such committees were authorized by the RDA's bylaws, but they had not been formed in Kita. Sissoko and his allies hoped to dominate these committees when they were formed, as they figured that they had the majority of Kitans on their side. They then expected that the choice of the political bureau would be left to the members of those committees, and so they would be able to sweep out their enemies and install themselves.

The petition they made to the BPN was granted after numerous delegations had travelled back and forth between Kita and Bamako. There was a great deal of controversy in Kita. Moussa Keita and his clique argued that the strong point of the RDA in Kita had always been unity, which was symbolized by the existence of a single committee for Kita; they should not wilfully destroy this unity by creating six committees for the wards of Kita. In 1965 it was still possible to hear people argue that the PSP ought not to have been disbanded, for competition was a good thing, and that the division of the RDA into ward committees had laid the seeds of dissension—all the quarrels, the cliques, and the clans had their origin in this decision. Those in favor of decentralization argued that Kita was too large, so a single committee was impractical; by having more committees the party would be able to maintain better contact with the people. Beneath all this argument was the fact that this was an attack by those not holding the seats of power on those in them.

Although the supporters of the creation of committees were successful, their expectation that this would lead to control over the BPL was not realized. The choice of the new BPL (when that occurred in 1962) was put in the hands of *all* the committees in the section of Kita, not just the six committees of the town. This change altered the political equation; for the first time people from outside Kita town had been invited to participate in the selection of the BPL.

Entry of Sylla and Kouyaté

The period between 1959 and 1962 was marked by a number of new factors and switches in alliances, which I want to summarize before describing the regional conference of 1962 and the events that followed. The few years following the granting of internal autonomy to the Sudan in 1957 saw the emergence in Kita of two new political figures. One was Moussa Sylla, a Soninké *dieli* from Mopti who was in charge of the Epidemic Diseases Service in Kita. He had always been active in the RDA. He came to Kita from Bafoulabé and ingratiated himself with the local RDA leadership by his willingness to do favors (for instance, when he went into the bush on official business he was prepared to carry out political or other errands for his allies). The other was Makan Kouyaté, a *dieli* from one of Kita's old *dieli* families who was a doctor. Kouyaté had served for many years in Guinea, where he had been active in the RDA. He returned to Kita following Guinean independence in 1958 and was put in charge of Kita's hospital.

Interpretations in Kita current in 1965 claimed that Sylla was successful in creating a split between Moussa Keita and Sissoko. Sylla allied himself with the former, and together they controlled the BPL. They were opposed to Sissoko, who was allied with Diawara and, increasingly, with Fatogama, as Fatogama switched from the PSP to the RDA after the collapse of the PSP. This was roughly the situation at the time of the two incidents—the Kita Natives' Association and the attempt to institute ward committees—described above.

When Kouyaté returned from Guinea, he was anxious to make a name for himself in local politics. He persuaded a *dieli*, a relative by marriage, to act as his advocate, and eventually persuaded the "kingmakers" in Kita (Moussa Keita and Moriké Sissoko) to slate him as deputy in the 1959 elections to the national assembly. At this point he was associated with the Sylla-Moussa Keita clique. He was especially closely allied with Sylla. Both were *dieli* and both were in the health service—their offices were only a few feet apart. There was talk of creating a marriage link between the two families. The other deputy was Dramane Diawara, who was closer to Sissoko and his faction. Following the 1959 elections, in which the RDA won every seat in the Sudan, the PSP disbanded itself and its members were absorbed into the RDA. The 1959 town council was elected after this disbandment and represented a fusion of all the political forces in the town. It was a period of harmony as far as PSP-RDA relations were concerned, but otherwise the struggle continued.

In 1960 the quarrel between the two factions over control of the political bureau was such that delegations were sent from the national political bureau to restore order. Sylla was so persuasive that he was named secretary-general of a provisional political bureau, and Moriké Sissoko and Fatogoma Keita were suspended from the party for a year for having intrigued. At this time, Kouyaté was still allied with Sylla and interceded on his behalf with the national level of the party. Sylla was also supported by a number of the younger men, including many teachers from out of town, for he was better able to convey a "progressive" image.

Sylla built up his position by his persuasiveness in speech; by his promises, both to individuals and to groups, not all of which were kept; and by his ability to place his friends and allies in strategic positions. Thus the SMDR's two top officers, Kader Keita of Samédougou and Moussa Keita, were both allies of his. Influence in the SMDR was especially important, for it allowed the clique to arrange financial deals favorable to itself. One of the clique members received a large sum of money on account from the SMDR to purchase peanuts. He was supposed to bring in the peanuts or return the money. Instead he used the money to buy a truck, and repaid only a small portion of it. His case was eventually discovered in 1965 when a new SMDR head was named; the clique member was tried and sentenced to six months in jail in addition to having to repay the debt. Sylla was also able to get allies of his into key positions on the youth bureau; his connection there, Mamadou Kamara, was still secretary-general of a provisional youth bureau in 1965. He also intervened on behalf of individuals to get jobs for them. An illiterate *dieli* was named "superviser" at Kita's Collège Moderne because of Sylla's intervention; and because of Sylla he was kept on in his job despite repeated misbehavior. When he was finally fired, it was a major political act requiring consultation between the school director, the secretary-general, and the commandant. Sylla was also adept at bypassing normal administrative channels. When the school director was impatient because of delays in getting approval through the administrative bureaucracy for new construction at his school, he appealed to Sylla, who was able to settle the matter in Bamako forthwith. Sylla also favored the ward in which he resided, Ségoubougouni. When the commune of Kita was established in 1959, exact boundaries between the wards had to be drawn for the first time. He managed to arrange it so that marginal land between Ségoubougouni and two other wards, Saint-Félix and Moribougou, was included in Ségoubougouni. Moribougou tried to protest the loss of "its" land, and pushed the quarrel up to the president (see chapter 8), who decided in favor of Sylla and Ségoubougouni. The Moribougou leader (Sissoko) belonged to the other faction.

After the period during which Sylla and Kouyaté collaborated in the faction that also included Moussa Keita, Mamadou Kamara, Tiémoko Diarra, and others, they split. Kouyaté's position was getting stronger, and he was no longer content to be subordinated to Sylla on the local scene, where Sylla controlled the political bureau. Finding himself unable to take over Sylla's position of leadership within the clique, Kouyaté left it and allied himself with his erstwhile enemies, Moriké Sissoko and Dramane Diawara. At this time he began to argue that Kita's affairs ought to be handled by Kitans, and not by outsiders—the argument that had been used some years earlier by the Kita Natives' Association.

THE 1962 REGIONAL CONFERENCE AND ITS CONSEQUENCES

As the regional party conference of 1962 approached, the two factions were led by, on the one hand, Sylla and Moussa Keita and their allies, including some young men from Makandiambougou and Ségoubougouni, and some young nonlocal teachers, and, on the other, by Makan Kouyaté, Dramane Diawara (the two deputies), Moriké Sissoko, and their allies, including most of Moribougou and Fatogoma Keita's clique in Makandiambougou as well as people from the smaller wards of Lenguékoto and Saint-Félix. (By this time the one-year suspension given Sissoko and Fatogoma Keita had expired and both were once again fully active party members.)

The 1962 conference of the section of Kita had as its central piece of business the election of a new political bureau, which would be the first elected political bureau since the RDA became a single, mass party: Sylla had been appointed, and those before him were chosen from and by a small group of activists who had traditionally supported the RDA. The contest was going to be between the "ins" and the "outs"—Sylla and his allies versus the deputies and their allies. Sylla's aim was to keep his post; the aim of the others was to exclude him from the bureau altogether. But those who opposed Sylla supported various candidates to replace him. At least a half-dozen different names were discussed: Diawara; Kouyaté; an administrative clerk from the imam's family, Alfa Cissé; the national minister of justice (originally from the northern part of the circle, but without any close ties to Kita town) ; Mamadou Kamara (the youth secretary-general) ; Sissoko; and Moussa Keita. Of these, only Alfa Cissé was actively lobbying for the post. One informant told me in 1965 that a consensus among the people of Kita had already been reached before the opening of the conference, but that it was kept secret (insofar as it really had been reached) so that the Bamako delegation would not be able to act against it (see chapter 5 for a similar story involving one of Kita's wards).

The conference had been preceded by intense political activity. Not only was there juggling for position; there had also been several visits from one of the six political commissioners of the party in Mali, who had attempted to "straighten out" Kita politics and to reconcile the various factions. The political commissioner had spent most of his time in the local rest house, and people came to see him alone or in groups. Most frequently they were complaining about the misdeeds of others. During this time, too, the various cliques held secretive meetings to decide on strategy.

Each of the 314 villages in the circle (including the six wards of Kita) had one delegate and one alternate to the conference. Fatogoma Keita was the delegate from Makandiambougou, and Moriké Sissoko the delegate from Moribougou: a demonstration that the anti-Sylla coalition controlled Kita's two largest wards. Although rural and town delegates theoretically had the same powers, the town delegates expected that the rural ones would follow their lead.

The choice of a new political bureau was not made in open session. A nominating committee consisting of representatives of the various geographical subdivisions of the circle, chosen from among the delegates from those subdivisions, plus the outgoing political bureau and the delegation from the national level, made the choice. The inclusion of Sylla and the rest of the outgoing political bureau in the nominating session was a setback for the anti-Sylla coalition, for it meant that people could not attack Sylla as openly as they otherwise would have: if he won, they would suffer. In what is perhaps a representative case, the delegate for the eastern part of the central arrondissement went into the nominating session with instructions from his fellows: get rid of Sylla and put Fatogoma Keita onto the bureau.[7] When the nominating committee had made its

---

7. This is the old man mentioned in chapter 8 who served as an arbitrator in personal quarrels and whose opinions on the precolonial structure were cited in chapter 3.

choices, it reported back to the plenary session, which approved the nominations.

The result was a compromise worked out under the aegis of the national delegation. The top post (secretary-general) went to Diawara, deputy since 1957 and a former secretary-general (at a time when the post had a different meaning). Sylla was given the number two post. Table 9 shows the faction affiliation of the new

TABLE 9

Faction Affiliation of BPL Members (1962)

Post	Sylla	Neutral/Unknown	Diawara/Kouyaté
No. 1			x
No. 2	x		
No. 3	x		
No. 4	x		
No. 5	x		
No. 6			x
No. 7			x
No. 8			x
No. 9			x
No. 10		x	
No. 11	x		
No. 12			x
No. 13	x		
No. 14		x	
No. 15		x	
No. 16		x	
No. 17		x	
Total	6	5	6

BPL members. Altogether six were associated with one faction, six with the other, and five were neutral or unknown to me. The "compromise" was seen by Sylla, however, as a defeat for himself. Not only was he removed from the leading post of the political bureau, but three of his leading enemies were given posts on the bureau. In compensation, some of his major allies were also on the bureau. From the point of view of the Diawara-Kouyaté clique, they had won a victory over Sylla, but he was still on the bureau and there was thus some dissatisfaction, for the victory was still incomplete.

Sylla's troubles were not over. Once the conference was finished and the national delegation had returned home, the quarrel sprang up again. Sylla was intriguing to regain his old position by discrediting his rivals. The deputies were worried by his intrigues and were disappointed that they had not been able to exclude him from the BPL at the conference. The deputies and their clique used the argument that Sylla had misused public funds and had taken bribes to suspend him from the party. Sylla appealed to his friends in Bamako, and the national political bureau refused to approve his suspension. He also made counteraccusations against his rivals. At the same time Sylla tried to find new allies in Kita, and sought out Mamadou Tall, a teacher from Mopti, of noble Toucouleur origin, who was fairly well known by the national party hierarchy (see chapter 4).

To cope with this new outbreak of quarrelling, the BPN sent a delegation headed by its political secretary to Kita. This delegation toured the countryside to sound out local opinion and to try to see who was right in their facts. Tall (who was not widely known as an ally of Sylla) managed to become part of the delegation. He first tried to persuade the delegation head that the population supported Sylla in this quarrel and not the deputies. The delegation head was perhaps all the readier to believe this as he was widely thought to be Sylla's chief ally in Bamako. In each village, the Bamako representative would first make a speech and then retire to rest. While he rested, Tall would contact the village leaders and persuade them to support Sylla in talking with the BPN delegation. The village leaders were led to do this mainly by the reflection that once the dust had settled, they would have to deal with Sylla. This idea was partly inspired by the rumors circulating that the BPN delegation would favor Sylla and exile the deputies; in fact, however, it seems that the BPN delegation came prepared to exile both Sylla and his rivals.

As a result of the BPN delegation's visit, it was decided in Bamako that Sylla was right and had the support of the people, and that the two deputies ought to be sent away from Kita. They were said to be "inadaptable." The reasons for deciding this were that the deputies were causing dissension in the section and that they had made false accusations against Sylla. (Sylla had managed to demonstrate that he was innocent of any misuse of funds or receiving of bribes.) Kouyaté was sent to Gao, where he was given a medical mission to carry out. Diawara was sent to Yélimané, but he never actually went there as he kept travelling between Bamako and Kita while protesting the decision.[8] With the secretary-general gone, Sylla as number two on the BPL became acting secretary-general.

At this point, although Sylla appeared victorious, his downfall began. For one thing, he turned against some of the younger men who had supported him in the showdown with the deputies. They reciprocated by turning against him; one wrote a letter to the BPN saying that he had supported Sylla in good faith, but now saw that he had been mistaken. For another, there was a complicated incident involving the organization of a subsection of the party to cover the central arrondissement.

This was the same time at which another of Mali's political commissioners was sent to supervise the political reorganization of Kita—exactly the kind of external interference that Kitans most dislike. When the political commissioner was looking into Kita's affairs, he noticed that the central arrondissement was less "developed" politically than the other arrondissements in the circle. This underdevelopment was attributed to the lack of a subsection organization, with political and youth bureaus.[9] So it was decided to create a subsection organization in the central arrondissement. The first step was to elect a bureau, which could then handle the rest of the organization. Sylla would have dearly loved to be elected secretary-general of the subsection bureau, as that would have compensated for his being only the acting secretary-general in the section bureau, and would have increased his power.[10] However, the people of the villages (the town of Kita was not to be covered by the new subsection) refused to elect him as secretary-general and chose instead Douga Tounkara (age twenty seven; Kouyaté's secretary at the hospital). At the same time they chose a somewhat older man

8. Gao is in the Saharan northeast of the country, and Yélimané is a small village, seat of a circle, in northwest Mali on the edge of the Sahara. Both are isolated spots, as far away from Kita and from each other, and as physically disagreeable, as possible.

9. This was in fact the pattern throughout Mali: the central arrondissement in each of the circles depended directly on the section's political bureau (see figure 5).

10. As he did not have to surrender one post to get another, he would combine the functions.

from Makandiambougou (age thirty-eight) as the secretary-general for the subsection's youth bureau.

When neither he nor his allies had been chosen to head the new bureau, Sylla's response was to try to hamper them in their operations. One of his actions was to withhold a large part of the money that it had been agreed would be handed over to the new subsection from the section's treasury. Despite these handicaps, the new leaders of the bureaus undertook an intensive organization campaign to set up a committee in every village in the arrondissement. They apparently found that village party organization was not in good shape, despite the optimistic reports on the subject that Sylla had frequently sent to Bamako during the period when he was secretary-general of the BPL. They met with a great deal of enthusiasm in the bush and felt that they were making progress in settling some old inter-village quarrels that had impeded proper political organization of the countryside previously.[11]

About a month after the new bureaus were established, a national-level delegation of youth leaders was expected in Kita. Sylla passed on the responsibility for welcoming them to the subsection officials. They prepared an especially warm welcome for the visiting delegation, in which the high point was a speech by the secretary-general of the subsection political bureau in which he spoke of what he and his associates had done and of what they hoped to do. Implicit in much of his speech was a criticism of Sylla: Tounkara said they had for the first time organized committees in every village, while Sylla had for years claimed already to have done this. In the tension following this speech, Sylla sent off a letter to Bamako, accusing Tounkara and his associates of working to recreate PSP strength in the countryside, of sabotaging socialist policies, of making propaganda in favor of the exiled deputies, and so on. The BPN sent a delegation to inquire into the matter, and found how isolated Sylla had become in Kita and how incorrect his accusations were. After this, even his friends in Bamako could not

11. One case involved two villages where three Keita lineages lived in close proximity to one another, forming what to the eye would be three wards of the same village. Due to quarrels over precedence, however, one of the wards was a separate village while the two others were joined. The rivalry between them also impeded cooperation in economic development schemes. The goal was to have them forget their quarrels and come together in a single village with a single committee.

continue to support him; within a couple of months he was assigned elsewhere, and the two exiled deputies were recalled to Kita.

As a result of this experience, however, the experiment with the central arrondissement's subsection was also abandoned, for it became apparent that if there were two bureaus in a single town (for example, the BPL and the subsection political bureaus, both in Kita and both reflecting much the same constellation of political forces) they would either have to have identical personnel or there would be so much rivalry between them that the overall situation would deteriorate. The reminiscences of this effort were in much the same tone as the memories of the Kita Natives' Association; both efforts were seen as Kita movements to fend off the influence of outsiders. Perhaps this element, too, entered into Bamako's decision to abandon the experiment.

THE DEPUTIES DOMINATE (1964–65)

In early 1964 the faction headed by the two deputies was once more dominant in Kita. Sylla had been sent away in disgrace, and the leadership of his faction had fallen to Mamadou Kamara, now school headmaster as well as youth secretary-general. Elections for the national assembly were held in April, 1964. The nominating committee which met to choose Kita's candidates consisted of the BPL, the bureaus of the subsections, and delegates from the wards of Kita town and from the central arrondissement. The possibilities mentioned were the two outgoing deputies, Mamadou Kamara, Aliou Keita, and Fili Ba of Toukoto. The committee voted in favor of retaining the two outgoing deputies, with Kamara a poor third. One of the reasons given for the continuing support of Diawara and Kouyaté was that they were of local origin and thus somehow their actions were predictable.

One story that circulated concerning this election is that the remnants of Sylla's faction tried to split the alliance formed by Diawara and Kouyaté. The story goes that Moussa Keita approached Diawara to suggest that if he consented to favor Kamara rather than Kouyaté then "all Kita would know who the senior deputy in Kita was." Diawara rejected this suggestion. The votes that Kamara and to a lesser extent Aliou Keita received in this election represented the supporters of the old Sylla faction, but with Sylla gone many of his supporters on the BPL and the subsection bureaus switched to the dominant side.

For a while after this period, the faction led by the deputies was so dominant in Kita that there were none of the reversals that characterized earlier periods, though there were some flare-ups. One of these involved the renewal of the subsection bureau in Sagabari arrondissement. The secretary-general of the political bureau there had been the original founder of the RDA in the area in the 1940's. He had originally been a supporter of Sylla, but abandoned him after the exile of the deputies. When a touring BPN delegation was in the area, in May, 1965, it heard so many stories of discontent that it instructed the Kita BPL to organize the election of a new bureau. The stories of discontent were being passed around by supporters of Kamara's faction (the former Sylla faction), who hoped to replace the old secretary-general of Sagabari with a new one more favorable to Kamara. As people expected a new BPL to be chosen shortly in Kita, this would have aided Kamara's cause for that effort. However, the attempt to replace the old secretary-general failed; he was returned to office. The threat from some local political figures was counterbalanced by the delegation from the Kita BPL which attended the meeting and which included one of the two deputies.

In August, 1965, a quarrel broke out between Kouyaté and one of his in-laws. The in-law had been one of Kouyaté's main supporters when he first returned from Guinea but when Kouyaté switched factions, the in-law had remained with Sylla and was still in Kamara's faction. The quarrel broke out into the open when Kouyaté allegedly made a threat to his in-law that he would cause him to disappear. The in-law was frightened, but not so frightened that he didn't counterattack. He went to a typist and had a letter of formal complaint drawn up in about eight copies. He sent the copies to various political bodies: the Ségoubougouni committee (of which he was a member), the BPL, the BPN, the local judge, the commandant de cercle, and so on. This was construed locally as an attempt to discredit Kouyaté. After a few months, the incident seemed to have blown over.[12]

Also during August, 1965, rumors began to circulate that both the commandant de cercle and the police chief, two of the most

12. As with many stories from the realm of political gossip the causes for dissension and opposition, and the moves of men against one another, were much more widely known than the resolution of the conflict, which perhaps no one had an interest in making known.

powerful civil servants in Kita, were about to be transferred. The commandant left for a new post in September, and the police chief left towards the end of the year. This was widely believed to be the work of Kouyaté, who was afraid that the two men were too close to Kamara's faction and would support it in the upcoming elections for mayor of Kita and for a new BPL. One of the leading members of Kamara's faction, a trader-trucker who had been behind the attempt to dislodge the Sagabari secretary-general, went to Mali's president to protest the reassignment, claiming that the retention of the police chief was necessary if the circle of Kita were to export as many peanuts as in the previous year. (This appeal was based on the fact that the police chief was in charge of organizing the trucking to bring peanuts from the villages to the railroad lines—see chapter 5). The police chief himself, however, was reported to feel that there was no point fighting the decision since once people had decided to get rid of you they would keep trying until they had. Perhaps he was thinking of Sylla.

THE FUTURE

Except for these incidents, the competition between competing factions was relatively quiet during my field stay. In part this was due to the fact that no elections were held during this time; factions usually spring to life when there are posts to be filled. In part it was due to the fact that the factional competition had reached a point where one faction was completely dominant. As long as there were no new elections to cause dissension in its ranks, it could remain both united and dominant and could deal easily with any minor threats that the subordinate faction might mount. However, it seemed likely that as soon as there were new elections or any other cause of strain, the dominant faction would split, as happened in the past, when Sissoko and Moussa Keita split around 1957 after the victory over the PSP became obvious. Indeed, this is what many Kitans expected to happen. They expected that the two new faction leaders would be Diawara and Kouyaté, the two deputies.

Diawara had been active in the RDA in Kita from 1947, being secretary-general of the RDA for most of that time. He became deputy in 1957. Kouyaté had been active in the RDA for as long a period, but the early part of his career was in Guinea. He became a deputy in 1959, but the fact that he was a *dieli* always counted somewhat against him, and through 1965 he had never held a position where he was in charge of anyone else. The two men maintained an alliance from the late 1950s and were successful in destroying the influence of Sylla. After my departure from Kita at the end of 1965, there was an election that may have indicated which way events were heading. The election was for the town council of Kita, and then within the council the councillors had to elect Kita's mayor—the first time the mayor had been chosen this way. Makan Kouyaté was elected mayor, the first time he had been chosen for an executive post in Kita.[13]

The two decades whose history is summarized in this chapter can be divided into four periods. First there was the conflict over the post of canton chief betwen Fatogoma and his supporters and the Tokontana and their supporters. The second stage was the conflict between the PSP, led in Kita by Fatogoma Keita, and the RDA, led by Moussa Keita of the Tokontana, Moriké Sissoko of Moribougou, and one or two civil servants. The third stage came after the defeat of the PSP and its elimination as an effective political force. At this point the RDA split into two factions, which competed for preeminence over the next decade. The main issue was the question of the degree of influence nonlocals should have in Kita's politics. After a period when the Diawara-Kouyaté faction dominated the Sylla faction, the fourth stage seemed to be shaping up as a conflict between the followers of Makan Kouyaté, perhaps including most of the leaders of the remnants of Sylla's faction, and the supporters of Dramane Diawara, perhaps including some of the rank and file of the old Sylla faction. At each stage there were two factions. As soon as one became dominant it split into two new factions, so that the dualistic system of opposing factions was always maintained, despite the tremendous shift in politics from traditional chiefship politics to populistic politics within the town arena.

---

13. Some people remarked that being the envoy of Kita as deputy was an appropriate job for a *dieli*, but that Kitans would never approve putting a *dieli* in a position where he could "command." So much for traditional prejudices.

7

Factions

I have tried to bring out the shifting patterns of alliances and rivalries in two decades of Kita's political history and to show what were the issues and goals that motivated the actors. Now it is time to push the analysis further and grasp the structure behind these events by isolating the recurring patterns of social relations such as the factions and cliques based on a system of asymmetrical relations. The system of factional conflict provided a rationale and a model for organizing interpersonal rivalry in the town of Kita. Factions also, like many other systems for regulating internal conflict, paradoxically served a unifying and integrating function; they set the limits to Kita's arena by defining that arena as the totality of participants in its system of factional conflict, and they limited more primordial kinds of conflict in that arena by cutting across the other divisions of society.

Kitans frequently talked of factions. Still one must be cautious not to give such conceptions too much concreteness, however present they may be in people's minds, for the sociological reality is seldom as neat as the conception of it. It is nonetheless possible to discuss the categories of social relations on which factions are based and to show the ways in which alliances are built up. It is also possible to show the ways in which local politics is filtered through the factional system and to discuss the roles that factions and factional conflict played in Kita's pattern of popular government. In this chapter I turn to these topics.

THE STRUCTURE OF FACTIONS

Factions in Kita were very loosely structured alliances of people who helped each other attain posts and work towards certain goals. They were organized around one or several key leaders who were the center for a halo of lesser leaders and for increasingly vague rings of followers. The chief links between the members of a faction were political in the sense that factions did not build on other ways of segmenting society, but cut across all of them. The links between actors in the political arena were formed on the basis of what people could do rather than on who they were, and what they could do resulted from achievement in the state or party hierarchies. The factions were not permanent, visible groupings; they did not involve everyone in Kita; and their limits were fluctuating and unclear. Insofar as it was possible to speak of membership, their members were varied in their social origins, and this diverse membership mirrored the many ways in which people were linked to the men at the core of the faction.[1]

Social patterns with roots in the precolonial Maninka culture supported this pattern of factions. One such pattern provided a model for individual rivalry in the political sphere which the traditional culture expressed as a rivalry between half-brothers, known as *faden*—men who share a common father but have different mothers.[2] In postindependence politics, the term *faden* was used to refer to political rivals who were anything but half-brothers. This pattern of rivalry was based on a value which encouraged people to achieve prominence in the community through participation in public affairs. Anyone in Kita who felt that he was at all important had to measure himself against others in terms of prestige, and prestige was gained primarily in the political arena. It was suggested to me by an informant that politicians who profited from their political positions usually "reinvested" the money in politics through largess and other techniques to build up a clientele. Both Moussa Keita and Moriké Sissoko were said to have ruined themselves financially by investing too much of the money they earned trading in peanuts in their political careers; yet both, of course, were quite prestigious. As the example of Abraham Keita given in the previous chapter shows, one can't try too hard. For a man to consider himself important in Kita, whatever his occupation might be, he had to be the kind of person to whom others turned for advice and to whom they listened. He had to be able to see himself as a man of influence.

Another such pattern was that of asymmetrical ties between people of different social status—citizens and noncitizens, freemen

---

1. This analysis owes much to Mayer (1966), Nicholas (1965), and Wolf (1966).
2. The early life of Soundiata was marked by his rivalry with his *faden* (Niane 1960). See also Hopkins (in press).

and *nyamakala,* more powerful and less powerful people politically. This pattern was linked with the idea that one should always approach a powerful person through an intermediary. Deriving from the *teriya* relationship between merchants and peasants (see chapter 3) and undoubtedly harking back to the host-guest and *diatigi-nyamakala* relationships (see chapter 4), a system with three tiers—petitioner, broker, and grantor—developed in Kita in the years following the colonial installation. The peasant or townsman who wanted a favor (the petitioner) sought out someone he knew, and whom he also knew to have access to the seats of power (the broker). This was a person with whom he had diffuse relations, which might involve many other aspects besides brokerage. The petitioner tended to seek out the same broker for all his problems. The broker, then, if he accepted the petitioner's request, had to seek out the relevant grantor and convey the petition to him.

The grantors were people with administrative positions, though of course they could also hold party positions. They were people with some degree of control over entry into schools, distribution of jobs, assignment of building lots, and so on. The school director, the police chief, the commandant de cercle, the mayor, the town clerk, the head of the SMDR, the head of the livestock service, the stationmaster were all possible grantors. The brokers were usually people with party positions, typically the secretaries-general of the ward committees or of the BPL.

The relationship between the petitioner and the broker was often expressed in terms of *teriya* and was the postindependence version of the relationship between merchant and farmer. Unlike the earlier version, the relationship between petitioner and broker did not have an immediate material correlate: the broker, for example, was not also in a position to offer credit and other favors to the petitioner in order to build up a clientele, nor did he have the advantage of possible material profit to spur him on. His only hope was to generate enough popular support so that he could become a grantor himself. My impression was that most political brokers found their role onerous. In a system where overt political ambition was liable to get one into trouble, the broker could not maximize the role's potential. For many reasons, the broker had to agree to act as intermediary in a certain number of the cases presented to him (the cases came from people with some kind of claim on him, and he had to be somewhat active in order to maintain his role), yet he got no material advantage from this and it restricted his own freedom of activity, since it required him to maintain good relations with the grantors. A ward committee secretary-general who was also a schoolteacher had to maintain good relations with the school director, a leader of the faction he opposed politically, because parents frequently came to him for help in arranging the affairs of their children. He could do nothing himself, and the fact that he needed the school director's good will meant that the school director retained some kind of control over him.

Petitioners claimed friendship with brokers, but brokers did not reciprocate. This contrasts with the earlier situation where the brokers (the merchants) did reciprocate in the claims of friendship. Although the vocabulary remained the same and the structure of petitioning did not change, there was no continuing relationship in the postindependence version, primarily, I believe, because the material factor was absent. Petitioners did not seek to establish a permanent relationship with a broker on the basis of being dependent on him, for there was no permanent return, such as credit, and they did not want to limit their freedom of maneuver. Structured dependent ties gave way to this looser situation, where the main function of the system was to provide a network for dispensing favors rather than for distributing resources.[3]

It can easily be seen how this emphasis on the role of the intermediary and on asymmetrical relations combined with the desires of individuals to be considered prominent to produce the loose alliances here called factions. The grantors and the brokers attempted to derive personal capital from their ability to grant favors, to get Bamako to do things, and generally to be generous with their time and capacities; at the same time, this ability was dependent on the continuation of the popular support needed to maintain them in the posts from which they could operate. Thus the factions were temporary configurations of these asymmetrical

---

3. It may be that the absence of any material reward for participation in the patron-client situation is an artifact of inadequate data. Bribes and other material benefits were mentioned in connection with the past in Kita and with the present in the higher ranks of the national society, but perhaps because of Kita's poverty they were never evoked in this context. It may also be that the constellation of relations around the merchant-broker was less permanent than I report, for my account is a reconstruction based on interviews. The way I present the analysis here, however, corresponds to what informants told me in Kita in 1965.

relations, bound together by alliances between the figures at the apex of each bundle of lines. No given composition of a faction lasted, as people shifted around in accordance with their interests and goals. Despite the tendency of Kitans to conceptualize their politics as conflict between two opposing camps, the reality was more complex and more elusive.

The most striking symbol of the existence of a faction was that it had a name. Kita's factions were referred to as if they had a single individual at their head. They were called, for instance, "Mamadou's people" or "Sylla's people," after their presumed leaders. In fact, the summary of Kita's political history shows that at each stage the faction was headed by an alliance of several different individuals, representing different segments of the town's population. When Sylla was the head of Kita's most powerful faction, it was still necessary to qualify his leadership by pointing out that he was closely allied with Moussa Keita. The alliance was important because it represented an alliance between the modernizing civil service tendency and a representative of the traditional chiefable family in Kita, who was at the same time one of the leading peanut merchants in the town and a key figure in the SMDR. Similarly, the faction that opposed the Sylla-Moussa Keita faction was headed by Diawara, Kouyaté, Sissoko, and at a later stage Fatogoma Keita. Again, these individuals each brought a different clientele to the faction. Sissoko was a peanut trader, with strong influence in his home ward of Moribougou. Fatogoma Keita had been the canton chief and was widely respected; as a Keita of chiefly lineage he could call on the traditional political alliances. Kouyaté had his initial support largely from his fellow *dieli* and from his subordinates at the hospital, while Diawara had built up an audience from his long period as secretary-general of the local party and later as deputy. Thus the factions themselves in Kita were composed of small cliques of men centered around a single person who was frequently the broker between the other members and the overall faction head. If the relationships between petitioners and brokers sometimes were based on primordial ties, those between broker and grantor were purely in terms of political advantage and personal compatibility.

The various cliques allied to form factions. In a sense the relations between clique leaders and faction leaders repeated those between clique leaders and followers: those involved might be kinsmen, friends or associates, or clients. The bonds between leader and follower were in each case consensual. No clique leader could promise to "deliver" his followers' support to another; his leadership of a clique was always dependent on the extent to which he expressed the views of clique members. When Sissoko broke away from Fatogoma to join Moussa Keita in founding the RDA in 1946, he "led" a lot of people in Moribougou to do likewise. Yet he was "following" public opinion in Moribougou in making the switch, for Moribougou had always prided itself on its progressiveness, and the RDA was the more progressive of the two parties. On the other hand, when Kouyaté switched factions around 1960, he did not carry all his supporters with him, for this was a more personal thing. The in-law who had been one of his strongest supporters in 1959, when Kouyaté returned to Kita, remained with the Sylla-Moussa Keita faction—where he had been before the return of Kouyaté.

The disparate reasons for recruitment into a faction meant that the factions were basically indistinguishable in their social composition, although the ambiguity of faction affiliation, except in the case of core members, makes this hard to demonstrate in detail. Looking at the core of each faction, it appears that all the major categories, whether ethnic group, ward of residence, occupation, or age, were represented among the supporters of each faction. Kitans themselves remarked on this, saying there was no real difference between the two factions. The dominant faction during my field work was alleged to be overly favorable to former PSP members because several of the more prominent of the former PSP members in Kita were associated with the faction, yet it was led by two old RDA men including Diawara, who had been secretary-general of the Kita RDA for most of its life. The other faction was alleged to be the faction of the nonlocals because two of its major leaders fitted that description, yet it also had the support of the lineage that had dominated the canton chiefship from the French conquest to 1942 as well as of other more recently established but indisputably Kitan families. Note that both these stereotypes are based on negative images—allegiance to a discredited party and not being a Kitan.

People who were closely enough allied with clique or faction leaders so that they could be considered as "members" of that faction were a minority of the population. Many people preferred to remain aloof from the factional struggle. Political leaders could only count on their loyal supporters for a part of the support they felt they needed; beyond this they were dependent on the general impression of good or evil that people had of them. Generally, politicians felt that the more support they had the better, and they were concerned with behaving so as to increase their support by increasing their popularity. They had to pay attention to public opinion; they could not afford to get a reputation for high-handedness or for refusing to listen to people; they could not argue too strenuously in favor of unpopular government projects. The people, in turn, were aware that their support was important to leaders, and they wanted to support the man who could do the most for them. A favor done was important both for the persons who benefited from it directly and for the politician who gained a general reputation for being "nice." The central fact about the structure of factions was the nature of the links between men, for this remained constant while all else was in flux.

PROCESS: FACTIONS AT WORK

There have essentially always been two factions within the Kita political arena. In recent times only in the period immediately following the collapse of the PSP in 1959 was there anything like complete dominance by one faction. The balance of power in a relatively complicated political system was such that no one faction came to dominate the political structure entirely, and thus the political institutions (BPL, town council, and so on) could not be used by one faction against another. Both factions were always represented on key bureaus. In 1959, following the collapse of the PSP, some of its representatives, recently absorbed into the RDA, were nonetheless given places on the town council and on the temporary political bureau. Membership on the 1962 BPL was consciously divided between members of the two rival factions.

The reasons for the maintenance of the two-faction system, despite the changes in personnel of the factions and the switches in alliance, were complex.[4] There were two competing trends. One was

4. Barth (1959) suggests the applicability of the theory of games to the problem of why there should be only and always two. One of the conditions that Barth lays down for Swat and that seems to be applicable here is that the prime motivation for involvement in competitive political activity must be the ambition to be the most powerful person in a given system. Any other motivation than sheer ambition—loyalty to relatives, desire for peace and quiet, material gain, ideology or principle—disturbs the equation.

147

for people to switch to the winning side. If one faction seemed to be increasing its strength at the expense of the other, some members of the less powerful faction sought to better their personal position by switching to the majority faction. This trend was limited by the fact that some members of the defeated faction would not switch for personal reasons, such as personal loyalty or the fear of looking ridiculous. The other trend was for the winning faction to split if its domination became too sure. I have shown how the splits in the RDA only began after the defeat of the PSP. Many people in Kita thought the process was about to repeat itself in 1966 following the great reduction in influence of the faction headed by Moussa Kamara (formerly Sylla's faction).[5] The reason for the split in these circumstances seemed to be that the competition between individuals for prestige continued and inevitably led to the split of a dominant faction into two competing factions. As Barth suggests, one reason for this is that it is better to be a leader in the second-ranking faction than to be a minor figure in the dominant one.

Despite the existence of two factions competing for support during the first decade of Malian internal self-government, and the rather general unpopularity of many governmental programs during the second half of that period at least, no faction tried to make political gains by adapting a stance opposed to government policies. Such a stand would have been suicidal, as the example of the Kita Natives' Association shows. If either faction had tried to curry favor by opposing central government policies, the other faction would have been able to call down the wrath of the central government on it and destroy it, for the rhetoric, if not the practice, of politics was socialist, and whatever went against that rhetoric was condemnable. So everyone maintained a generally favorable position with regard to central government policies. At the same time there were moments when both factions, carefully choosing their ground, stood against certain details of government policies.

The best example of this that came to my attention centered around a 2 percent cut in the price paid to peasants for their peanuts. This cut was presented to the peasants as having been authorized by the government to cover inevitable wastage in the process

5. Information gathered during a visit to Kita in 1970 suggests that this split did in fact occur, but the intrusion of national politics into the local scene with the "active revolution" of 1967 and the military coup of 1968 obscured the details of the process. Neither deputy was in Kita in 1970.

of transferring peanuts from the village to the railroad line. The peasants grumbled, but accepted the cut. Later on, the question was brought up again by Kouyaté, who claimed that there was no need for such a cut in price and that if he had been in Kita at the time the decision was made, he would have discouraged it. Faced with this position, Diawara backed down from his earlier position (it was he who had presented the decisions to the peasants originally) and said that he had never supported the decision either. This was a clear demagogic appeal to the peasants for support by Kouyaté, leaving Diarawa with the choice of defending an unpopular decision or switching to Kouyaté's point of view. In either case, Kouyaté got credit for righting the wrong.[6]

This example shows the limits of local dissension, at least in public; acceptable dissension dealt with the application of policies, not with the policies themselves. This case is also somewhat unusual, for in its suggestion of a split between Kouyaté and Diawara it brought a local issue into factional politics. Other local issues, such as the manner of integrating PSP members into the party, the running of the cooperatives (see chapter 5), the rights and wrongs of school crises, the proper duties and obligations of leaders, even (except for the period of the Kita Natives' Association) the question of the involvement of nonlocals in Kita's government, did not become bones for factional contention. In part this was because other interests, cutting across factional lines, were involved; and in part because attempts to mobilize factions along these lines laid Kita all the more open to interference from the national level—or so Kitans feared. Finally, the case of the price of peanuts revealed one other thing: no one in town had any interest in maintaining the 2 percent cut.

A great deal of the competition between faction and clique leaders took the form of specific acts, such as arranging favors for individuals, persuading the central government to do something in Kita, or intriguing against one's rivals. Many questions of personal interest were brought to the attention of the politicians, and these had to be dealt with if the politician was to maintain or improve his position. Such questions included parents who wanted their children accepted into school, young men who wanted jobs, a newly

---

6. This case suggests something of the broker role the town can play for its rural constituents.

FACTIONS

arrived family which wanted a house lot or an old family which
wanted another, legal problems concerning individuals which had
to be solved, destitute people who had to be helped, people who felt
they had been dealt with unjustly by the government, and so on.
All these were occasions for favors within the political hierarchy,
and they all fed into the petitioner-broker-grantor schema. The
success of political leaders in acting as brokers, or their generosity
in acting as grantors, in these matters had a direct bearing on the
amount of popular support they could command.

Kita as a whole had also to cope with the national government.
This meant that the national government had to be persuaded to
provide Kita with the things that benefited everyone, such as
schools, dispensaries, pharmacies, trains, and more teachers and
nurses. It also meant that the policies established by the national
government had to be applied in Kita, perhaps with slight variations to suit local conditions. Politicians who were successful in
petitioning the central government for the things Kita wanted, or
who were successful in shielding Kita from the worst aspects of
government policies, thereby increased their stature and prestige.
I have given the example of Sylla intervening on behalf of the
school director with the national government; Kouyaté, too, was
adept at this, and was mainly responsible for the decision to place
a people's pharmacy in Kita (see chapter 8). One of the criticisms
of Dramane Diawara, on the other hand, was that he did not have
such influence in Bamako.[7]

Intrigue against one's rivals seemed to be endemic in Kita.
The success of intrigue depended largely on the existence in Kita
of a political arena within which public opinion had a role and
individuals were concerned about their prestige. Intrigue was directed at making the victims look ridiculous or powerless. This
intrigue was mostly either gossip or speeches in public meetings or
bureau meetings. Kitans were sensitive to talk denigrating themselves, which they referred to as "ruining one's name" (ka togo
tinye). Intrigue also took the form of obstructionism. Thus it was
said that every bureau was divided into opposing factions. Members
of the minority faction would argue against all proposals made by

7. The most frequent way of evaluating a deputy throughout Mali was in terms
of his success in dealing with the national government for the advantages his
constituency wanted.

the majority faction, thinking of reasons why the proposals were unlikely to work. Once the meeting was finished, these same minority members would leak unfavorable accounts of the discussion in the bureau meeting and would thus try to direct public feeling against the majority.[8] Other forms of intrigue consisted of taking advantage of the blocks in the flow of information in the country to present the national level of the party with a one-sided view of the situation in Kita. Thus people with a highly-ranked contact in Bamako tried to give a version of Kita events that favored them.[9] A variant of this was once attempted by Sylla. He wanted to get rid of a male nurse assigned to one of the smaller towns in the circle of Kita. Since he was frequently asked to intervene on behalf of civil servants wishing transfers, no one found it strange when he informed the health ministry that this man, too, wanted a transfer. In this case, however, his duplicity came out, and the incident was one of the causes of his downfall. Another technique of intrigue was to sow dissension among one's enemies. A favorite method was to start gossip that X had said something uncomplimentary about Y (X and Y being allies, opposed to the gossipmonger). If Y fell for this, he might break off relations with X; even if neither ever came to the other side, the gossipmonger stood to gain something. This technique was said to be the speciality of the *dieli*. Some people took this kind of political activity with deadly seriousness; for others, especially in retrospect, it was the sporting, "game" aspect that was most appealing; some people enjoyed recounting with gusto the maneuvers, intrigues, and political derring-do they had been involved in.

The processes of factionalism worked on two levels. On one level there was the competition between individuals and between coalitions of individuals, involving intrigues, attempts to garner support by winning friends, and so on. And on another level there were the processes that kept this competition focused in the political arena and that pushed it to coalesce in a two-faction structure.

8. It is a principle of the party in Mali that all discussion must take place within the meeting. This is also a central canon of Leninist political organization; the Leninist conception struck a very responsive chord in Malian values.

9. To combat such tactics, the party developed the role of political commissioners. These commissioners tried to make contacts with all cliques in order to get at the truth.

FACTIONS

THE MACROSOCIOLOGICAL APPROACH

It is apparent that factions and the patron-client relations out of which factions are built performed certain functions for Kita society as a whole. Factions affected some aspects of Kita life more than others. They were concerned primarily with the relative prestige of the leading citizens of the town and with the way in which the people were able to participate in Kita's politics. Thus factional conflict essentially concerned the ability of different individuals to exercise influence in the town's government.

Factions in one sense were the concrete form that the general pattern of competitive politics took. Out of the mass of individual strivings for prestige and position, two rival groups emerged, which we call factions. The factions were a coalition of cliques and the cliques in turn were formed of people each of whom was individually ambitious as well as eager to support the clique leader. The atmosphere of competition meant that any dispute, no matter how banal, was liable to be interpreted as having relevance for inter-faction competition. But this is not the same as saying that every dispute automatically became a bone of contention between the two factions. Rather it means that each person involved in a dispute was risking his prestige in doing so; a loss or gain of prestige on the part of one of the principal figures in town affected the relative positions of the factions the next time that some issue arose in which the factions were set off against one another.

Factions and the kind of ties that made up factions were primarily called into play when there was a struggle for the positions of day-to-day power in the society, such as an election to some bureau or council. They also came to the fore when it looked as if the central government were going to intervene, and people jockeyed for position and tried to convince the government's emissaries of the correctness of their position. Rarely it involved a movement such as the Kita Natives' Association, an open attempt to constitute a political bloc in order to use it to take over the leadership positions in the town.

Factional affiliations were of some relevance in the number of small and large favors that were necessary to keep the system moving. On the one hand a faction leader rewarded his supporters by arranging jobs and other advantages for them: Sylla was a master at this and did it more systematically than either Kouyaté or Dia-

wara. On the other hand, politicians were encouraged not to re-
strict their favor-doing to people who already supported them,
because a large part of their success depended on gaining new, if
temporary, supporters, and this in turn depended on their reputation for being "nice" or "mean." Doing favors for people outside
one's immediate clique was a good way to develop a favorable
reputation. The existence of a system of factional rivalry provided
the reference institution for the pattern of demands for favors and
their acceptance as legitimate by the "brokers" and "grantors" of
the society. Without the prestige that accrued to the successful
"broker" or "grantor," the process of favor-doing would have been
less functional as a means for circumventing bureaucracy.

The factions enabled a skein of relationships to exist which
wound through the other divisions of society. Associating men in
ways that had nothing to do with primordial ties, factions were a
network of ties that served to bind the whole together. Material interests might divide society in two,[10] but if both factions contained
some adherents from each side of the division, and if political competition were channeled into competition between the two factions,
then the division remained merely a potential one. Faction affiliation was based on something like the free consent of the individuals
involved, so it was possible for faction members to transfer their
allegiance as the individual leaders rose and fell, or as they came to
stand for different things. This gave a certain flexibility to the
system which it would not have had if the competing groups corresponded to other ways of segmenting society.

The factions permitted many people to become involved in
politics. This was of key importance in Kita, where every self-
respecting man felt he ought to have a political role. Factions allowed a man to grant or withhold his allegiance; however insignificant his position, he felt he could negotiate and bargain with his
support. Support played a vital role for the politician, too. When a
national level delegation was investigating the roots of a quarrel in
Kita they inquired of the people in the villages and in the town
which side they supported. The people themselves were well aware
that their support was important to leaders, and they were usually

10. Meillassoux (1965:134) argues that such a split existed in Bamako between
the merchants and the civil servants, and something of the kind occurred in
Kita with the cooperative issue.

not shy about approaching them with demands for favors. They also explicitly conceived of expulsion from office as a sanction for a man who performed badly in their eyes. The atmosphere of competition engendered by the two equally balanced factions allowed every citizen to make his voice felt and to feel that he had at least the potential to participate in politics.

The atmosphere of competitive politics also played a more concrete role. It allowed the expression of certain demands, both individual and collective. The most notable example was the dispute over the influence in Kita politics of nonlocal civil servants. Expression of demands worked in cases like these because, as politicians sensed what the feelings of the mass of the people were, they might espouse these positions in order to increase their followings. This path of demagogy was also followed by Kouyaté when he came out against the 2 percent cut in peanut prices. There were of course many issues that did not become a part of this process; however, even the expression of the demands associated with such problems as the method of distributing food among the cooperatives took place in an atmosphere where everyone's prestige was always "on the line"—as was shown by the attempt of the secretary-general of Moribougou to embarrass the president of the Moribougou cooperative, with whom he disagreed, by bringing up their disagreement in a public meeting where he hoped to mobilize public opinion on his side. It is a fair but unprovable hypothesis that if the constraint resulting from the central government's positions had not been a factor, the factions would have played much more fully than they did the role of providing a structure through which individual and collective demands could be made.[11] The factions were the key to the participation of the mass of the people in local politics.

The factions in Kita were a particular crystallization, at a given time, out of the general pattern of personal competition for prestige and esteem. The political relations between the leaders and followers within the factions were modelled on the "friendship"

11. On the other hand, the central government controlled the use of force and other major sanctions, and so these were not available to a faction wishing to consolidate its position. This could be said to have equalized the factions and maintained a certain level of competition. It would be interesting to see whether the disappearance of the party following the 1968 coup has led to a different role for factions.

type of dependent relations. The dynamics of factions in Kita involved both the attempt of some to join the bandwagon of a winning faction and the tendency of a dominant faction to split. At most periods of Kita's recent history there have been two opposing factions competing for the top political position in the town. Because of the constraints imposed on them by the attitudes of the central government, the factions quarrelled more over political posts than over issues, and did not develop into a progovernment and an antigovernment faction. The analysis of the factions alone would not give us a complete picture of the government of Kita; the faction system concerned mainly the choice of those who occupied positions of power in the political hierarchy. The type of social relations which went to make up the factions were not tied to any primordial factors. Each faction involved representatives of all social groups and categories in the town; they represented links between these categories, thus aiding the social integration of the town. Furthermore, the social system of the town was coterminous with the extension of the factions, so that the factions were defining characteristics of the nature and identity of the town itself. The factions also fostered popular government by enabling a large number of individuals to participate in the political process through the leaders' need for support; in some circumstances they provided the means through which demands were expressed.

8

The Dynamics of Agreement

The key to self-government is the ability to make the choices necessary to keep things going and to generate enough popular support for those choices so that they can be implemented. When a more or less permanent political arena corresponds to the community,[1] then popularly supported decisions are possible, for the ebb and flow of discussion means that the consensus behind each decision eases its implementation. Kita town frequently acted as an arena within which every Kitan could have an effect on the decisions that were being made. It was an arena where consensus could form through free and open discussion (as long as the major government policies were not questioned) and through confrontation of different points of view. It was an arena where leaders competed for advantage by espousing popular causes while ordinary citizens cast their support one way or another, or tried to arouse public feeling on a question so that leaders would be forced to take action. It was an arena in which only projects that had ample popular support could be realized, for there were no institutions able to enforce locally made decisions on more than the recalcitrant few.

This chapter is concerned with the dynamics of agreement, including making decisions about projects for the future, raising questions about the way in which leaders were leading, and settling disputes. The resolution of all these quandaries took place in an arena—not necessarily the same in each case, but always with a

1. For a discussion of the concept of arena and the related one of field, see Bailey (1963), Swartz, Turner, and Tuden (1966) and Swartz (1968).

tendency for the arena to correspond to the town of Kita—through the working out of the balance of forces, including the desires of the central government and its local representatives and the pressure of public opinion. Each time one of these issues had to be settled, the balance of forces in the town was called into question, for the resolution would be bound to favor the ambitions and status of one or another individual or group.

There was always a tendency for the main arena in Kita to correspond to the town's social network, although in some cases the influence and role of the central government or of the town's rural dependencies were more apparent, and in other cases only a part of the town, such as a ward, might be involved. One of the strengths of the town as a social unit was that it so frequently formed an arena within which forces worked towards the resolution of the crises that arose, for this meant that the assimilation into a single system was not simply formal but had a basis in the interaction patterns of the town's citizens. That the town was so often an arena was related to the Kitan obsession for running one's own affairs. Whatever the hostilities and rivalries, there was an interest in maintaining the relative tranquility of the social system so that the central government would have no excuse to step in. Whether the problem was the need to apply a new central government program or to settle a potentially explosive quarrel before it got out of hand, this tendency to seek solutions by calling on the internal resources of the system was what made it possible to think of Kita as a more or less permanent arena.

MEETINGS AND ARENAS

The interactions within the Kita arena leading to the formation of a consensus and eventually to the emergence of a new direction in policy might range from the casual encounter of two friends to the exceptional circumstance of a regional conference for the entire section. But the key occasions were ones where a number of people gathered to discuss the affairs of the town, a ward, or some professional or other group. These meetings were the chief physical expression of the arena, for here all the leading competitors in the faction-prestige system were brought face to face in the presence of those whose support was essential for their success; in other words, whatever happened here happened in public. These meetings, especially those of the whole town or of its BPL representatives, played the same role in the postindependence system that the assemblies of the *diamana* had played in the precolonial system.

Meetings of one kind or another were an almost daily occurrence in Kita. The most important ones were the various party meetings, with the weekly sessions of the BPL first in consequence. There were also bureau meetings and general assemblies in each of the committees. There was a series of "information meetings" for the whole town during 1965; they seemed to be emerging as a new element in the town's political structure, although they did not correspond to any level in the party hierarchy. Once, in June-July, 1962, there was a general assembly for the entire section, involving both the town leaders and representatives of all the subsections and committees in the circle. This general assembly, as I showed in chapter 6, was a key turning point in the history of Kita politics. There were occasional "Conférences des Cadres" for all civil servants, in other words, for everyone who counted in the new system. And there were ad hoc meetings, such as those called to settle cooperative affairs or those where teachers discussed their professional affairs or settled disputes in the school. And finally, there were meetings, held on a monthly basis, that brought together the principal figures of the state and the party in Kita with the representatives of all the villages in the central arrondissement; these, although held in the town, were chiefly of importance for the rural areas and their relations to Kita and to Mali.

Of these meetings, the only ones I was allowed to attend, because of their uncertain status, were the "information meetings." These meetings differed from the other kinds of meeting enumerated above in that they were not called in order to take decisions, but simply to facilitate the dissemination of information to the townspeople. But, as the following description shows, they soon escaped from that narrow purpose, and I feel that, except for the fact that they did not make decisions, these information meetings were typical in their dynamics of most of the other kinds of meeting which were held in Kita. They served the functions of allowing rank-and-file members of the party as well as leaders to try to marshal public opinion to their point of view, of permitting the exchange of information and attitudes between leaders and people, and of providing an opportunity for ambitious people to make political gestures in public in the pursuit of their private ends.

I attended four out of the five such meetings held between April and November, 1965. They were formally organized, with a bureau constituted for the meeting consisting of a president, a secretary, and two assessors. The meetings usually had an agenda of items which the leaders wished to bring up. There was a definite spatial separation made between the leaders, who occupied either a platform of some kind or an open space in which a table was placed, and the people, who were ranged in front of them on the level. The people who associated themselves with the leaders and with the policy about which the people were being informed (which they usually knew about in advance of the meeting as the policy had been discussed in the BPL meetings and privately) stood behind the table at which the bureau sat, or perhaps slightly to one side. When they spoke in support of the government's plans, they were speaking from the platform to the people. The mass of the people, together with some political leaders who preferred to dissociate themselves from the leaders, at least in this public circumstance, sat in a rough semicircle in front of the platform or table. When they talked, they had to talk *to* the leaders sitting or standing there. Generally those who placed themselves in the audience intended to take exception to what the leaders were going to say, or wanted to raise a new question which they believed the leadership would rather not have raised. Often as the meeting progressed, the relationship of confrontation which was maintained during the informative period was shifted to one where people were arranged in a circle in the question period, when discussion heated up.

The meetings had two parts. In the first part, the leadership discussed the topics it wished to raise; in the second part, the people raised the questions they had on their minds. In theory, they were only supposed to ask for clarification on the issues raised by the leadership; but in practice, as we shall see, they often raised new and potentially embarrassing ones. After all, these were the only occasions on which the town's leaders exposed themselves publicly to the people.

The first meeting of this series, held in April, 1965, began shortly after 9 P.M. in the main market shed. Among those present were the commandant de cercle, the department heads, the two deputies, Diawara and Kouyaté, and many, if not all, of the members of the BPL. Most of these men were gathered at or behind the table on a raised platform. A few men of the same category were mingled with the audience. Most notable of these was the newly arrived head of the SMDR.

Kouyaté opened the meeting by explaining the new commerce law, which the national assembly had just passed. (The general effect of the law was to put such strictures on private merchants, including especially large financial bonds they would have to post against their honesty, that the merchants would be forced from business.) As he explained the minimum sums that were necessary for each category of merchant, the people gasped in astonishment. Diawara spoke next, bringing up a variety of different topics. He said that Kita would have to build some new classrooms by *faso-bara,* that a new arrondissement would probably be created in the circle, that the government wanted everyone to register their cattle (this meant compliance with an existing regulation rather than a new one) so that the government could plan logically to organize the export of frozen beef to earn foreign exchange, and that now was the time for everyone to get their new party cards. To bolster his argument, he carefully explained why it was that the party needed money: to give subsidies to the theater troupe, to finance Kita's fair, and so on.[2]

Then the floor was opened for questions and discussion. The first speaker was the new SMDR head, who attacked the whole BPL for being rotten, and said that the meeting was a pretty sorry example of a general assembly. He also expressed some reservations concerning the commerce law. He was answered by Kouyaté. Then a young man (who had always made his living from commerce and had been an RDA supporter from the earliest days and was a BPL member) objected to some aspects of the law. He was answered by the stationmaster, Aliou Keita—also a BPL member. Aliou said that the sense of the law was that merchants should leave commerce for farming, for they had no hope of complying with the law. People expressed appreciation for his frank talk. He was followed by the head of the local agriculture service, a native of Bamako, who said that everyone should farm. Some people had come to him for advice on how to return to the land, which he had given, but the people had become discouraged too easily. Next spoke a *nyama-*

---

2. He had discussed essentially the same topics before a meeting of farmers in a village near Kita that same morning.

kala whose father had been an early and prominent RDA supporter, and who earned his living from commerce. He said that he was one of those who had gone to the agriculture service for advice, but that he had found the advice impractical as it called on him to do things beyond his means (appreciative laughter).[3] The director of the Somiex defended the rights of the smaller merchants and said that something ought to be done to ease the transition for them rather than simply to drive them out of business. Kouyaté said the BPL would look into this. He pointed out that people should join the consumers' cooperatives (which had not started operations at this time) for, once they were open, the Somiex would no longer sell retail. As for the commerce law, they should remember that only 135,000 of Mali's 5 million people lived in the circle of Kita, so they had better be prepared to go along with the majority. A peanut oil refinery originally scheduled for Kayes had been moved to Toukoto in the circle of Kita (it was not yet built) because the circle of Kita produced so many peanuts; now it was up to them to work hard to justify this move.[4] Kita was also a major exporter of millet, so there was also reason to work to maintain this position. Diawara rose to point out that one had to follow the majority, and the majority had voted this bill into law in the national assembly. Returning to his concern with *fasobara* he said he would close the market on Sunday if people didn't come voluntarily to the *fasobara* sessions.[5]

The final incident of the meeting came when one of Kita's better-known smiths raised a topic of personal interest to himself. He had made two rifles which had been exhibited at the Annual Kita Fair some six weeks earlier. When the fair closed, the police confiscated the rifles, claiming that he did not have the right to make guns. At the time of this meeting, the guns were in the police

3. It is interesting but perhaps coincidental that here Keita spoke as a chief, explaining what had to be done, and people reacted to him accordingly, by calling out his clan name; the *nyamakala* spoke as a *nyamakala*, pointing out the existence of problems, and people reacted to him accordingly, for the problems were real and it is the role of *nyamakala* to say what others dare not.

4. Delegations of Kita notables had had audiences with the president of Mali as early as 1962 in an attempt to get the refinery built in Toukoto where there had once been a sizable railroad repair yard.

5. Since many of the shops in the market served as men's clubs for lounging and gossiping, the idea was to give these men no place to gather so they would have to come to the *fasobara*.

chief's office. The gunsmith wanted to raise this question before this general Kita meeting because he felt a wrong had been done to him. Either he ought to be paid for the guns or they ought to be returned to him; he had put a great deal of work into them, and the circle had been proud to exhibit them at the fair where people from out of town could admire them. Why were they confiscated afterwards? Both deputies and the police chief quickly contradicted him, saying he had acted against the law in making the guns. Besides he was out of order, for the matter wasn't on the agenda. The meeting had gone on long enough. At this point, the new SMDR head took the floor to say that everyone was wrong, people ought to be encouraged to take initiatives like this. As for him, he was going to give the gunsmith 10,000 francs ($40) from SMDR funds the next day. This angered Kouyaté who inquired what business this was of the SMDR's. On this inconclusive note, the matter was left. The meeting closed on a note of harmony, however. An old man asked an innocent question about the commerce law, which Kouyaté answered. The old man replied that now he understood, whereupon Kouyaté clapped his hands to applaud this show of intelligent good will, and the meeting was over.

There are several interesting observations that can be made regarding this meeting. The first is that the people were discussing the commerce law as if it were something in their power to decide, whereas in fact it had already been passed by the national assembly; the point was no longer whether one approved it or not, but whether one understood it and its implications. This is the point that Kouyaté tried to make. Nevertheless, it is equally true that eventually the application of the law's provisions to the lowest class of merchants, to which practically all those in Kita belonged, was postponed and softened, so that perhaps expressions of dissatisfaction such as were made at this meeting were not completely without effect. The second observation is that by and large the supporters of the law took the position that they were not so much arguing in favor of it as they were explaining it. The opponents of the law (many of whom were old RDA supporters who made their living from commerce) spoke as if they were trying to manipulate public opinion in their favor. The third observation concerns the role of the SMDR head. He came a little late, placing himself ostentatiously at the opposite end of the market shed from the platform, and took the floor several times, speaking quite aggressively.

He seemed to be trying to show himself not as a troublemaker, but as a man opposed to hypocrisy and injustice, prepared to denounce them wherever he found them. (He was later named to the BPL, less than six months after his arrival in Kita.) The fourth observation concerns the expectations of the gunsmith, who spoke from the floor and was trying to force a decision in his favor by arousing public opinion. Finally it is interesting that this was the first Kita-wide assembly held for some time (at least none had been held since September, 1964, when my field work started). The innovation seemed to reflect the feeling that the complicated commerce law should be explained to all of Kita's merchants at the same time by a man well qualified to do it. The normal procedure would have been to leave this explanation to the ward general assemblies; this would have resulted in six different explanations being given, and some of them would have been less well-informed than others. But the innovation of town-wide assemblies also seemed to reflect the feeling that the town, unrepresented in the formal structure, was the key social unit nonetheless. Certainly these meetings were perceived as "general assemblies" for the town.

The other meetings of this type followed the same format, with an initial period when party leaders explained some aspect of government policy and a subsequent period when new subjects were raised from the floor. Among the topics which the party leaders brought up were the need to turn out for *fasobara* sessions, the advantages of using fertilizer, the question of sending money to flood victims, questions related to the opening of the schools and especially to school fees and school discipline, and the cooptation of new members onto the BPL. Many of these questions were more specifically local problems than the commerce law discussed in the first meeting. But challenges were also raised in these meetings. In one meeting the question of school dues was raised. Why were different sums collected at different times ? What had happened to the money ? and so on. The first part of the following meeting, two months later, was given over to answering these questions and in general concluded that everything was in order. But further questions were raised. Kita had gone to a lot of trouble to have all its streets straightened, in the hope of getting water and electricity, but so far there was no sign of either; and the method of distributing scarce grain among wards and individuals was unfair (see chapter 5).

A meeting held in May, 1965, to allow the leader of a delegation from the National Political Bureau (BPN) to speak to the population was similar in many respects. The BPN member's speech covered practically every issue then of concern to the government: the historical role of the party in freeing Mali from slavery; the need for people to work, farm, pay taxes, and buy party cards; the marriage law of 1962 and the commerce law of 1965; the advantages of sending one's daughters to school; and the desire of the government to earn hard currency by exporting frozen beef by air. But the question period, as usual, brought the unexpected. Kouyaté gave an impassioned plea to the delegation to help persuade the national government to give Kita running water, a people's pharmacy and a people's bookstore. Then a *dieli* known for his drunkenness and uninhibited speech made a vague and ambiguous speech about how the problem in Kita was the large amount of quarrelling between persons, hinting he could tell many tales. He then turned on his heel and walked out before the leader of the BPN delegation could question him. When he was brought back, he refused to give any of the details he had hinted at, saying that they would have to get him to Bamako first. A teacher then complained that many teachers had missed a month's salary through an administrative error which had never been set right. The delegation head said he would have the matter looked into. Then a young man complained of the youth organization in Kita; the youth, he said, was dead. This attack on Kita's youth leaders created a furore, and there were passionate denials from them, particularly on an accusation of misused funds.

These information meetings were exceptional events in Kita's political structure because they were among the few occasions when the whole town was gathered together and because, having no formal place in the party organization, they were not qualified to make decisions. General assemblies were frequently held in committees, the basic locus of party activity. At these meetings, the secretary-general or, in his absence, his deputy, acted as the chairman. Together with the other members of his political bureau he would present new policies and the information and instructions that were being passed down the party hierarchy. These meetings usually also included a question period, when the ordinary citizens of the ward could bring up the matters that concerned them, and apparently—though I was unable to attend meetings of this kind—

the discussion could be quite lively. It is indicative of this that one committee secretary-general told me that when a man from his ward rose to speak in one of the information meetings described above, he knew in advance what the man was going to say, because he had raised the question so insistently in the committee meetings. The people were jealous of their right to speak their minds in such meetings, and a secretary-general and bureau who did not hold them regularly were likely to be accused of "dictatorship."

General assemblies were impossible at the levels of the sub-section, the section, or the nation, because of the numbers of people involved. Comparable meetings at these levels involved delegates, typically chosen on a committee basis for the subsection and section conferences. These meetings were held sporadically. The conference that was held in Kita in 1962 was in theory restricted to the delegates of each of the 314 committees in the section; as it was held in the open-sided market shed, however, anyone in the immediate vicinity could easily follow the proceedings, and many came especially to listen. The market place was filled with perhaps several hundred people listening intently, so that a vast number of Kitans had a sense of participation in the meeting, though they could neither speak nor vote. The main order of business at this meeting was the election of a new BPL. Reports on the section's activities over the preceding period were also presented. There was a great deal of discussion from the floor, including open criticism of the outgoing secretary-general (Sylla) and his allies, who defended themselves. Because of the intense discussion of all the various issues involved in the months preceding the conference, it seemed that when the delegates of Kita's six committees spoke they were in a real sense expressing the consensus of town public opinion. People in Kita were looking forward to the next regional conference as a chance to air their displeasure once again at the way things were going.

These general assemblies and similarly structured meetings played an essential role in the political organization of Kita. They were the chief formal means by which communication between leaders and the mass of the people was effected. The general assemblies were used by the leaders to communicate the new policies and decisions to the people and to exhort them to greater efforts, for instance in *fasobara* projects. They were also a forum where the people could communicate to the leadership their points of view and where they could bring topics of concern to them to the attention of the leaders. Both leaders and people were conscious of the importance of these meetings for communication. Such meetings also served as climaxes in the continuing process of readjustment of the scale of personal prestige that occurred in the Kita arena. People's prestige would rise or fall according to the popular support they could attract or demonstrate during these meetings. People tried to take political stands that would enhance their positions in the ongoing political quarrels and differences of opinion in the town. Such meetings were important in this process precisely because they were public: a gesture that would have no sense in a BPL meeting became a fruitful maneuver when carried out in a public meeting. This element of the meetings was more significant in its political consequences than any decisions that might be made.

Thus, for instance, the secretary-general of the Moribougou committee brought up the question of the division of scarce food among consumers' cooperatives and individuals, in the hope of marshalling public opinion not only against the section leadership, which largely favored the policy he opposed, but also against the president of the Moribougou cooperative who also favored this policy. He was playing first to those people from his own ward who were present (to show them that he was standing up for their interests), and then to those from other wards (to persuade them that the policy he favored was more just). It was a gesture he could only have carried out in a public meeting for the town; in his ward meeting he was constrained as secretary-general from advocating a partisan viewpoint (in any case people in Moribougou largely agreed with him, for he was expressing popular sentiment in the ward), and in a more limited meeting such as the BPL or an ad hoc meeting for cooperative leaders he found the leaders arrayed against him and no public to appeal to. This was his last chance to sway the decision his way. Although his effort did not succeed, it reaffirmed his political position publicly.

This mixture of genuine concern about an issue and the need to confirm a personal political status characterized many of the other questions and comments at such meetings. The head of the SMDR who spoke out in favor of the gunsmith provides an example. On another occasion, when the question of bringing water and electricity to Kita was brought up, a young man rose to take a very belligerent position in favor of the questioner and thus against the leaders. An explanation offered to me for this young man's attitude was that he was determined to take the floor on some issue, in order to gain the notoriety derived from speaking out in a public meeting, and it just happened that this issue presented itself. True or not, this explanation illustrates the way in which Kitans conceive of these meetings. A few speakers, such as the gunsmith, did not have these political motives; the gunsmith had purely personal motives.

The 1962 party conference and the meeting held at the time of the 1965 visit of a BPN delegation took on a slightly different cast due to the presence of people from outside the Kita arena. In the 1965 meeting described above, Kita's leaders were in the same position that the Moribougou secretary-general had been in when he raised the question of the distribution of food in the cooperatives. They could, in effect, petition the national level on behalf of all Kita in the presence of all Kita. Kouyaté seized this opportunity. He was the first speaker in the question period, and he demanded that the national government provide Kita with three things that any respectable town ought to have. He spoke in an emotional way, as if to indicate that he was just an ordinary citizen taking advantage of the presence of the BPN delegation to make certain claims. However, it seemed to me that he was speaking more for the benefit of those in the audience—his constituents as Kita's deputy— than he was to the BPN delegation. When it was announced a couple of days later that a people's pharmacy would indeed be opened in Kita, the general assumption was that Kouyaté (who was also the town's doctor) already knew when he made his speech that the pharmacy was coming and had simply taken advantage of the opportunity to demonstrate how effective a petitioner on behalf of Kita he could be.

The criticisms levelled against the then secretary-general at the 1962 party conference, and those against Mamadou Kamara and the BEJ in the May, 1965, meeting were also related to the presence of national personalities. When powerful figures from outside the arena are present, people may try to bring certain issues to their attention in the hope of inciting them to intervene in local affairs. The public nature of such an attempt makes it also a move in the local arena. Needless to say, this is considered by many Kitans to be a very dangerous tactic, and it is indicative that those who tried it at the 1965 meeting were politically insignificant loners, however much they may have expressed majority feeling in the town. Sometimes, however, such a tactic is accepted, as when Kita's delegates to the 1962 conference tried to discredit Sylla in the eyes of the national delegation so that they would abandon their support of him and he could be replaced by a local figure.

I have noted the tendency of the information meetings for the town to take the form of a discussion of issues, as if the meeting was able to make a decision concerning them, and have pointed out that this was not in fact the case, although the expression of public sentiment might have a long-term effect on decisions. The crucial decision-making body in Kita was the BPL: the bureaus of the ward committees essentially only decided on housekeeping details. I have no direct information on the processes by which the BPL or the ward committees reached their decisions. On the basis of a few comments that were made to me, and on the observation of the decision-making process among teachers and among farmers in a rural cooperative (Hopkins 1969a), I offer the following comments.

Everyone had the right to speak. Speakers were likely to take extreme positions with an emphasis on oratory and turning the catchy phrase. The same double emphasis on the issue and on the speaker's place in the political network was apparent. Positions taken, therefore, often reflected the relations of the speakers to their publics. The discussion would continue often with several people talking at once and would perhaps break down into several smaller partial discussions, until everyone had had his say. Then someone would sum up what the sense of the meeting had been, and this would be agreed upon.

Everyone present was involved in the decision taken; there could neither be going back on it later, nor any legitimate minority viewpoint once the decision was made. A person objecting to the decision should say so at the meeting; if he failed to win people over to his point of view, that suggested that he had been wrong. Because those present were associated with the decisions made, even if they had opposed them, a presumptive majority tried to assure perfect attendance. Conversely, people knowing that a decision they opposed was liable to be made at a given meeting usually avoided attending. Then if taxed with the decision, they could dissociate themselves from it.[6] In one case a man was particularly anxious to

6. As Kouyaté did with the decision to lower peanut prices by 2 percent.

avoid being present because he did not want to be associated with the making of what he felt would be an unpopular decision. So on the morning when the meeting was scheduled, he went hunting. The meeting was postponed till the afternoon, in an attempt to maneuver him into coming. But he went back to the bush in the afternoon as well, leaving word that he had lost his glasses. The meeting was postponed till the following morning, and finally he had to come (by this time he had made his point anyway). When the decision was made, it was his job to implement it. He did nothing to implement it. After several days this was discovered. Since this was in an administrative context, his stubbornness rated him a critical letter in his file. His motive seemed to be to avoid any connection with what he was sure would be an unpopular decision for fear that it would jeopardize his political career.

Voting was rarely used as a mechanism for reaching decisions.[7] I heard of only one instance of its use. This was in a meeting, attended by the members of Kita's BPL and the subsection political bureaus, at which the two candidates for deputy from Kita in the 1964 elections were chosen.

Thus the meetings were central to the ongoing political process in Kita. They provided the essential forum where the political consensus could form through the confrontation of different points of view. They also provided a physical expression of the abstract Kita arena where political moves could be made in public to increase one man's prestige or attack another's, and thus were essential to the continuous processes of factionalism. By providing a field for the political processes inherent in the town's social system, they helped to sharpen the definition of the limits of that system.

KEEPING THE PEACE

The meetings where rival personalities clashed represented the boundedness of Kita's political system in one way; and the settlement of disputes expressed the same fact in another. As in the meetings, there was an effort to utilize local resources to solve the

---

7. In Bailey's terms (1966) the BPL was an arena council for it had to implement its own decisions without any effective sanctions; it stood in an elite position in contrast to its public; and it was concerned (at least partially) with external relations. According to Bailey, such a council is likely to make its decisions by consensus, and Kita's BPL certainly bears out his contention.

disputes whenever possible, particularly when the disputes brought the fragile structure of the political system itself into question.

Most of the disputes that arose, of course, were domestic ones where the integrity of the town was in no sense threatened and where the appeal to legal forces outside the framework of family and neighborhood violated only that most local of arenas. Most of the cases that Kita's judge heard involved disputes over marriage: either the wife was requesting a divorce or the husband was bringing a suit for "abandonment of the conjugal home" against a wife who had left him. Other cases involved wounds inflicted and fighting, and, less frequently, thefts and swindles. One judge in several months of work in Kita had seen no cases involving land or inheritance, and no murders.

Before independence, these domestic quarrels had been arbitrated by many informal figures in the town, such as Muslim marabouts or old men respected for their "wisdom" and knowledge of traditional lore. In 1965, these men were seldom approached to arbitrate quarrels, although in rural areas this was still done, and the practice extended sometimes to rural people living in Kita. One old man had spent most of his life as a farmer in the bush; although he had moved to Kita (where he frequently filled the role of court advisor on traditional law under both the French and at this time) he was still approached by people from the rural areas with problems. The case I witnessed involved a man whose daughter wanted to marry a boy of whom he didn't approve. The father wanted the old man to persuade his daughter not to do this, but the old man refused because he knew it would be futile to try to dissuade the girl, although he agreed that the marriage was not likely to be a good one.

Cases that arose within the town were supposed to be taken to the police. The police chief or one of his assistants inquired into the case and tried to effect some kind of compromise between the disputants. If he found it impossible to settle the case informally, he then passed the dossiers on to the judge. The judge then inquired into the facts of the case a second time—sometimes differences appeared—and again tried to arbitrate it, especially in cases of divorce. If he failed in this second attempt to arbitrate the case, there was then a public hearing, at which the principals and their witnesses testified, and the judge handed down his decision. A loser dissatisfied with the decision would appeal to higher courts in Kayes and eventually in Bamako.

The open hearing was not prescribed by the legal code for most of the cases that the judge heard, but the judge who was assigned to Kita during the latter part of my stay felt that it served a useful purpose, that of educating the people. By attending cases heard in public, the people would learn more about the law they lived under. It was also for this reason that the judge preferred to work in Bamana as much as possible, although as a Sonrai from Timbuctoo he spoke only a little Bamana himself. He also felt that public sessions helped reduce suspicion of the court's activities. However, he found that Kitans took relatively little interest in the legal process; in Douentza, where he had been before Kita, there was a crowd of regular listeners at court sessions.

People who took their cases to the police and the courts did so less out of a spirit of litigation than simply in hope of enlisting the police on their side.[8] Violating the family or neighborhood arena usually represented a quantum jump in the seriousness of the quarrel, for although the legal dispute might be settled, the principals were much less likely to return to friendly relations than if they had settled the case themselves.[9] There was a high value placed on settling family quarrels in the family, village quarrels in the village, and so on. When marriages in the town were formalized, the heads of the respective families often made an agreement not to submit any dispute arising from the marriage to the government but to settle it among themselves. Similarly, villagers often

---

8. It is interesting to note that in skits and in the *kotéba* theater the police often appear as a kind of deus ex machina to punish the guilty. This role is also played by fetishes in the *kotéba*. In a play entitled *Fanta* produced in Kita in 1962, the police appeared at the end to punish a double-dealing girl immediately, without waiting for any legal proceedings (see Hopkins 1965: 178–79; Labouret and Travélé 1929; Meillassoux 1964).

9. In one case, two out-of-town teachers lived next door to one another. At first they got along very well together, but the difference in age between them and between their respective wives amounted to a generation gap: the younger man had once been the pupil of the older. When the older wife began to order the younger one around—treating her as if she were a daughter or a daughter-in-law—she rebelled. A quarrel ensued, and eventually the younger one went to the police. That was the end of any amicable relations between the husbands as well, and the younger family found it expedient to move to another part of town.

boasted that all their quarrels were settled within the village, without involvement with the civil authorities.

It was because they were aware that the best resolutions of disputes came without this interference that the judge and the police chief tried either to arbitrate them or to ignore them. The police chief was prone to "ignore" quarrels between women, which in Mali have a reputation for being unsolvable. Once a large crowd arrived at the police station. The wives of one man were quarrelling with those of his neighbor; this had been going on for some time, and it had finally reached the boiling point. Both sides came to the police station (about two hundred yards from the respective houses) with their supporters and accompanied by many curious onlookers. The police chief berated everyone, telling them to stop quarrelling and keep the peace, and then refused to have any more to do with the matter.

Other disputes went beyond this domestic frame and escaped the abilities of the police and the judge to work out solutions. Such cases involved not individuals but the conflicting interests of various segments of the community. By this token, they were typically resolved politically within the Kita arena or some segment of it, and a lot of politics went into defining the proper arena for working out a settlement. The eight disputes summarized here show the importance of local public opinion, of the involvement of the national level, of having a neutral figure to use as an arbitrator, and of the struggle to define the limits of the group concerned in a quarrel.[10]

1. In 1959 the municipality of Kita was created, and for the first time it was necessary to draw physical boundaries between the villages which were to become wards. Previously people, regardless of where they lived, had remained attached to the ward where they were born or into which they were integrated because their *diatigi* lived there. The boundary between Moribougou and Ségoubougouni was drawn to follow the stream that runs between them, although there were many people from Moribougou living on Ségoubougouni's side of the stream, and the traditional boundary between the two was a road that ran along the low ridge on Ségoubougouni's side of the stream. The quarrel over the jurisdiction

---

10. See also the description of the disputes centering around the establishment of the consumers' cooperatives in Kita (see chapter 5).

over this land became so acrimonious that it could not be settled locally. When the president of Mali came to Kita on a visit, he was asked to decide the matter. He decided in favor of Ségoubougouni, saying that if anyone living in the disputed territory didn't like this, they could move.

2. During the heyday of the conflict between the PSP and the RDA, in the early 1950s, each party organized an orchestra to play dance music in an effort to compete for supporters among the young people. When the PSP disbanded, its orchestra remained intact. In 1961 the party organization decided to end the semi-autonomous status that both orchestras had enjoyed until then. This had meant that the orchestras were essentially run as commercial enterprises for the benefit of the musicians and of certain individuals who had put up the money for the purchase of instruments. The PSP orchestra accepted the new status, which meant that the BEJ got any profits that might be earned from dance admissions and so on. The RDA orchestra objected to this, despite the pressures put on them. So the BEJ sent around its political secretary with some Brigadiers de Vigilance to seize the instruments. The leaders of the RDA orchestra made no attempt to prevent the seizure. The BEJ then had instruments but no musicians, since the musicians refused to play. Eventually the BEJ worked out a compromise with the leaders of the musicians according to which the BEJ could call on the musicians whenever they wanted to but the musicians would be free to play on other occasions as well. When the musicians played for the BEJ, they would be paid ahead of time, so they would get their money even if the dance was a bust. This quarrel was marked first by an attempt to persuade, then by an attempt to force a solution, and finally by a negotiated compromise.

3. In the early 1960s there were two directives which were the subject of constant disputes between the rural people and many townspeople on the one hand, and the party on the other. One order forbade the practice of burning off the dried bush after the fields were harvested; the other forbade people to grow maize in or near their compounds. The first order was based on the agronomists' theory that the annual burning destroyed the soil; the second on the theory that mosquitoes were encouraged by the presence of maize, and so it was a public health measure to keep maize at a certain distance from people's houses. These orders were largely

ignored by the people, despite the best efforts of the BPL to enforce them. In both cases, people disputed the scientific basis of
the prohibition. When the BPL investigated a bush fire, they might
be told that it had been started by a certain kind of antelope believed to breathe fire. The BPL tried to set an example by rushing
out to extinguish some bush fires, but even some BPL members
refused to participate in this, for they felt ridiculous, and many
people laughed heartily at the spectacle. Eventually, the BPL had
to give in, since the orders were unenforceable, and they told people
they could burn what they wanted and grow maize inside their
huts for all the BPL cared.

4. In 1965 the six ward chiefs of Kita appealed to the commandant de cercle in his role as mayor of Kita to pay them the
share of taxes collected in their wards which had traditionally
been theirs. The commandant refused on the grounds that there
wasn't enough money to do this. The chiefs appealed to the secretary-general of the section, who intervened on their behalf with
the commandant, and the chiefs received some money, although less
than their customary share.

5. In 1965 a theatrical contest between troupes representing
the subsections of Toukoto and Sébékoro was organized in Kita by
the BEJ. The Toukoto troupe, which was expected to win, arrived,
but the Sébékoro troupe was unavoidably detained by the failure of
trains to run on schedule and had not arrived in Kita by curtain
time. The Toukoto troupe wanted the contest declared a forfeit
and refused to present their program unless they were declared
winners. The BEJ argued that it was not the fault of the Sébékoro
troupe and that Toukoto ought to agree either to hold the contest
the following night or to present their program one night and let
Sébékoro present theirs the following night. Toukoto responded that
they didn't want to stay an extra night in Kita, that a contest
spread over two nights would not be fair, and that it was Sébékoro's
fault they were late, as they could have come by road. All this argument was held between BEJ members and Toukoto youth leaders
on the stage in front of the audience, many of whom had entered
to see a play and stayed to enjoy the argument. Small knots of
people on the stage were arguing back and forth, gesticulating,
shouting, and drawing people aside. Eventually the Kita BEJ pre-
vailed over the Toukoto leaders, and Toukoto agreed to present
their program that night and to allow Sébékoro to present theirs

the next night. As everyone expected, Toukoto's program was much superior to Sébékoro's.

On another occasion, in a scheduled contest between troupes representing the Pioneer troupes of the sections of Kita and Bafoulabé, the argument over procedure was such that the Bafoulabé trouple simply refused to perform. The argument here involved the method of choosing which section in the Kayes region had the best Pioneer troupe. The Kita youth leaders had understood that three troupes would compete in Kita and the other three in Kayes, with the winners facing each other. The Bafoulabé troupe suggested a different interpretation, according to which the troupes in Kita would compete and be scored.[11] The following week the other troupes in the region would compete in Kayes and be scored. The highest scorer would be the winner. The Kitans sensed a trap. They had won the contest in the Kayes region between youth troupes already, and thought they saw a scheme to prevent them from winning the Pioneer contest as well. If the other three circles in the region were being judged by a different set of judges a week later (when Kita's score would already be known), it would be only too easy to doctor the scores to defeat Kita. Kita refused to compete according to the new rules suggested by Bafoulabé and presented its program under its own rules. Then Bafoulabé refused to perform.

All this is rather complex, but apart from illustrating how much emotion is put into the theater when one town is competing against others, these cases illustrate the importance of having a fairly neutral figure to arrange an acceptable compromise. In the case involving Toukoto and Sébékoro, it was Kita's BEJ, as the parent organization, which was able to arrange the compromise. In the case of Kita and Bafoulabé, the parent organization was headed by the regional youth inspector in Kayes, and he was suspected in Kita of having organized the whole scheme. So the contest just broke down.[12]

6. The butchers' strike. In December, 1964, the government decided to apply a law already on the books concerning the taxes

---

11. The third troupe scheduled to come to Kita had forfeited.

12. A quarrel between Kita's troupe and Kayes's troupe in 1962 over who had won, in which the honesty and impartiality of the judges were called into question, was settled by the national level of the youth organization (Hopkins 1965:186).

butchers paid on the animals they slaughtered. The effect was to raise the tax. At the same time, the butchers were given permission to raise the price they charged their customers by 20 percent, but this did not satisfy them. The meeting at which the butchers were informed of these changes was held on a Monday; in the absence of the commandant de cercle, the police chief chaired the meeting. When the butchers protested, he told them that if they refused to accept the new situation he would throw them all in jail. They refused and said that they would not butcher under these conditions. Then they all went to see the deputy commandant de cercle, and he too was unable to persuade them to accept the change. As a result of this, only one cow was slaughtered on Tuesday and none at all on Wednesday.

There the matter rested until the commandant returned to Kita on Thursday. On Friday he told the butchers that not only would they have to pay the tax if they wanted to butcher, but furthermore he now discovered that they were behind in their license fees; they would have to pay up the fees before he would let them begin butchering again. At the same time, the commandant arranged with the SMDR to provide money to buy cattle and obliged one of the butchers to slaughter and dress the meat under police supervision. This continued for several days, and eventually the butchers gave in. They had exhausted their capital during the two weeks or so when they were receiving no income, and thus found themselves in a very awkward position in their relations with those who supplied them with cattle. They already owed money to these men, who after the strike raised the price of the cattle they were selling, alleging there was an added element of risk, and refused the butchers credit. The result of this situation was that there was room for a new middleman who bought the cattle from the suppliers with cash and sold them at a higher price to the butchers on credit, a development in no way foreseen by the government.

This incident shows how some people attempted to resist an administrative decision. The butchers (mostly long-term supporters of the RDA) hoped to get public opinion on their side when they refused to butcher under the new conditions. They failed, and there was no wide support for them. When the commandant returned, he was able to take sufficient measures within the administrative framework to oblige them to concede their defeat and accept the new administrative measures.

7. A case involving school discipline. A teacher in his first year of teaching was having trouble with one of his pupils who was the son of Kouyaté the deputy. Kouyaté himself was absent at this time. The boy allegedly threatened the teacher that if his father were in Kita, the teacher would not be able to treat him in such a manner, or, if the teacher dared, he would be transferred away. The teacher was driven to slapping the boy, who then went home straightaway. His grandmother was at home, and she got very excited about the incident and took the boy to the police station where a complaint was filed against the teacher. The police chief sent a summons to the teacher, ordering him to come immediately—although he was still in class at the time. The teacher reported the matter to his headmaster, who reported it to the senior headmaster, Mamadou Kamara. The teachers felt that this was an unwarranted intrusion into their affairs and that the young teacher was not accountable to the police for his disciplinary methods.[13]

The impasse between the teachers and the police became a question for the BPL to decide. The senior headmaster and the boy's father were both BPL members. The BPL indirectly settled the matter in favor of the teachers' point of view, though not before they had liberally cast blame in all directions. The BPL sent a delegation, headed by a former teacher who was one of its most respected members, to make the rounds of the schools to talk to the pupils. The general theme of this talk was to emphasize to the pupils the need for discipline and hard work; if they were not well behaved, they would be expelled, and they needn't think they could just go to Bamako and enter school there, for Bamako would be warned against them. The head of the delegation explained that he was talking first because he was the oldest man on the BPL and because he was a former schoolteacher. He spoke of the deference which his former pupils who had now become ministers still showed him, citing this as an example for the younger people to follow.

13. It is against the regulations of the Ministry of Education to use corporal punishment. It should also be recalled here, though I am not aware that it had any relevance for the dispute, that the deputy, Kouyaté, and the senior headmaster, Kamara, were among the leading figures in the opposing cliques. Also that the teacher involved here was on friendly terms with the commandant.

The deputy commandant, representing the administration, struck a positive note, saying that Mali could only be built with discipline and so self-control was necessary.

After stressing the need for discipline to the pupils, the BPL delegation met with the teachers. The delegation criticized the teachers generally, bringing up the points that the younger male teachers (such as the teacher in question) were flirting with their female pupils, and that the female teachers (who mostly taught the younger pupils) sometimes used vulgar language in scolding their pupils. Then the quarrel between the young teacher and Kouyaté's son was brought up. The teachers complained of the interference of the police into an internal school affair. They redefined the affair as a matter of one brother striking another and argued that such a family matter ought to be settled within the family. Closing ranks under the threat of police intervention, the teachers argued that they ought to present a united front, for otherwise the pupils would learn how to exploit the differences between them, and that the three headmasters ought to set a good example by agreeing among themselves. At this, Kamara, the senior headmaster, claimed that the quarrel he had had with one of the other headmasters the previous year was due to the misrepresentation of others (intriguing by carrying false stories), a version which, if not unanimously accepted, nonetheless set a mood of reconciliation.

At this point the BPL delegation left, and the teachers' meeting continued under the direction of Kamara, who claimed the right to chair the meeting as he was the oldest man present (and not because he was the senior headmaster). He brought up a number of things which teachers ought to avoid: they ought not to flirt with one another (it was all right to talk, but no roughhousing) ; and they ought not to interrupt one another while teaching, even if they had found a way of occupying their own class. At this the matter was closed. Except that nine months later at the beginning of the following school year, Kouyaté was talking at an information meeting about the need for better discipline in the schools. While talking he was looking straight at his son, who was so embarrassed he fled.

This dispute started out as one of school discipline and came to involve the teachers as a whole and the police. It was settled through the intervention of the BPL, which took the matter very seriously, and treated it as a political situation that had to be calmed. This was for two reasons. First, it involved a quarrel between two segments of the bureaucracy (schools and police). Second, it involved the deputy's son, and the father was not there to show what his attitude would be. The BPL basically took the side of the teachers in concurring that this was a school matter, and that the teachers were justified in calling for more discipline. At the same time, it was at pains to point out to the teachers (but not in front of the pupils) their own shortcomings, which were notorious, and the teachers themselves held a self-criticism session. The original issue of the teacher versus young Kouyaté was all but forgotten as everyone discussed broader issues. Neither the teacher nor young Kouyaté was punished or even publicly criticized. The BPL saw the problem in general terms: indiscipline in schools and lack of conscientiousness among the teachers.

8. The Brigades de Vigilance. Towards the end of 1964 the BV stopped operating in Kita. Various stories were told to explain this, but all of them had in common that they suggested a difference of opinion between the BV and the BPL about the attributions of the BV (see chapter 5). The BV remained quiescent, except for a ceremony in honor of the "Best Brigadier Day" in June, until the Independence Day celebrations of September 22, 1965. For this occasion the BPL asked the BV to march in the traditional parade, along with the Pioneers, the "peasant girls" and other groups. It had become usual for the BPL to provide uniforms for the marchers so that they might all appear in the same dress. These uniforms would then become the property of the marchers. In 1965 the BPL provided the entire costume for the Pioneers and the peasant girls, but only provided shirts for the BV. When the BV discovered after the parade that they had been "shortchanged," they protested, and said that they would cease to cooperate altogether with the BPL if they were not given trousers and shoes as well. They backed up their claim with pious statements on the difficulty of their work, their value to the community, and the amount of sleep they had lost.

Within a few days, the BPL and the BV had worked out a compromise. The BV would return their shirts, and the BPL would see to it that the entire outfit was given to them eventually. The BV members were to be favored in getting jobs, especially the jobs seen to be available at the Somiex warehouse then under construction. In return, the BV was to pick up its normal operations again and patrol the streets during the small hours of the night. This compromise was discussed in general meetings which all the Brigadiers and the BPL representatives as well as the police chief attended. In effect the BPL gave in to the pressure from the Brigadiers, but put sufficient conditions on their concessions to make them look like a compromise arrangement. I asked one person why the BPL bothered to maintain the BV; he answered that they did so in order to look good in Bamako.

The analysis of these eight incidents shows that the major institutions that were called into play when a dispute arose were the administration, particularly the police and the commandant, and the Party structures—the BPL for disputes affecting the town in general, and the BEJ for those concerning youth activities. The administration on occasion enforced its decisions (which were always taken, one must remember, with the implicit approval of the party at the national level) by refusing to compromise and by putting the objectors in an untenable position. This was the case with the butchers. Although the government threatened to use force, its ultimate victory was due to the fact that public opinion did not support the butchers. The administration had the financial and organizational resources to show the butchers that they were not indispensable and would only suffer if they kept on in their path. Thus the major method by which the administration settled disputes arising from its policies was by standing firm and enforcing them by whatever means were available. Actual physical force, it ought to be mentioned, was practically never employed.

If, however, there was enough public sympathy opposed to the administration's decision, then the matter became a political one and was handled by the BPL. In some cases, the BPL would simply press for a revocation of an administrative decision, as in the case of the "salaries" allowed the ward chiefs. In other cases, the BPL might decide to abandon an attempt to enforce an administrative decision, as in the maize and field-burning cases. In the quarrel over the boundary between Moribougou and Ségoubougouni, an administrative decision became politicized and demanded a political solution. In this case, because the solution came from the national level, it was presented as an arbitrary one which people would have to recognize or else. Sometimes a quarrel was handled by the BPL because it became too "hot" for the administrative apparatus to handle. This is the explanation for the interest of the BPL in the school discipline case. In other cases, the dispute arose from within the party apparatus, and so the BPL was naturally the organism which tried to settle it. This was the case with the dispute between the BV and the BPL, and it was the case with the disputes involving the youth—the orchestra and theater incidents— which were handled by the BEJ. But when a dispute was settled by the BPL or the BEJ, the solution was never simply "imposed," as in the case of many of the administrative solutions. When a problem was handled by a branch of the party, it became a political problem and the solution was reached by discussion, with often vigorous debate, and by something which at least had the appearance of a compromise.

The remarkable aspect of the settlement of these quarrels arising from administrative or political decisions, or stemming from conflicts of interest built into the system, was how many of them were settled after a public airing by a solution reached through negotiation and give-and-take. This was particularly striking in cases like the school discipline case and the BV case. There were few cases where the administration was able to be arbitrary and accept no compromise in the application of its decision, and all these cases were ones in which the role of public opinion was unimportant.

The analysis of the process of political confrontation in meetings, the manner in which decisions were made and disputes were resolved, reaffirms the existence of a solid social system corresponding to the physical town of Kita. Because of this, there was a tendency for the Kita arena to predominate, and for it to be the main one in which prestige was sought, projects for the future were made, and quarrels were settled. Kitans were very aware of the different levels at which there were arenas, as the reaction to official justice showed, and they were very keen on keeping town affairs to themselves, just as the teachers wanted to keep school affairs within the school confines. This is not an absolute, however, and there are examples where the central government was appealed to on an issue. Within the Kita arena, the main organized forces, especially the BPL and its members, played key roles in the processes described here. The relevance of the BPL was certainly due in large part to the fact that it was itself an arena reflecting the various points of view in the larger arena. Popular support and participation were continuing factors in the equation, and there was a tendency for significant political events to occur in public where the people could follow and judge them. Particularly striking here are the town "general assemblies," the use of a similar tactic to settle the school crisis, the feeling of the judge that there would be less suspicion of his court if it were open. But public opinion did not need a formal circumstance such as a meeting to make itself felt. The resentment against Sylla in 1962 as well as the determined opposition to the party's schemes to abolish bush fires and maize in compounds shows how this opinion expressed itself. Similarly, the butchers counted on something like this to manifest support for them, but it was not forthcoming.

In the last two chapters the processes of factionalism and personal rivalry, and the institutions for channelling popular sentiment, have been described. Now it is time to turn to a cultural analysis of these political structures.

9

Ideology and Pragmatism: Alternative Orientations in Kita Politics

At various points in the course of this book I have referred to the attitudes that Kitans themselves had toward politics and political activity; the time has come to pull all this together. The argument so far has dealt with the economic and social bases of politics and the dynamics of politics as an interaction process. This information on the institutions and processes of government needs to be completed by a discussion of the views that Kitans had on politics, on the nature of man and society and on the role of man in society, of the ways in which they evaluated their leaders, their ideas of the goals and purposes of political activity, and of the ways in which recent political history is mythologized to serve as a comment on the present. This culture of politics lies behind the structures of politics.

The culture of politics in Kita is best treated in terms of two separate bodies of ideas, which I call the ideological orientation and the pragmatic orientation. An ideological orientation to politics is one which takes as its central point the idea that there is an ideology in terms of which everything ought to be done, that there is only one correct ideology and that it has been determined, as have all the details deriving from it, by a rational procedure based on an objective interpretation of reality. A pragmatic orientation to politics is one which is characterized by a spirit of compromise in discussion, by a recognition of the individual character of people and social units or categories, and by an acceptance of such political "realities" as ambition, rivalry, and individual self-interest as natural.

These are two quite separate approaches to politics, and much political behavior can be better understood if the distinction between these two bodies of ideas and attitudes is kept in mind. These orientations involve both existential premises and value elements (how things are and how they ought to be), each of which affects the other while blending together to form the whole (Kluckhohn 1951:411). I regard these orientations as ideal types, and I suggest them for their heuristic value in providing an explanatory framework for this complex aspect of Kita society.

This analysis is meant to suggest a new way of looking at the relationship between ideas, ideology, and political behavior. I am suggesting that these alternative orientations were simultaneously available to actors in the political arena. Some individuals made use of one, some of the other, and some switched from one to the other or made use of elements of both, depending on the context. These ideas were derived, of course, from ideas of the nature of the world (including specifically the institutions of politics), but because they influenced behavior, they were crucial in forming new institutions such as parties and cooperatives as well as in the less deliberate organization of factional conflict and the making of decisions. That there were alternative orientations rather than a single one suggests that there was a corresponding duality in the conception of each of the resulting institutions. Because everyone was familiar with the premises of both orientations within the tightly knit Kita arena, the duality did not lead to a failure in communications, a fundamental split in society; rather they lent a richness and a flexibility to political discourse that served to stabilize the political scene by making the institutions more responsive to changes in popular sentiments.

There is some tendency for the distinction between the ideological and the pragmatic orientations to correspond to one between values and behavior—between a universalistic normative system and everyday behavior. Yet it would be incorrect to interpret the material in this way. People who acted in the manner of the pragmatic orientation did so with reference to the value elements of that orientation, not in spite of the existence of possibly contrary elements in the ideological orientation; and conversely, when people referred to the ideological orientation as a guide to action, they were not thereby inhibited from acting.

These alternative political orientations corresponded only in a limited sense to groups of people. The pragmatic orientation to politics was closely related to the institutional structure of preindependence and especially precolonial Kita; consequently those individuals who remained essentially oriented toward these institutions tended to be associated with this orientation almost exclusively. The ideological orientation was clearly derived from the new social and political system introduced into Mali after 1945, and especially after independence, and for which "socialism" is a shorthand expression. Those individuals who felt that they were modern or would like to be, or who were primarily involved with the workings of the political and administrative bureaucracy of the state, tended to be associated with the ideological orientation. Logically there should have been three classes of people with regard to these two political orientations—those who followed one or the other almost exclusively, and those who followed either according to circumstance. In practice there were but two classes of people— those who followed the pragmatic orientation exclusively, and those who followed either according to circumstance. The ideological political orientation had insufficient representation in Kita society to have a class of people who thought only in terms of it, though it is likely that there were more such persons in the relatively sophisticated society of the capital.

Furthermore, since these alternative orientations are ideal types, actual behavior in particular instances could represent a blending of the two orientations. For instance, in the argument between the wards concerning the proper way to divide up scarce goods among themselves, the argument took place in terms of the ideological political orientation—abstract criteria, applied equally to both sides, and so on—but the goal sought by either side was more in terms of the pragmatic political orientation—the maximization of benefits for one's own ward.

Each faction contained people who thought or operated primarily in terms of either orientation. In practice, the leaders of each faction, especially those leaders who had the educational back-

ground to be effective in the top posts, tended to think and operate more in terms of the ideological orientation than did their
followers. The cut was horizontal, not vertical.

The pragmatic and the ideological orientations were both
concerned with such problems as national sovereignty, the best
kind of local organization for economic development and for increasing the material well-being of the people, and the organization of effective self-government at the national and local levels.
The ideological orientation had no monopoly on the civic virtues,
and the pragmatic orientation had none on domestic virtues. The
ideological orientation had its blueprint for family life, as did the
pragmatic; and the pragmatic orientation was as concerned with
the affairs of the town and state as the ideological was.

It might be thought that the ideological orientation, because
of its universalistic nature, would be the same throughout Mali,
being associated in many ways with the action of the national levels
of the party and the administration, while the pragmatic orientation, being derived from the traditional institutions found in a
particular locality, would vary from one part of Mali to another.
But the ease with which people from one part of Mali fit themselves
into the political life of another part suggests that the specific
pragmatic orientations of the various parts of Mali had a great deal
in common. Certainly the SMDR director had not undergone a
crash course in Kita's political values before making such effective
comments in the town's general assembly (see chapter 8).

THE IDEOLOGICAL ORIENTATION

The basic assumption of the ideological orientation to politics
was that there was an objectively correct way of looking at things.
This correct viewpoint was derived from a rational, scientific analysis of the various elements involved and was concerned primarily
with economic factors and questions of efficiency. Once the objectively correct viewpoint had been established, there were two possibilities. Either one recognized that it was correct and agreed with
it, or one did neither. In the former case, one was said to have
"understood"; in the latter, one was said to have "not understood." Those who understood—the enlightened—then attempted
to persuade those who hadn't—the unenlightened—to change their
point of view. It was recognized that it was neither sufficient nor
good to oblige people to change their opinions, or to accept insti-

tutional change while remaining convinced that it was wrong or bad. The first requirement for a successful program was felt to be the "understanding" enthusiastic support of the people.

This objectively correct doctrine was formulated in meetings, either general assemblies or bureau meetings, where free discussion led to a conclusion. This conclusion was not seen as a compromise, however, but as the triumph of right in a free and open discussion. Once the decision had been made, there should be no further discussion; that would be opportunism—in effect, acting according to the pragmatic orientation to politics. The decision was then presented to others as party policy and an attempt was made to persuade them of the correctness of the decision. Consequently, when a decision made in Bamako or in the BPL meeting was presented to the people at a general assembly, the meeting was structured not as a council to decide—the decision had already been made—but as a session at which the new policy was to be explained. Anyone who hadn't understood could ask questions as to detail, but the policy itself could not be called into question. If there was a lot of opposition to a policy, the attitude of the politicians was to say that the people hadn't understood it yet. If they had understood it, they would support it.

The BPL secretary-general explained to me that he normally tried to persuade people. He added that it was necessary to do this at the level of understanding of the people, which meant that one should emphasize the practical side of the issue, as the people were unable to grasp the theory behind the decision. What this meant in practice was that the new program was explained to the people as something they were obliged to accept, although considerable effort might be displayed to explain to them all the implications of the new program. No attempt was made to use the party as an educational tool, to increase the doctrinal awareness and political sophistication of the people. There were two categories of people with whom the secretary-general felt he could not talk rationally: pupils and religious believers. Pupils were too young for rational discussion, so for the moment they should just obey.[1] Belief in religion was irrational; neither rational arguments nor concrete proof would convince believers to change their minds, so the best thing was to leave them alone.

1. This was said after one of the periodic disciplinary crises.

The logic of this political style implied that policies are advocated, supported, or followed on the grounds that they are right. Conversely, failure to follow a policy suggests that one has not (yet) understood. The following comments made by civil servants, many of whom were especially concerned with rural economic development, illustrate this logic: "Villagers who don't work to repair their roads haven't understood the necessity for it." "Kitans understand the need for reducing spending on circumcision ceremonies better than villagers do." "The problem with the peasants was in making them understand the new agricultural marketing policy. As soon as they saw that the bonus price for their peanuts, sold through the Association of Village Cooperatives, could help them buy goods for their village store, they understood." "Villagers are reluctant to talk about the village committee because they fail to understand." "More associations of village cooperatives would have been founded if the people had understood." "The peasants haven't understood yet that the role of the government is to help them and not to exploit them, so they remain suspicious." "If the Maninka don't understand, they must be forced." Failure to understand on the part of villagers or townspeople was thus taken as the main reason why a policy had not been acted on more readily. The remedy was to be more persuasive—or, as is suggested in one of the comments above, to use force.[2] But this explanation often was used as a crutch by those who did not want to analyze further the reasons why people might not want to go along with a certain policy.

It was, of course, not only the ideas concerning the acceptance of new policies that were characteristic of the ideological style of politics; the policies themselves were, too. Here, however, the formation of the policies occurred mostly at the national level. These policies were formulated through the decision-making institutions in Bamako. After independence most of the policies were inspired by Mali's socialist option. Some of the main bodies of laws that were renewed after 1960 covered marriage, the conduct of commerce, the organization of the school system, the establishment of a series of state enterprises, the reorganization of the administrative and social structure of the village, and the production and marketing of peanuts and other crops. These laws and regulations reflected the

2. This then contradicted the recognition, mentioned above, that persuasion is more effective than compulsion. It reflected an impatience with the unpersuadable.

attempt to create the institutional framework for a new national society and culture, where the new Malian man would be active in society according to the ideological style (see chapter 2).

One of the most important tenets of the ideological style in politics was the elimination of special privileges and the institution of equal opportunity for all (cf. Fallers 1963). There should be only one kind of man, and the functional specialization and structural differentiation of the traditional society should no longer play a role. One informant remarked that the goals of Malian socialism were this equality and the gathering of all the means of production into the hands of the state. Everyone should be treated identically by the administration; everyone had the same right to participate in politics and to speak up in public meetings; everyone had the same rights of access to schooling. Two specially thorny problems for the proponents of equality were the *nyamakala* and the merchants. The government's policy towards the *nyamakala* was ambiguous for, on the one hand, they wanted to liberate them from their age-old oppression, while, on the other, they wanted to eliminate their special privileges. The anti-*nyamakala* attitude that formed part of the ideological political style had its origins in the traditional low opinion of *nyamakala,* reinforced by the more exploitative role that many *nyamakala* had come to play in the urban setting. In Kita *dieli* were seen at worst as a disagreeable but permanent phenomenon, and the *dieli* themselves seemed in no hurry to change their status. But the central government had taken some measures considered to be anti-*dieli,* such as suggesting that most of the expenses surrounding all life-crisis rites (except funerals) be drastically reduced. Since the *dieli* were thought to be the main beneficiaries of gifts given on these occasions, the general feeling was that the government was trying to crack down on them.

One young civil servant and politician said that the *dieli* were generally of bad character, and that they were not compatible with socialism, for socialism required everyone to work, and the *dieli* would not work. On the other hand, he did not think they would disappear in his lifetime. Another party official defended the measures taken against the *dieli* by saying that the purpose was to ease the burden on families who felt called on to give more than they could afford to the *dieli*. He felt that *dieli* who served as intermediaries or who were historians justified themselves, but that there were a great many who were parasites. A play entitled *Mass*

Education, produced in 1965, showed how touring *nyamakala* were first ridiculed and then persuaded to change from entertainer-parasite to productive farmer; this play reflected accurately the official attitude toward the *nyamakala.*

The merchants were another group troublesome to the conceptions of the ideological political style. They were distrusted mainly because they were suspected of making undue profits, or of benefiting from the work of others. They were criticized for being useless middlemen, prone to profiteering. One leading political figure dismissed them by saying, "The merchants are a recent development in Kita, since the end of World War II, and this shows there is no inherent reason why they should continue to exist. They are not essential."[3] One civil servant, in a report, described Kita as "the bastion of a mercantilism and of a speculation born of colonialism, and whose defects have tarnished the mentality of our people, both urban and rural." As in the case of the *nyamakala,* the thrust of the ideological orientation was to eliminate the special privileges that men had because of their position of middlemen (social in one case, economic in the other). People should be reimbursed for the work they do, either as primary producers or as bureaucrats organizing the economy of Mali; there could be no room in the scheme for merchants, who were seen as earning their money without working.

This attitude toward the merchants was dramatized in a play given in April, 1965, by the Kita theatrical troupe. The play was called *Reconversion* and recounted the story of a prosperous merchant dealing in peanuts in the late 1950s, who owed much of his prosperity to his unfair practices. He was shown trying to cheat the illiterate peasants by reducing the weight of their peanuts; then, when a literate peasant came to sell his peanuts, he tried to bribe him into silence by raising the price paid to him alone by one franc a kilo. The literate peasant sensed the deception and refused to sell the merchant his peanuts; instead, he informed the other peasants of the merchant's practices, thus striking a blow for justice by taking business away from the corrupt. The second part of the play showed the postindependence situation, with a delegation from the party visiting the village to explain the new arrangements for marketing peanuts and meeting with an enthusiastic reception from the

3. See chapter 3 for a history of the merchants in Kita.

villagers. The final scene of the play showed the dastardly merchant back in the village, shouldering a hoe and ready to take up a new life as a farmer. This was the "reconversion."[4]

People operating in the ideological orientation stressed the need for work, sacrifice, discipline, cooperation, and organization. This was all part of a view of a world where everyone should work hard to do his share, without worrying about immediate self-interest, and where everything was well organized and people obeyed orders. These ideas were prominent in the speeches made on public occasions by party and administration officials. "One for all, all for one" was frequently cited as the socialist principle. Officials emphasized that "Mali must be built on discipline." "We must all work together in order to make the load light." "The most important thing is to work hard," and so on. Sometimes planning was given a most extensive role: one administrator stated that it was a shame that villagers were allowed to build their cooperative stores wherever they wanted; this led to chaos. In other words, the administration should not only require the construction of those stores (and the method of construction) but should also specify the location within the village.[5] Similar ideas also sprang up in conversation. One young political leader argued that "A good political system demands discipline." Another youth leader said that his was the generation that would have to be sacrificed. The secretary-general of the BPL said that one of the most important criteria of a good militant was his discipline. Sometimes the ideas were expressed by others, as in the case of the peasant who argued (in a meeting with the representative of the agricultural service) that "Since we are all brothers, let us all work together." A final note from the theater: the organizer of Kita's dance troupe argued that inasmuch as the dance was meant to be a collective enterprise, people should not be allowed to show off their individual talents but should melt into the group effort.[6]

4. One of Kita's biggest peanut traders of the 1950s did just this. He went to a village nine kilometers from Kita and started a garden for the rainy season of 1965. He was, however, a charter member of the RDA in Kita.

5. In fact, almost every village built its cooperative store next to the village chief's compound, but this was not the kind of order that the administrator had in mind.

6. In most Malian male dancing, the men compete on a personal basis to see who is the most graceful or the best acrobat. For another view of the problems of staging African dances, see F. Keita (1957).

There was also latent in a lot of the thinking along the lines of the ideological orientation a disapproval of high living, a kind of puritanism. This was associated with the Islamic puritanism brought back from Arabia by pilgrims influenced by what they saw there, but it had authentic Malian roots as well (cf. Ba and Daget 1962). This puritanism was most explicit in the organization and ideals of the Brigades de Vigilance, which in a sense were trying to preserve the morals of the town. Puritanism and austerity were more honored in the breach than in the observance, however, despite the occasional manifestations of these traits in official circles. The most striking incident of official support of morality during my field work was the speech given by the leader of the BPN delegation in which one of the topics covered was the new marriage code. He took a moralistic, egalitarian, modernistic point of view, which was appreciated by the women present.

The ideas in the ideological orientation dealing with the process of politics emphasized that discussion should only take place in meetings, that rivalry was a bad thing ("The Kitans should know better than to have all these personal vendettas" was one comment), and that democracy was the prime value. Democracy meant that everyone was equal and had equal rights of participation, that decisions should be taken following open discussion of the issues, and that no one should try to give orders to anyone else arbitrarily. Many of these ideas were also part of the pragmatic orientation; the ideological orientation differed by attaching a greater formalism to the decision-making process. "Everyone has a duty to participate in discussions, and a duty to respect the decisions that result from those discussions." "There should be no discussion outside meetings." "One should respect the opinion of the majority." These were some of the comments that reflected this concern with the modality of decision-making. On the other hand, I frequently heard people sympathetic to the ideological orientation claim that a two-party system would work better. One such informant told me, "If there are two competing parties, then the 'ins' have to work hard to stay in, and the 'outs' have to work hard to get in."

The ideological orientation to politics also included an idea of the role of education. Education was seen as coming about above all through participation in political meetings, rather than as the result of a specific effort to teach anyone anything. I was told that women should participate in committee general assemblies so they would learn about politics. Another young man told me that the youth-organized theater was better than the traditional *kotéba* because it was more educational. He went on to say that the Pioneer theater (involving pupils) gave its plays in French so that the points would not be lost.[7] The judge stated he held open court sessions "to educate people." When the party organized some classes for its cadres, on the other hand, to teach the doctrine formally, they were poorly attended.

The notion of being "civilized" was associated with the ideological orientation. The notion was essentially a cultural one: being civilized was defined by the kind of clothes one wore, the way in which one behaved toward other people, one's knowledge of the latest dances. Being civilized was behaving like the sophisticates of Bamako. One did not have to wear European clothes to be "civilized"; the criteria were that the clothes should be clean and ironed and that the colors should match. Although it was never expressed to me, I suspect that the extent to which the clothes covered the body was relevant, too. One never sees educated Malians in short trousers, a favorite European costume in Mali, and only rarely does one see them in short sleeves. One Kitan, on seeing pictures of Ghanaians in their bare-shouldered dress, concluded that the Ghanaians might have more knowledge than the Malians but they were less civilized. This notion of civilization was associated with the idea of a national Malian culture, to which people, especially young men, became acculturated, and it was linked with the other elements of the ideological orientation. Politically, the young men who best exemplified the virtues of civilization supported the party and the ideological approach to politics, at least superficially, but their orientation to consumer goods was of course antithetical to the notions of sacrifice and discipline discussed above. Although the type case of the civilized person was the young sophisticate, the same notions of what civilization was and where it fit were found among other kinds of people, such as middle-aged civil servants and farmers.

The people who were most associated with the ideological

7. This may seem a rather curious contention; my point here is that he was concerned with having the theater be as effective as possible in conveying its message, both to the audience and to the actors.

orientation were the party and administrative officials, especially when acting in their official roles. Such people were the conduits through which the policies and ideas of Malian socialism entered the local community. Then there were a number of people who perhaps had long been associated with the RDA and who often spoke French—merchants and artisans for the most part. In many ways the most interesting type was a kind of young man who had achieved some degree of literacy and was anxious to associate himself with something as civilized as this in order to raise his social status. They often were the most doctrinaire, the most categorical in their opinions, precisely, of course, because they were the least sophisticated. Not having had enough education to help them move up the ladder, they attached themselves to the modern, ideological approach to politics to symbolize their separation from traditional ways.

THE PRAGMATIC ORIENTATION

The basic assumption behind the pragmatic orientation to politics and government was that rivalry epitomized the political process. The pragmatic orientation, in contrast to the ideological, was derived from the kind of politics that seems always to have been characteristic of Kita; it contained far more existential elements. Politics was seen as a many-sided struggle for prestige in which all participated. In striving for prestige, factions formed around strong leaders who were at the apex of the pyramid. Individual differences in status, both ascribed and achieved, were recognized and considered to be part of the order of the world. The stress was on individual effort and success rather than on the common good; at the same time, everyone was seen as having a right to take part in government, although in different roles according to status. A part of the pragmatic orientation was an uncertainty as to the worth of the kind of factional, intrigue-ridden politics that people saw as characteristic of Kita. The usual alternative was not necessarily the ideological orientation; people might wish simply to eliminate the abuses in the system, without thinking that the abuses were the system.

The crucial aspect of politics, as seen by Kitans, was competition among individuals for prestige, which in the present circumstances meant competition for the various posts in the hierarchy of party bureaus. Kitans had mixed feelings about this process. On the one hand, there was the idea that competition was a good thing; on the other, Kitans frequently complained that competition for posts had ruined the town. They were convinced that competition for prestige and reputation involved a lot of intrigue and skulduggery, that a lot of money changed hands, and that there were many shifting alliances usually involving two groups of people joining to eliminate a third. People felt that such practices resulted in an unhealthy atmosphere which was personally corrupting and degrading. One BPL member described the path to success in Kita politics in the following terms: "The way to get ahead in politics is to observe who the leaders are and what their allegiances and methods are. Then you can figure out a way to defeat these methods."

Numerous Kitans expressed the idea that competition was a beneficial as well as a natural part of life. Competition was enshrined in the organization of the theater and of sports where collectivities at all levels from school classes to nations competed. There were two football teams in Kita; efforts to merge them into a single team, which would be more powerful in competing against rivals from other towns, were always rejected on the grounds that it was necessary to have both teams in Kita to maintain the level of rivalry that would encourage each to do its best. One old RDA hand stated that he had been opposed to the merger of the RDA and the PSP in 1959 because it eliminated competition, which he felt was healthful. Younger men, too, expressed this idea. One said that if he were in charge of the country, he would allow an opposition party because it was better to have two parties. In the previous section I cited the case of another long-time RDA supporter who stated that political competition made everyone work harder at doing things for the people. Competition for prestige and position could be regarded as a laudable course of action.

Politics was looked down on because of the effect that the effort to gain prestige in the competition had on the morals of those involved in it. One man, active in politics, said:

> Some people are eager to have their names on everyone's lips. To accomplish this they must spend money. And if they get the money illegally and are discovered and jailed, what is the use of it all? It is better to remain quietly at home, taking care of one's house and family, than to get mixed up in all this.

Not only did people say they avoided political activity because of its "dirty" aspects; they also felt that anyone who was overtly politically ambitious was not to be trusted. This was especially true of those who seemed to be trying too hard to advance, as in the cases of Abraham Keita and Alfa Cissé described in chapter 6. The distrust of the ambitious was expressed by a young farmer, who asked, "They lie to advance their careers, so how can we trust them?" He added that as farmers had no political ambitions, they could be trusted.

Some people said that their withdrawal from the political arena, or the fact that they never became prominent in it, derived from their fundamental dislike of the "dirty" aspect of politics. The man who made the comment cited above about the path to political success said that he was disillusioned with politics because of the failure of the government to keep its promises—as one who had relayed these promises to the people, he had been put in an awkward position. He concluded, echoing the other quote just given, "The best way to lead a quiet life is to stay out of politics." A village leader, commenting on the relatively recent involvement of villages in the party structure, said, "Now that we see what politics is, we want to get out of it."

The remarks about the contrast between political activity and the "quiet life" illustrate a second reason why politics was in disrepute among the younger civil servants: because it was time-consuming. Some people stated that while they were reconciled to some degree of involvement in politics, they hoped to remain in a marginal role—to be one of the bottom political bureau members rather than a leader. This reduced the demands on their time and put them at a certain distance from the center of political intrigue. Just as staying in one place for some length of time was a prerequisite for real political influence, so moving around from place to place was a protection against being obliged to have more political work than one wanted. Some people claimed that they had come to Kita from Bamako to avoid political activity there; others felt that it was easier to escape involvement in a large town like Bamako where there were many qualified people. In a small town, all literates and civil servants were under considerable pressure to take on a political role.

Another reason for a reserved attitude towards involvement in politics was the feeling that such positions were impermanent.

A teacher who was also a committee secretary-general said, "I feel it is more in my best interests to become a good teacher than a good politician, for politics is transitory, but a career skill is always with you."

Being involved in politics meant that one had to be concerned with one's reputation, as a matter of self-interest. A good reputation was important because it led to increased support in the case of factional conflict and at election time, and thus had a direct bearing on political success. The importance of the link between reputation and support meant that local politicians had an interest in making local modifications to national-level policies when they thought that these policies would not be well received locally. Politicians also tried to become the exponents of popular feelings. In the competitive situation, this meant that leaders "bid" for support. Politicians avoided taking any direct action against anyone of any group.

People preferred to let things drift rather than try to discipline anyone or to oblige them to do something, for those who used force or punishment as a method were attacked for being evil, of bad character, and so on. According to one young politician, the reason for this laissez-faire attitude was that "everyone in Kita is related to everyone else, so no one is willing to harm anyone else, or even to take strict measures against them." This affected various aspects of life. When the BEJ was instructed by the national party to choose "The Best Brigadier" (from the Brigades de Vigilance), they chose thirty instead (five from each of the six committees) in order to hurt no one's feelings.[8] The only pupil who really received a serious punishment (and many were threatened) was one who had no family in town. A teacher tried to avoid giving a professional examination to his fellow teachers, feeling he would be blamed if any failed—and indeed he was, although he successfully placed the burden of decision on the two out-of-town examiners by stating his opinion last and making it such that it did not affect the average of the other two grades.

Ultimately politicians felt that their personal reputation for being "nice" was more important than whatever might come from enforcing discipline. Many Kitans also felt that any coercive au-

8. A "Best Brigadier" was also supposed to be chosen in most other Malian towns at the same time. In many cases, including Bamako, the oldest member of the BV was chosen, presumably as a way of avoiding the delicate task of choosing a single person on the basis of achievement rather than ascription.

thority was illegitimate in Kita because it had no precedent. Anyone who tried to dominate others created resentment against himself. When President Modibo Keita visited Kita in 1961, he tried to order the Kitans around (or so they said), and the result was only to create a reaction against himself. The dislike of orders and the atmosphere where competition often expressed itself by systematic obstruction of opponents' projects made it hard to suggest an innovation and have it accepted. In the traditional society, *nyamakala* were able to suggest certain courses of action and have them accepted, whereas if ordinary citizens had brought them up, they would have given rise to competition. The alternative was to maneuver public opinion in such a way that the decision appeared to be based on consensus.

Politicians had to walk the tightrope between favoring certain people and treating everyone equally. One way to gain support was to favor certain segments of the community, but this was equally sure to alienate the other segments. Politicians were always watching to detect any sign of favoritism on the part of their fellows. One BPL member commented:

> In the old days, considerations of relationship played a role. For instance, if a leader had to name someone to a post, he would tend to favor a relative. People gave in to these considerations even though they knew they ought not to. But at present people are more sophisticated. Besides, if anyone tried to operate in this way, his colleagues would learn of it, and prevent him from doing so by ganging up on him. Everyone works together, and keeps an eye on his fellows—each knows what the others are up to—and so people are afraid of trying to favor friends and relatives because of the sanctions against it.

People demanded equal treatment, especially if they thought that someone else was specially favored. If there were *fasobara*, everyone had to go. If there were a contribution for something, everyone had to give the same amount. If there were a distribution of scarce goods or foods, then every effort had to be made to ensure that the distribution was equitable.

Generosity was also favored as a personal quality, and conceptions about the role of generosity colored local interpretations of people's behavior. A man who seemed to be unusually generous was thought to be trying to improve his reputation with an eye towards political advancement. Giving a lot of money to a *dieli* was symptomatic of political ambition; the stereotype of the political parvenu was that he tried to convert wealth into political position through his generosity to *dieli* and others. People saw him as "buying" allies through his openhandedness. In any case he was trying to build or hold a reputation. Those who favored the ideological orientation felt that the obligation to be generous in order to maintain their position was a particularly onerous one; this discontent was at the root of a lot of the measures taken against the *dieli*. The need to be generous in order to maintain one's position was believed by many Kitans to be the cause of a lot of financial funny business, as the quotation given above demonstrates.

There was a generalized suspicion of one another's motives that made it hard for people to work together. Anything was potential grist for the political mill; and any position taken, even outside the strictly "political" domain, might reflect a calculation of political advantage as much as any other factor. One teacher, who had been in Kita about a year, commented that he had never seen so much intrigue and duplicity as he had found in Kita: it was impossible to work frankly and openly with anyone. A member of an old Kita family divided people into three types: those who work sincerely to accomplish something (the fewest), the saboteurs, and the apathetic. He decried the attitude of the saboteurs, who try to make all programs fail. A member of a subsection bureau made this analysis:

> Every political bureau is divided into rival cliques. Each bureau has its malcontents, who try as hard as they can to overthrow the secretary-general. They can do this by attacking him subtly during the meetings (that is, by thinking up reasons why the secretary-general's plans won't work), or they can do it by agitating outside the meetings, revealing what the bureau's plans are and suggesting tendentiously where their disagreements with the plans lie.

People's motives were often interpreted in the worst possible light. Self-interest was cited as an explanation for most actions, both in politics and in other fields of endeavor. People frequently explained the difficulties of cooperative projects by saying that individuals were more interested in pursuing their own interests than in working together. "It would be good if people could work together," said a peasant, "but the Maninka are incapable of this; they only work for their own self-interest." Management of cooperative enterprises (including *fasobara* programs) was a delicate task, for it had to appear that everyone was getting the same benefits for the same work. Kitans sometimes expressed the idea that, in earlier times, people were less exclusively motivated by self-interest, and so cooperative projects fared better.[9]

Self-interest, like competitiveness, was neither entirely good nor entirely bad. People found it natural that merchants and others should work for their personal interests in trying to earn a living and that they should be rewarded on an individual basis for this. Merchants themselves have always been highly regarded in Kitan society, and the developments under the RDA did not change that regard much. A merchant was more highly regarded than a farmer and, until after independence, more so than a civil servant. Before independence, many merchant fathers took their sons from school as soon as they learned to read, write, and do arithmetic, for this was all that was thought necessary for a successful merchant.[10] A successful merchant was always admired not least for the standard of living he was able to maintain; the attempt, in the play *Reconversion,* to attack a merchant by showing him living in luxury was too subtle a point for most Kitans.

At the same time, people rarely justified their own behavior in terms of self-interest. They preferred to argue, in the ideological orientation, that their behavior was based on principle. One of Kita's leading politicians stated that, along with the people of his ward, he always saw what was right and acted accordingly. The RDA interpretation of its electoral victory in the late 1950s was that it was right and that other people gradually came to realize this (see below). People also liked to think of themselves as "frank" (that is, as saying what they thought regardless of the consequences) in their dealings with others. One man suggested that, because of his notorious frankness, he was better suited to a job on the cooperative's overseers' committee than to one on the administrative coun-

---

9. It would seem doubtful that this was true, except within the structure of the extended family or lineage where cooperation, in any case, was on a different basis. Instead of being between equals linked by interest, it was (and is) between hierarchically differentiated people under the head of the lineage.

10. The resulting lower educational achievements of merchants worked against them, for most merchants were not sufficiently educated to shift into the administration after independence.

cil where, according to him, he would not be able to speak his mind.[11]

Kitans were aware that little got done without pull—without passing through intermediaries. This awareness was expressed in several ways. There were disgruntled people who felt that others had gotten special privileges because they had friends in the right places. A shopkeeper who felt himself to be on bad terms with the town's leaders remarked, "If you are on good terms with the local politicians, forget about needing papers. But make sure your papers are in order if you and they are on bad terms." Some people made a virtue out of not having, or using, pull: a teacher who got the reassignment he wanted boasted that he had gotten it strictly through regular channels, without trying to enlist powerful supporters. On the other hand, there were those who wanted to accomplish something and sought out "brokers" to support their request; by their actions they stated their belief in the existence and importance of pull. This category was the most common. Others thought they had pull and boasted of it. An example was a civil servant who regarded himself as the protector of an out-of-town pupil living in his father's house. When the pupil failed to pass his exams, the civil servant expressed the opinion that, had he been in town and able to bring his influence to bear, his protégé would not have been failed.[12]

Kita's political leaders also complained about the attitudes of their followers, who frequently failed to act as good militants. One man, active in Kita politics from the late 1940s, commented that the young men of 1965 were much less interested in politics than had been true fifteen or twenty years earlier, when he was a young man. A committee secretary-general remarked, "Kita is a difficult town for political leaders now because the people are uncooperative. They do not follow the leaders, and even say unpleasant things about them, which the leaders just have to put up with." One of his specific complaints was that people never came to meetings on time so that they dragged on interminably. Another political leader in Kita complained about the lack of enthusiasm shown by Kitans

11. It is also true that he would have to act on the administrative council, and would run the risk of irritating people, whereas on the overseers' committee he could support any complaint that aroused the people of his ward.

12. As far as I know he did nothing to rectify the matter; at any rate, the pupil stayed failed. I refer to his instinctive reaction rather than to his behavior.

and added, "It is hard for leaders to do their job because the people won't cooperate." A common attitude was expressed by a school-boy who held an office in a pupils' recreational club: "If you have responsibilities in an organization, you also have difficulties."[13] The difficulties of leadership in 1965 might have been partially due to the beginnings of disaffection with the RDA government, but prob-ably leadership has always been uncertain enough so that these complaints might have been heard at any time. The new element was a different idea of what leaders ought to do, based on the ideo-logical orientation.

The most effective way to ensure that no one's interests were neglected was to make all decisions in more or less public session to which all parties concerned had access. Frequent general assemblies were seen as an antidote to dictatorship; a secretary-general or other leader who did not convene such meetings frequently was thought to be running everything by himself—and, people suspected, for his own benefit or that of his clique. Publicity and face-to-face meet-ings of the maximum number of the people concerned were thought to be the best guarantee that things were done properly. "Open discussions are held in meetings," an active youth member said, "So everyone will agree and there will be no opportunism"—mean-ing no criticism outside the meeting aimed at stirring up trouble against the leaders. People regarded the general assemblies and other open meetings as a chance to exert some control over leaders' activities. Whatever is done in public everyone knows about; if something is done in a restricted group, others might become sus-picious and rumors might start. The judge in Kita favored open court sessions not only for their educational value but also because they allayed any suspicions people might have about the court.

Concentration of power in the hands of a single individual was believed to lead to the abuse of that power; the natural rivalry of individuals kept the system in balance. A young intellectual remarked, "If the village chief and the secretary-general of the village party committee are the same person, this is dictatorship." One of Kita's leading politicians was regarded with suspicion by some because they felt he "kept things to himself too much." (In

13. See Meillassoux (1968:132–5) for the political problems of leadership in a Bamako youth club.

another connection, but revealing for the general attitude, men who attempted to make a decision regarding their daughter's marriages alone, without consulting any other family members, were thought to be arrogant and egotistical.) Kitans saw frequent assemblies and a dual authority system as the remedy for "dictatorship."

Behind these considerations lay a deeper value: everybody should participate in political decisions. In the traditional political structure, every adult male or at least every head of family was expected to participate in the assemblies where Kita's affairs were discussed. They were expected to attend, and entitled to voice their opinions. In the postindependence period, people in Kita expected to be able to take part in politics, even if at the lowest level, and everyone considered that he had the right to make his voice heard. The primary meaning given to "democracy" by Kitans was that everyone should be able to take part in politics.

The idea that decisions should be reached by collective discussion, gradually arriving at a solution acceptable to all, led to a different conception of the role of meetings than did the notion, discussed above as part of the ideological orientation, that meetings were where the enlightened instructed the unenlightened on their duties. There was a certain tension at meetings because of the two concepts of what they were and how they should proceed. The leaders were unwilling and unable to accept any discussion of the policies they were presenting, for these policies had already been decided upon; the people did not react properly unless they could discuss a matter openly. The people brought up questions on topics not on the agenda that often forced the leadership to change its posture.

Kitans viewed the national government and its local representatives at times fatalistically, at other times opportunistically. In the fatalistic vein, they assumed that the government was capable of doing whatever it wanted and that nothing could prevent it. If it decided to collect taxes twice, all one could do was pay them twice.[14] One young farmer told me, "We had better do what the government tells us to do voluntarily, otherwise they'll force

14. In one case, a part of the difficulty was that most merchants were unable to produce the receipts given them for the previous tax payments and so no one was sure whether the government was indeed collecting the tax twice or not.

us to do it." The same man who told me it was both counterproductive and without precedent to use force to establish a policy in Kita argued, on a different occasion, that plows would spread because the government would insist on it. In the opportunistic vein, people saw the national government as the dispenser of good things, especially pork-barrel projects of all kinds (schools, dispensaries, wells, pharmacies, warehouses, and so on). One young man argued that the government should build all schools itself, without calling on human investment or local participation of any kind. Thus the national government is seen at different times as omnipotent and malevolent, as omnipotent and benevolent, and as powerless except when implementing popular decisions.

Whatever the attitude towards the national government, however, the prevalent view in Kita was that a local unit should run its own affairs as much as possible. I have already discussed this attitude at length and given some examples, such as the case of the Kita Natives' Association and the other attempts to eliminate non-Kitans from responsible posts in Kita. This attitude also covered other situations, such as the dislike of what was seen as interference by the national government in Kita's affairs, or the attempt to take Kita's grain during a famine to feed other areas which were even more affected. One of the best methods for protecting oneself against such interference was to make sure that the authorities at the next level were ignorant of the details of local organization. Hence, in a reverse way, we can see the importance of fact-finding missions led by political commissioners, and the tendency of the national government to use local cleavages, in the absence of accurate information, as the best way to gain access to local knowledge and local influence.

Leaders were referred to as *mogoba* in Maninka, a term derived from the traditional political vocabulary, where it meant a big or important man. Other words were occasionally used: *nyamogo,* which means roughly the same as *mogoba,* and *fama,* which means "chief." In French these people were referred to as *patrons,* with the implication of "boss." The *mogoba* were conceptually a distinct social category, although there was some dispute about the exact membership. Political intrigue and competition for posts were seen as involving only *mogoba;* the rest of the populace were somehow interested bystanders, no more.

One man commented that "Laws such as the marriage code are for the common people, *mogoba* do what they like."[15] Another claimed that a plane designed to carry ill people to Bamako for medical treatment "was only for *mogoba*." A farmer pointed out that *"fama* don't work." When building lots were distributed in Kita, it was stipulated that they would revert to the town government if people didn't build on them within a certain period. People noticed that the *mogoba* were not building on theirs, so they concluded that the regulation would not be enforced. A mechanic, on hearing that a certain BPL member he knew well "was tired of politics," reacted by saying that, after all, the man had a position, so he ought not to be tired of it. Thus the ordinary people regarded the *mogoba* as the Establishment, bound by different rules and with their own way of life.[16]

Kitans had various standards by which they judged the *mogoba*. Several people argued to me that some of their leaders were *tubabu* (Europeans) and others were *farafing* (blacks). The criteria seemed to be that the *tubabu* ate in the European style and held themselves aloof from the mass of the people, while the *farafing* were more approachable. These people obviously felt *farafing* leaders were better than *tubabu* ones, perhaps because they were more "human." Among some people it was considered good to be "civilized," which implied a certain adherence to some styles inspired by Europe, but I heard no one argue that being "civilized" made one a better leader.

Good leaders were supposed to be approachable. Of one of Kita's leaders it was said that he was approachable, that he listened to what people had to say, and that he tried to reason with them to persuade them that his point of view was right.[17] It was also said of him that he was good because of *o te kuma* ("he doesn't

15. Several months later, the judge told one of the leading political figures in Kita that he could not just divorce his wife by sending her away, he would have to follow the marriage code. If the man persisted in ignoring the law, he, the judge, would prosecute him, no matter what his political position. The man took his wife back (she was one of three).

16. There were of course many links of all kinds between *mogoba* and others, and considerable movement between the various statuses.

17. He was certainly available in the physical sense as he spent much of his time in Kita in the party headquarters in the marketplace, where everyone had access to him.

speak"), meaning that he wasn't always after people to get them to do something. Contrasted with such leaders were those of whom it was said that they tried to boss people around too much, that they tried to force people to do things, perhaps by threatening them, and that they tried to keep information from people in order to rule them more ruthlessly. Such leaders were not liked.

Another trait praised in a leader was that of being wealthy and generous. This attitude presumably derived from the precolonial situation, where many leaders served some kind of redistributive function. On the other hand, leaders were criticized for seeking only money and position.

A good leader should be *yere wulu*—a term that means both being a "citizen" (neither a *nyamakala* nor a slave) and being born into a legitimately constituted family. Locally born leaders were also preferred, because they were believed to share in local values and to be controllable through the many personal ties they had in the community. Some people expressed the idea that *dieli,* other *nyamakala,* and descendants of slaves ought not to have the top positions in Kita, but the success of *dieli* in particular shows the limitations of this attitude. Leaders were also praised for their frankness and courage, two traits associated with being *yere wulu.* One leader remarked that those who had left the RDA during the "repression" of the late 1940s showed lack of courage and ought not to be allowed to have the top positions now. A leader who had been suspended from the RDA for attacking Malian socialism in the presence of the president was nonetheless admired in Kita for his courage and his frankness.[18]

Kitans also liked their leaders to have some influence with the higher levels of the national government—in the regional capital of Kayes or the national capital of Bamako. This allowed them to operate effectively as lobbyists for the things that Kita wanted. I have summarized above an incident in which one of Kita's deputies seized an occasion to advertise his success in getting Bamako to organize projects in the town. On the other hand, several people complained that Kita's leaders did not lobby enough in Kita's favor, or did not have the kind of contacts needed. They lacked "pull."

18. In 1970 he had regained his social position, though not his economic one.

One leader was criticized for being "proud"; not a native of Kita, he knew that he was not liked in town yet he would not leave voluntarily and insisted on sticking it out. He was also criticized for saying bad things about people; he had been quite popular, it was said, until he began "ruining people's names." A leader might also lose favor if the people felt he was giving bad advice, which might simply mean that he was consistently on the losing side. This happened to an old RDA stalwart in one of the rural areas of the circle.

Kitans had a fairly consistent standard of what they looked for in a leader. They wanted one who would leave them alone as much as possible, who would operate by persuasion rather than force, and who would be effective as a lobbyist with the national government. In their view, however, not all their leaders fitted this pattern. They explained this discrepancy by saying that they retained long-time leaders because of gratitude for their actions in the past, specifically in the struggle against the colonial government and the PSP. Kitans complained of leaders because they found them arbitrary, bossy, and demanding, or because they were lazy and ineffective. Yet it seemed that those who were criticized for being bossy and demanding were the most effective in dealing with the national government and in mobilizing the people of Kita. Their very success made them suspect, as Kitans feared too great a concentration of power.

The pragmatic orientation contained more existential elements than the ideological orientation; it was much more the view held by people of how their system worked, with some notion of which parts of that system they considered worthwhile and which ones they saw as disadvantageous. Rivalry was seen as a natural phenomenon with both good and bad consequences, with everyone striving for prestige and reputation on an individual basis. People were suspicious of one another's motives so that a situation of intrigue arose where rivals often felt compelled to compromise principles in order to increase their popularity and thus improve their competitive position. "Pull" was a normal means of achieving personal or community goals. Mass participation in public meetings with open discussion was the best way to reach a decision binding on all participants. Everyone ought to be treated equally but at the same time many people succeeded in being granted special privileges. Generosity and frankness were valued as personality traits. Every locality should be left to govern itself as much as possible. The people tended to see the best leader as the one who stood up for them best to the central government, yet left them in peace the rest of the time.

Almost everyone in Kita at some time operated by the pragmatic orientation to politics. Some people operated only by it, particularly farmers, merchants and others who had never been at all acculturated to the ideological orientation. However, some merchants and farmers had assimilated certain tenets of the ideological orientation, and almost all of them responded to moralistic appeals based on that orientation. The pragmatic orientation offered a system of values derived essentially from the social structure of pre-colonial Kita, but it also offered an existential view of how politics worked which was hard for Kitans to drop in favor of the more austere vision of the ideological orientation.

Values and Myths

The pragmatic orientation dominated in Kita. This can be seen from the much more elaborate discussion of it that it has been possible to give, if it were not already obvious from its reflection in the patterns of rivalry and the patterns of discourse discussed in the last two chapters. Yet the ideological orientation continued to exist in Kita, providing an alternative model for politics which undoubtedly was especially attractive to those whose expressions of dissatisfaction with the corrupting and debilitating aspects of real Kita politics are cited above. People who felt the need to get things done became very resentful of the hypocrisy and the inability to deal with others in a straight-forward manner which were too frequently characteristic of Kita politics. The continuing attraction of the ideological orientation for certain Kitans, especially the young men, meant that the ideas of the party and the state retained some degree of influence in Kita no matter how great the dominance of the pragmatic orientation. The existence of these two strains of political thought in the small community corresponded to two diverse needs, one that of the people who remained fully committed to the town's values and standards, and the other that of the people who were alienated by such a system and who at the same time felt the need to improve Mali's conditions.

Both these sets of ideas were available to Kitans, and were variously brought to bear on such problems as dealing with the national government, working cooperatives in a way satisfactory to the populace, settling quarrels between local personalities, and so on. The duality enabled a certain ambiguity to settle over the key institutions in Kita, and in particular over the relations to the national government. Debate over the correctness of one or the other orientation was in part in terms of the past, for interpreting the past is one of the principal ways in which Kitans argue about the present. The past in question here was the period from 1946 to 1959 when there was competition between the RDA and the PSP. The RDA myth and the PSP myth are versions of this period that "explain" why things happened the way they did. The differences between them correspond closely to the distinction between the ideological and the pragmatic orientations.

According to the PSP myth, the PSP dominated Kita during the entire period from 1946 to 1957. The RDA won through trickery. Specifically, the RDA made promises to the people and thus gained their sympathy, but then they couldn't keep those promises. The PSP refused to outbid the RDA in making promises and instead warned the people of the probably dire results of an RDA victory, emphasizing that the road to success in the future was long and that people would have to work hard. They warned the people that, if the RDA won, everyone would become slaves and would lose control over their women, children, and property. PSP people felt that the RDA had been unfair in making these demagogic promises, and especially in posing as the champions of the rural areas and the oppressed. One ex-PSP leader stated that there had always been some people opposed to the chief; the RDA merely championed them, benefiting from the greater degree of free speech after World War II. PSP people also felt that the final victory of the RDA in 1959 was due in large part to an unfair stratagem on the part of the RDA-dominated central government whereby all leading civil servants who supported the PSP had been assigned to distant posts in the bush shortly before the election in order to minimize their influence on election results. The PSP myth saw the RDA as operating entirely according to the pragmatic orientation to politics and in a rather cynical fashion violating norms of fairness. The myth saw the PSP as taking a pragmatic view of politics in the sense of seeking practical solutions to concrete problems.

According to the RDA myth, the party started off as a distinct minority which furthermore was required to remain clandestine to survive. Because they stood for correcting injustice and because they inspired conviction in the justness of their cause, the RDA members gradually won more and more support. In essence, they won because they were right. One of the founders of the RDA in Kita claimed that the RDA saw the truth and acted on it while others, even if they saw the truth, were afraid to act on it. Another old RDA militant listed some of the points which he said the RDA had emphasized: the RDA would open opportunities to all, so that anyone might become a commandant de cercle or a doctor; there would be no more head tax, because the revenue needed to run the country would be raised from taxes on the French companies; the peanut price would be high; and there would be no more slavery.[19] According to a civil servant who had also been an early RDA supporter, the main theme of the RDA's propaganda was that the RDA opposed injustice, particularly the injustice associated with the colonial situation. Thus the RDA was opposed by the traditional canton and village chiefs and by the administration's civil servants, all of whom supported the status quo from which they benefited. He also suggested that one reason why the RDA was successful so early in Kita was that, being on the railroad line, Kita was more open to outside influences.[20]

The second important aspect of the RDA myth was the glorification of the struggle against the PSP and the French administration. Like the exponents of the PSP myth, the old RDA hands liked to emphasize how long the PSP had really been in control of Kita.[21] While the PSP myth emphasized this to show what a fluke the RDA victory had been, the RDA myth did so to make more plausible the stories of heroism in the struggle against the PSP and

19. In 1965 this man no longer felt he had been right to support the RDA.

20. Morgenthau (1964:280) makes the same suggestion, but it is interesting that most of the railroad workers in Kita were said (in 1965) to have supported the PSP, led by a man (Fily Dabo Sissoko) who was of the same ethnic group (Kasonka) and region as most of them. On the other hand, everyone may be thinking of Toukoto, the second town of the circle where a railroad yard, since closed, employed many workers in the 1940s and early 1950s (Delval 1951:57).

21. The first election which resulted in a clearcut RDA victory was one held in August, 1956, for the French National Assembly. Earlier there had been victories with a plurality of the vote, starting with the election of an RDA man to the Territorial Assembly in 1952 (see chapter 6).

the colonial administration. There were stories of RDA propa-
gandists touring on bicycles, on foot, or on donkey-back while
campaigning in the villages and of being expelled bodily from
certain villages. Old RDA hands spoke with relish of the cantons
and the villages which they had not dared enter. One man talked
with pride of how he had converted a well-known and powerful
canton chief to the RDA. People also were apt to emphasize how
much they had had to sacrifice because of their association with
the RDA. One man spoke of losing his job, another of not having
been able to continue his education. There was sometimes competition in this respect: "I lost more than you." People also pointed
out the early RDA leaders who had given their fortunes to the
cause.

The difference between the earlier period and the present was
summed up by a young farmer who had been active in the RDA
since his late teens: "Politics under an African government is quite
different from what it was under European rule. Now if you do
something against the government and are jailed, people just laugh
at you." In other words, under a European government, anyone sent
to jail, no matter what the reason, got sympathy as a victim of the
Europeans. After independence it was strictly a question of rivalry
among Africans, and losers were mocked. The early period of
competition between the two parties under colonial rule had been
a heroic time, and people looked back to it with nostalgia.

From this period came two interpretations of the past: the
RDA myth, according to which a small group of people saw the
truth and eventually triumphed because they had been right, and
still were; and the PSP myth, according to which the RDA was
successful because of its unfair tactics, including demagogy. In other
words, the contrast was between the ideological point of view of
the RDA and the pragmatic point of view of the PSP. But if the
RDA's reasons for the final victory were put in ideological terms,
much of the analysis of what had gone on during the period of
rivalry was in pragmatic terms: people were proud of the "coups"
in which they had taken part.

These divergent images of the recent past justified feelings
about the present. They also served as background to the alternative orientations to politics that I have described in this chapter.
These orientations have been presented in an attempt to make
some sense out of my data on the attitudes towards politics I en-

countered during my field work, on the complex pattern of party and state institutions, and on the functioning of a political rivalry which only incidentally corresponded to the framework of the party. This approach assumes that the culture of politics—the values and the myths—is necessary to a grasp of the structures and processes of politics.

Kita appears as a community which was alienated from the policies and schemes of the central government, although continuing to support it for nationalistic reasons. Politics in Kita was very closely linked to the town as a community, and within that community institutions and values joined to create a kind of popular government. At the same time, the popular government that served Kita so well when it was a question of turning the engine over slowly bedevilled it when there was a question of moving decisively in any direction, even for the public good. The stress on consensus and the need of leaders for popular support meant that initiatives were rarely taken and were easily swallowed up and that leaders struggled for prestige rather than betterment. Without popular support they could not remain leaders, and popular support was not forthcoming to those who tried to mobilize the people. The implications of this dilemma are the subject of the concluding chapter.

10

The Past and the Future

The description of small-town political organization in Mali given here corresponds to a period only a few years after decolonization and independence. If one looks back on Malian history, the decade of one-party rule under the Union Soudanaise-RDA may stand out as a unique divergence from the general trend of Malian history and institutions, or as a necessary stage for the process of decolonization. But it is much more likely to appear as the first step on a long and arduous process of nation-building. This book, then, may be seen as dealing with one of the early phases of that development. Here is a classic case of a one-party system in its heyday, and much of the analysis deals with the implications of the single party for the political process. As such, the case of Kita has relevance for understanding social and cultural processes in broadly comparable situations around the world; it is part of the repertory of human solutions to the problems of organizing collective life. But there is no guarantee that such a system will come to be in Mali again, now that it has been overthrown and replaced by a military government. What I have said in this book relates to a system which is in the realm of history, whatever broad continuity there might be with the present or the future. I have tried to show the influence of the past on the situation that I knew, and I would like to conclude this book, after summarizing what I feel are the major lessons for anthropology and for the study of the new nations to be drawn from this material, by suggesting what the implications for an understanding of the present and the future of Mali might be.

POPULAR GOVERNMENT AND NATIONAL CULTURE

It is always exciting to look at situations where people are more or less spontaneously creating new social and cultural forms. One such situation is when a revolution occurs, as has happened in Russia, Yugoslavia—or the France of 1789 or the United States of the 1770s. The new nations are prime examples of this situation because political independence means that the institutions of the colonial period, themselves frequently only a couple of generations old, are necessarily modified when they are taken over by local people. Both at the national and the local levels, people are searching and experimenting with new institutional forms and patterns of relations, trying to develop an institutional framework that corresponds to their new political and economic status. Yet one does not enter this process empty-handed, but carries along with one a certain cultural baggage which one may then put to use either with or without reinterpreting it. The examination of the case of Kita has shown how there are strong threads of continuity that run through Kita society and politics from as far back as we can trace, but at the same time there have been many reformulations of these traditional elements, new elements have been incorporated, and the result has been that in a very fundamental way the society has been transformed.

Other anthropologists have shown how the creative ability of various peoples has enabled them to develop more or less spontaneously new social forms to cope with the problems of political independence and economic modernization. Janzen (1969a, b) shows how, in the absence of any sustained government policy or ability to penetrate and organize the rural areas, the BaKongo of the Manianga area (Lower Congo) have organized themselves into cooperatives and associations to deal with their economic and political problems, of which the overriding one perhaps is dealing with the national government in Kinshasa and the new economic situation subsequent upon independence. In Java, Geertz (1963a) has shown how people have sought economic opportunities and advances in accord with their basic values and habits of organization, noting especially the contrast between reformist Islam and Balinese Hinduism (again, with little or no government stimulus), and suggests that ultimately such efforts are likely to be doomed because of the unfavorable economic circumstances (1963b). Brokensha (1966), writing about Ghana, shows how, despite the strong central government of Kwame Nkrumah, the town of Larteh was left largely to its own resources, and how the national party organization was made responsive to local values in the town. This is the same area where a couple of generations earlier people had virtually exploded into a whole new set of social and economic relationships based on cocoa production (Hill 1963). On a somewhat different level, there are the cases of the farmers and merchants of Massachusetts, who were able to create imaginative new forms of government for themselves when British colonial authority withdrew to Boston in 1774, leaving a vacuum in the rest of the colony (Brown 1970); the Spanish anarchists in the 1930s who, taking advantage of a temporary absence of power, tried to reorganize their villages according to their idea of the Golden Age of the past (Hobsbawm 1959: 74–92); and one or two moments in French history, notably the first decade following 1789 (Brinton 1934) and the Paris Commune of 1871 (Lissagaray 1967).

In other cases from around the world we learn how local institutions have evolved under pressure from a modernizing national government. Abner Cohen (1965) has well documented this kind of situation for those Arabs who were left in Israel after the 1948 partition; and Antoun (1965) has shown that many of the same resentments of national policies and institutions, as being contradictory to local values and standards, exist in the East Bank Jordanian village he studied, which is located some fifty miles away. The case that Fernea (1970) describes for southern Iraqi farmers is more striking because these farmers have an organization where genealogy plays a larger role. Fernea shows the crucial role of the chief as a broker in this situation; this theme is also well documented from Uganda (Fallers 1956; Southwold 1964), and Mexico (Wolf 1956; Friedrich 1966, 1968). The southern French village that Wylie (1958) describes exemplifies the tension aroused by the presence of two quite different sets of attitudes, as does the Andalusian village analyzed by Pitt-Rivers (1961).

Comparable situations are also found closer to home. West's (1945) description of a rural community in Missouri provides one of the most sensitive accounts. In this community, the county agent was the main stimulus towards a broader view of the world and

more modern methods of farming, and the people opposed innovations in the school system that threatened the familiar social
fabric by preparing their children for a different kind of life. In a
small Texan community in New Mexico, the stress on individual-
ism and independence led the people to avoid any appeal to the
state police for settling local disputes and to resist all attempts to
resettle them on less marginal farmland (Vogt 1955). But it is not
only in rural areas that such variations in local institutional and
cultural patterns affect the schemes of central governments and the
spread of national cultures. Whyte's (1955) study of an Italian slum
in the United States shows both the problems that arise from the
differences in values and the important fact that despite this everyone is participating in the same social system. He argues that the
settlement houses, as representatives of the values of the dominant
middle-class sector of society, erred in not allowing leadership roles
in those houses to be taken by people who had emerged from the
local community and who might have offset the leaders who rose
through politics and the underworld. In a somewhat different
context, studies that have been done in factories (Zaleznick, Christensen, and Roethlisberger 1958) show how the creation of certain
values on a shop floor, arising from the pattern of ongoing social
relations, affects productivity when workers are oriented to those
values rather than to the standards set by the firm. Suttles' recent
study (1968) of the near West Side in Chicago focuses explicitly
on this theme, for Suttles argues that the various ethnic groups in
this community develop a kind of "provincialism," in other words,
a set of values and beliefs which are different from what he refers
to as "official norms" and which make it hard for local groups to
communicate with each other as well as with the society at large.
And for suburbia, Gans (1967) shows how the "local" values of most
of the people affect their relations with higher levels of government
and how people faced with an organizational vacuum on moving
into a new community created institutions that fit their needs.

Studies that analyze the interplay between spontaneous pressures towards change and government-planned initiatives toward
the same end are rare. Tunisia and Algeria provide two of the best
examples. In Tunisia, Zghal (1967a, b) has emphasized the per-
sistence of local values and customs, showing how traditional values
and especially economic power tended to reassert themselves in
newly irrigated areas where the government wanted to encourage

a more modern and egalitarian kind of social organization. Both Zghal and Zamiti (1970) have shown how the failure to allow for the spontaneity and strength of rural patterns was one of the sources for the disenchantment with Tunisia's cooperative system. In Algeria, too, there has been much interest in the forms of local rural communities. The farm workers spontaneously took over the land that withdrawing French farmers left behind in 1962, but the subsequent history of the self-management movement was one of successive and successful attempts by the government to reestablish control and impose standards on these cooperatives (Blair 1970; Porter 1968). Thus in Algeria a spontaneous popular movement towards new forms was checked and controlled by the central government, while in Tunisia the actualization of plans elaborated by the national government was impeded by the continued attachment to local patterns and older ways of doing things. In both cases it seems that the root of the problem lay in the tendency of the national government to equate real local government with loss of central control.

Most of these studies note the problem, analyze its contours, focus on the problematics of interstitial roles, and deplore the extent to which local variants of culture are being eliminated, or national unity and development are being impeded. But few deal with the problems of the wider meaning of this contradiction for change in the direction of modernization. National integration and development is a value, and so is the maintenance of patterns of local autonomy and integrity. Are these two values part of a zero-sum system, so that the realization of the one implies the denial of the other? Or is it possible to combine the two in such a way that greater benefits accrue to all? This is the kind of question that anthropology, with its concern for small-scale, intimate units and for individuals, should address itself to. What light can our knowledge of the range and variation of societies existing in the world throw on this problem? Can we, basing ourselves on our concrete knowledge of societies that exist or have existed, propose new models for social organization and cultural patterns that will enable societies, our own as well as others, to cope more effectively with the changing social, cultural, and technological environment? Even if prediction remains little better than a matter of chance, the implications of the present for the future must continue to interest us. Anthropologists need to use their knowledge of particular societies and of the social process in general to put forth ways in which the inevitable trend towards social modernization (if not economic development) can be channeled in such a manner that the participation of the people is assured; that whatever changes and policies are made, are made with and by the people, not against them or at some level so abstract that the people no longer count.

POPULAR GOVERNMENT IN KITA

The recurrent theme of this book has been the very high level of popular participation in Kita's government. What might seem to have been a monolithic, centralized one-party system in fact had a high degree of flexibility, as people and institutions were responsive to popular pressures. Political pressure from the bottom was far more important in Kita's government than initiative from the center, for the former never let up. Kita public opinion put limits on the range of activities that could be successfully sponsored in the town, and it had a role in dispute settlement. The people pressured the government to provide the things they wanted: schools, hospitals, water supply, and so on. Political leaders competed for public support, and to a great extent the retention of individuals in the major political roles reflected their success in obtaining more support from the public than their rivals were able to.

Another recurrent note in this analysis has been the significance of a "Kitan" identity as providing the basis for the major arena of political activity. The most important identities for political behavior were those based on locality—the identity of "Kitan" and the identities based on the various wards. Local identity was more relevant for government than ethnic affiliation, religion, social status, or any other type of solidarity. There is a mythic affirmation of this relevance in the story of how the Keita won Kita's independence from the Traoré king. This Kitan identity was translated into an urban particularism, in which the association with the town became crucial for ordering one's relations to the outside world. It was also expressed through the existence of a political community corresponding to the town and its hinterland. The community provided the arena where personal political ambition brought people together in factions competing for power and prestige. The pattern I found in Kita resembles the descriptions given of factions in Senegalese towns and rural areas (Robinson

1960: 340–45; Foltz 1965: 138) ; it may well be that when we know more of the processes of politics and government elsewhere in the Western Sudan that the presence of this kind of system of factions will become a diagnostic trait. Factional conflict, although deplored by many Kitans for its divisive effects, had beneficial as well as prejudicial aspects, and in particular furthered the integration of the community: factional rivalry made a physical community into a political community. This political community then acted as a unit in relation to the outside, and thus the importance of identity with the political community—that is, with the town of Kita—was reinforced.

Success in the Kita factional system was at least partially dependent on manpower, and so those desirous of exercising political influence had to compete, using all the means at their disposal, for this support. There were few economic means to this end in independent Mali, for even the relatively structured relationship between merchants and client farmers (to say nothing of precolonial slavery) had disappeared. Nor were there preconstituted blocks such as lineages or ethnic groups that could be manipulated by knowing politicians. The explanatory model that works best is one that assumes that each individual in the political field was able to decide what to do on the basis of his own personal interpretation of his advantage, and acted accordingly. Such a situation led politicians to appeal to people by taking up popular causes instead of allowing and encouraging them to work for what they might feel to be just causes. In other words, demagogy was a way of maintaining preeminence over one's faction; its importance was heightened by the requirement, in a factional system such as this where people could and did switch sides, for personal success and forward movement if allegiances were to be maintained.

The merchants, who were the most powerful group during the final stages of the colonial period, were eclipsed by the civil servants. The civil servants occupied most of the choice spots in the party hierarchy, so that something like an "Establishment" of those with sufficient education (and thus literate, urban-oriented, French-speaking) emerged. These civil servants/party officials also typically lived in, and experienced, more different areas of Mali than the merchants; their frame of reference was more likely to be national than regional. Success in the system nonetheless went to

educated civil servants of local origin; even the relative cosmo-
politanism of the civil servants did not eliminate regionalism.

But by far the major theme that has run through this book
has been the emphasis in both values and behavior on popular participation in the governmental process. This theme of intense involvement of a large portion of the population runs from the
precolonial Maninka social structure to the period described here.
In the early Maninka social structure, the only real leaders were
those who had achieved that position through their skill at manipu-
lating the values and processes of the society so that the majority of
the people supported them, and public opinion and consensus were
essential if any decision or policy were to be effective. By the period
discussed here, there were institutionalized general assemblies for
the wards and for the town as a whole, the replica of the meetings
formerly held for all the country of Kita; there were extraordinary
numbers of people with formal posts in the party hierarchy; administrative decisions were made and political disputes settled with
an eye towards the expression of public opinion; and leaders had
constantly to be aware of the currents of public opinion. This
theme of popular participation is also reflected in the values of
both the two major orientations, the ideological and the pragmatic,
and it is reflected in the organizational structures and operational
necessities of the institutions of politics, cooperatives, sports, and
so on. In the Kita political context, this popular participation gave
a legitimacy to actions undertaken by the recognized leaders.

While the ideology of the RDA and Kita's traditional political
values agreed on the central importance of popular participation
in the political process, this agreement stopped there. There was a
fundamental split between the two political orientations. The
ideological orientation saw politics as a tool to be used for profound
social reform, while the pragmatic orientation saw it as a means
for distinguishing between the relative prestige of different individuals. This split led to a kind of lack of cultural consensus on
the meanings of acts, but the underlying agreement, based on the
traditional style, was strong enough so that this lack of cultural
integration was limited in significance. Nevertheless, one can say
of Kita as Geertz (1965: 205) did of a Javanese town, characterized
by an even greater diversity of orientations, that it is possible to
perceive "the progressive articulation of social form—meaning—
through the medium of social action." The necessary interaction

of all the actors meant that there was a tendency for acts to come to have the same meaning for all concerned. This tendency was reinforced by the clearly defined boundaries around the town arena and by the active participation of so many people in the politics of that arena.

NATION-BUILDING IN MALI

One of the main reasons for being involved in Kita politics was to attain a position of power and influence. Such a conception was, of course, contrary to that of the RDA's national political culture, as expressed in Kita by what I have called the ideological orientation. And, as indicated in the last chapter, this contradiction between the two conceptions of politics was one of the major strains in Kita. What had happened by the time I carried out my field work in 1964-65 was that competitive, "pragmatic" politics had driven out nation-building, "ideological" politics.

It is interesting to reflect on why this should have happened, for to answer this question is to suggest the reasons for the failure of the RDA in Mali. There can be no simple response. A part of the answer is that the precolonial, traditional patterns of politics simply reasserted themselves. The difference between Tokontan Keita in 1880 and Makan Kouyaté or Moussa Sylla in the 1960s was not great at all. The major elements of this traditional pattern that reasserted themselves were a certain conception of the proper role of a successful man in guiding the affairs of his community, a certain pattern of asymmetrical relationships involving various forms of patron-client relations, and an emphasis on reaching decisions based on open discussion in assembly where some kind of consensus could be reached. In other words, there was a cultural support for competitive politics that did not exist for nation-building politics.

The success of Mali as a mobilization system (Apter 1963) in relation to the economic context is also relevant. The party structure, both in Kita and throughout the country, certainly had the potential to be a "mobilization system," and undoubtedly there were many, especially at the national level (cf. M. Keita 1960; Badian 1965; Diallo 1968) who dearly wanted it to be so. But people can be mobilized through enthusiasm only to a limited extent: beyond that they must be persuaded or obliged. Mali's government did not have the wherewithal to oblige people on any

large scale, and its leaders proved increasingly incapable of persuading people that collective action for economic development
was worthwhile. This failure to persuade was due in large part to
the lack of any results from earlier efforts, a lack that was all the
more critical because government leaders had on occasion unjusti-
fiably raised expectations. Mobilization for economic development
and social change seems to be the kind of situation that requires
immediate returns if enthusiasm is not to be dampened, and such
returns could not, in the nature of Mali's economic situation, be
forthcoming. People rapidly became disillusioned and resistant
when the RDA and the government tried to mobilize them. Most
of the indices that people judge by showed that their personal
economic situations were worsening.

The RDA government had asked for sacrifices and discipline
because it wanted not just to hold the line, but to pursue a utopian
policy of social revolution and economic development. Further,
the Malian government, itself demonstrating the independence that
was so high a value for village and town, wanted to be as free as
possible of foreign economic and political influence. This combination—trying to go it alone with an economic unit that was unequal
to the demands and attempting to mobilize the people for changes
at home which, for the most part, could only come slowly—led to
the dissipation of the enthusiasm of the period around independence. The failure of the regime to capitalize on the burst of
creative energy set free by independence meant that ideological
politics, devoted to nation-building, quickly lost favor as a source
of personal commitment. People ceased to respond to appeals based
on the higher values of the nation. If there were no quick payoff,
people lost faith in the value of sacrifice and discipline; yet without
these qualities, there could never be a payoff. This was the downward spiral in which the Malian government found itself.

The failure of the mobilization system for economic and
social changes left the door open for a return to the traditionally
validated system. People were no longer concerned with the national
good, but instead began to play the game of pork-barrel politics.
Politics in Kita became a question of who could do what for the
community, or even for specific individuals in the community. I
have given many examples of this: particularly such cases as the
deputy appealing for a pharmacy and a bookstore, or the ward
secretaries-general acting as brokers for their constituents with

town-wide authorities. Thus the system of patrons and clients could find a new life in a different political setting.[1]

If a government is unable to persuade people to follow the policies it advocates, it may also turn to the use of force. But it should be clear by now that the Malians did not have adequate government force for this to be a real possibility (in Kita the failure of the local party on the questions of bush fires and maize in the courtyards was indicative of the lack of capacity to oblige) ; even if they had had the force, the increasing narrowness of the base of power when government is based on force alone (Parsons 1963) would soon have become evident. Most important, the use of force in government is contrary to Malian political values. Malians react very negatively to anyone who tries to give them orders, unless it is from a thoroughly legitimate base; the most frequent response is to accuse the orderer of wanting to be a dictator. The legitimate Malian technique for obliging someone to do something is to make sure that that person participates in the decision to act. There are elaborate tactics to ensure that the people concerned by a decision, especially those who have to act on it, are party to it; there are equally elaborate attempts to avoid such participation by people who want to escape responsibility for a decision. The tendency of meetings to shift from explanations of a new policy to a discussion of the decisions themselves also illustrates this value.

Thus the dilemma of independent Mali: a functioning political system, based on traditional Malian values reinforced at key points by Leninist theory, could be developed, and could serve as an integrating and unifying political institution, proving effective for involving the very great majority of the urban and rural populations in the national political process, but at the cost of sacrificing chances for economic development. The hierarchies of party, union, and cooperative linked the various communities of the nation and provided a forum for discussion and activity that constantly stressed the national aspect, as these were national institutions.[2]

1. In a broad way, this trend had gone even further when I visited Kita in 1970, after the abolition of the party structure.

2. Conversely, the abandonment of the nationally oriented institutions seemed by 1970 to have contributed to a situation where purely local issues were once more becoming paramount (for example, quarrels over precedence among *dieli* and among Muslims) and where communication between the various parts of the national social system was becoming difficult.

But local leaders established themselves in part by implicit criticism of national policies and by making themselves the spokesmen of local special interests which might well go against a system of national priorities. At the same time, the failure of the system to generate an improved standard of living meant that popular dissatisfaction with central government policies increased and made people all the less willing to accept direction from the center. In certain respects, the Malian genius for associating people with every decision ought to have been eminently suitable for spreading new ideas and innovative techniques through the populace and for countering any opposition that might appear, but such a system places a very high premium on the persuasive ability of the bearers of the new culture and it presupposes a willingness to make the necessary sacrifices over an extended period of time. Also, a greater faith in the instincts and reasonableness of local populations might have led the central Malian government to allow more freedom for local initiative to solve the problems created by the new institutions; but this was not forthcoming. In the event, Malian townspeople and villagers lost faith in the political goals of the regime and were hardheadedly skeptical of the virtues of specific schemes for development. The regime had then either to renounce its plans for development and focus all its energies on political activities, or to turn to the use of force, which it was largely unable, for the reasons enumerated above, to do. The Malian government, caught on the horns of this dilemma, tried to reinvigorate the Malian polity through the "cultural revolution" of 1967–68, when it was declared that Mali had entered the period of the "active revolution." The hollowness of this attempt must soon have been apparent. The bankruptcy of the RDA regime as the leading force in Mali was evidenced by the turning of public opinion against it and the consequent shifting of the basis of power from persuasion and consensus to force and fear. When the RDA government was no longer accepted as legitimate, the stage was set for the military coup d'etat of November, 1968 (see Snyder 1969; Jones 1969; Comte 1969).

This ended the first stage in the history of independent Mali as a new nation in the modern world. The RDA regime had been an experiment in radical change. The RDA leaders proved unable to carry the experiment through to a conclusion—largely, I feel, because of the poverty of the country, although organization and political mistakes doubtless played their part. But one should not underrate the achievements of the RDA period, as we have seen them in Kita. They lay largely in the political sphere and consisted in the building of institutions such as cooperatives, party branches, government companies, schools, hospitals, and the like; in the creation of a Malian national identity, operating within a Malian political community; in the abolition of a large number of traditional roles such as the canton chiefship and statuses such as the castes; and in the avoidance of new statuses based on ethnicity.

The example of Mali shows that it is possible to move towards modernization through a social revolution, but that ultimate success along these lines is tightly linked to the economic success of the country. People must feel that they and their country are moving ahead; political successes can take the place of material advance for a while, but not forever. Mali has a particular significance in the Afro-Asian context, because it pushed ahead with certain types of reorganization that others may have thought of trying. There were probably more controls over economic activity than elsewhere in Africa and more government involvement with the economy. There was more of an attempt to create a social revolution according to the social philosophy of the RDA leaders. This deep commitment to change is what made Mali so relevant to other cases. If revolutionary mobilization systems are to succeed in changing the face and course of development in the Afro-Asian world, then the Malian case is certainly a thorough test. Given Mali's poverty, one is tempted to argue that if it would work in Mali, it would work anywhere. But the recent history of Mali does not encourage optimism that it would work in Mali, or that the Malian case is destined to be exemplary. The drama of Mali was always whether a poor country could obtain a rising standard of living and political independence by adopting a socialist policy. It seems that the answer is no; a poor country will remain poor regardless of regime, and a regime in a poor country that tries the radical modernization that Mali tried will succumb to the combined political and economic strains.[3]

3. A similar pattern is found in Tunisia. Under the guidance of a powerful minister for economic affairs, the Tunisian government pushed ahead energetically with the creation of cooperatives and other socialist institutions. But due to a combination of misjudgments on the part of the plan's promoters, and word-of-mouth propaganda on the part of its opponents, the mass of the population turned against this plan. The Tunisian government was faced with a choice

The case of Mali is relevant for the other underdeveloped countries, and even for the developed ones, from another point of view. The Malian political and social system, as we have seen it in one locality, represented one possible combination of elements (power, authority, consensus, participation), a combination that underlined the fact that power comes from the people in a very direct way. The description of the socio-political system of Kita in 1964–65 shows the desire of people to participate in politics and the ways in which their participation led to conflict between Kitans and the national government's schemes for social, economic, and political change. I have shown how this is worked out both in social organization and dynamics and in cultural patterns and values. Our knowledge of what is possible in the world is largely based on what can be shown to have been possible. Whatever its fate subsequently, the system described here was a fully functioning way of life for the people of Kita. It is not only admissible to the general repertory of societies, but is a prime example of the kind of social organization that can result from self-conscious attempts at modernization, when people treat the problems of institutions as a problem in technology. Anthropology should study the attempts by people in emerging societies to create new institutions, for these may turn out to be the institutions of the future. The comparative approach of anthropology can lead to an evaluation of the chances of different concrete proposals or alternatives in a given society. This concentration on logical possibilities and the implications of innovations must be one of the central tasks of anthropology today.

The story of independent Mali, as we have seen it here in the concrete case of a town of middle size in the western part of the country, is the story of an experiment in social organization. The analysis of Kita will cast light on other parts of Mali, where I believe the situation is much the same, and thus on the whole of the country. For all of the new nations, and perhaps for some which are not so new as well, the case of Kita raises the issue of the value, limits, and consequences of participatory government in a local community which is part of a national community. This study suggests that while participation can lead to popular government,

---

between repression and abandonment of the plan. It chose the latter alternative, in what amounted to a coup d'état against the minister for economic affairs which left the rest of the governmental structure intact.

it may also hinder effective action by a populistic national government. The problem of harnessing local popular government for national ends without changing its nature remains.

Bibliography

Amin, Samir. 1965. *Trois expériences africaines de développement: le Mali, la Guinée, le Ghana.* Paris: Presses Universitaires de France.

Amselle, Jean-Loup. 1969. Rapport de mission sur l'économie marchande au Mali (octobre 1967–juin 1968). In *Cahiers d'Etudes Africaines* 9:313–17.

Anonymous. 1890. Recensement effectué en février et mars 1890. Ms. in National Archives of Mali, Bamako. File 5–D, Kita.

———. 1967. Mali–six years after. In *West Africa* 2590:79–81; 2591:115–16; 2593:208–10.

Antoun, Richard. 1965. Conservatism and change in the village community: a Jordanian case study. In *Human Organization* 24:4–10.

Apter, David. 1963. Political religion in the new nations. In *Old societies and new states,* ed. C. Geertz. New York: The Free Press of Glencoe, pp. 57–104.

Ba, Amadou Hampaté, and Cardaire, Marcel. 1957. *Tierno Bokar, le sage de Bandiagara.* Paris: Présence Africaine.

Ba, Amadou Hampaté, and Daget, Jacques. 1962. *L'empire peul du Macina.* Paris and the Hague: Mouton.

Badian, Seydou. 1964. *Les dirigeants africains face à leur peuple.* Paris: Maspéro.

Bailey, F. G. 1963. *Politics and social change: Orissa in 1959.* Berkeley: University of California Press.

229

——. 1966. Decisions by consensus in councils and committees: with special reference to village and local government in India. In *Politics and the distribution of power*, ed. M. Banton. London: Tavistock, pp. 1–20.

Barlet, Paul. 1942. Chronique du cercle de Kita de 1880 à 1920. Ms. In possession of M. Seydou Sy, Kita.

——. 1944. Renseignements et statistiques concernant le cercle de Kita. Ms. in National Archives of Mali, Bamako. File 1–D–7.

——. 1966. Personal communication.

Barth, Fredrik. 1959. Segmentary opposition and the theory of games: a study of Pathan organization. In *The Journal of the Royal Anthropological Institute of Great Britain and Ireland* 89:5–21.

Bayol, Jean. 1881. Voyage au pays de Bamako. In *Bulletin de Géographie*. 7th series. 2:25–61, 123–63.

——. 1888. *Voyage en Sénégambie*. Paris: Baudoin.

Bechet, Eugène. 1889. *Cinq ans de séjour au Soudan français*. Paris: Plon.

Bernus, Edmond. 1956. Kobané, un village malinké du Haut-Niger. In *Cahiers d'Outre-Mer* 9:239–62.

Blair, Thomas L. 1970. *'The land to those who work it': Algeria's experiment in workers' management*. Garden City: Doubleday-Anchor.

Brasseur, G. and Le Moal, G. 1963. Note de présentation, cartes ethno-démographiques de l'Afrique occidentale, feuilles 3 et 4 nord. Dakar: Institut Français d'Afrique Noire.

Brinton, Crane. 1934. *A decade of revolution, 1789–1799*. New York: Harper.

Brokensha, David. 1966. *Social change at Larteh, Ghana*. London: Oxford University Press.

Brown, Richard D. 1970. *Revolutionary politics in Massachusetts: the Boston Committee of Correspondence and the towns, 1772–1774*. Cambridge: Harvard University Press.

Brun, Joseph. 1907. Notes sur les croyances et les pratiques religieuses des Malinkés fétichistes. In *Anthropos* 2:722–29, 942–52.

Chanteaux. 1884. Rapport sur l'hivernage 1884: observations, statistiques, moeurs. Ms. in National Archives of Mali, Bamako. File 1–E (Rapports politiques: Kita).

Chéron, Georges. 1931. Le dyide. In *Journal de la Société des Africanistes* 1:285–89.

Chirot, Daniel. 1968. Urban and rural economies in the Western Sudan: Birni N'Konni and its hinterland. In *Cahiers d'Etudes Africaines* 8:547–65.

Cohen, Abner. 1965. *Arab border-villages in Israel.* Manchester: Manchester University Press.

Comte, Gilbert. 1969. Comment Modibo Keita a été renversé. In *Jeune Afrique* 464:28–33, 465:20–26.

Delafosse, Maurice. 1912. *Haut-Sénégal-Niger* (first series). 3 vols. Paris: Larose.

Delmond, Paul. 1941. Le cercle de Kita, zone d'influence de l'Islam. Ms. in Centre des Hautes Etudes sur l'Administration Musulmane, Paris. Document no. 514.

———. 1953. Dans la boucle du Niger, Dori ville peule. In *Mélanges Ethnologiques.* Mémoires de l'Institut Français d'Afrique Noire, no. 23, pp. 9–109.

———. 1966. Personal communication.

———. 1967. Personal communication.

Delval, J. 1951. Le R.D.A. au Soudan français. In *L'Afrique et l'Asie* 16:54–67.

de Wilde, John C. 1967. *Experiences with agricultural development in tropical Africa.* 2 vols. Baltimore: Johns Hopkins University Press for the International Bank for Reconstruction and Development.

Diallo, Demba. 1968. *L'Afrique en question.* Paris: Maspéro.

Fallers, Lloyd A. 1956. *Bantu bureaucracy.* Cambridge, England: W. Heffer and Sons for the East African Institute of Social Research.

———. 1963. Equality, modernity and democracy in the new states. In *Old societies and new states,* ed. C. Geertz. New York: The Free Press of Glencoe, pp. 158–219.

Fernea, Robert A. 1970. *Shaykh and effendi.* Cambridge: Harvard University Press.

Foltz, William J. 1965. *From French West Africa to the Mali Federation.* New Haven: Yale University Press.

Friedrich, Paul. 1966. Revolutionary politics and communal ritual. In *Political Anthropology,* ed. Marc J. Swartz, Victor W. Turner, and Arthur Tuden. Chicago: Aldine, pp. 191–220.

———. 1968. The legitimacy of a cacique. In *Local-level politics,* ed. Marc Swartz. Chicago: Aldine, pp. 243–69.

Gallais, Jean. 1962. Signification du groupe ethnique au Mali. In *L'Homme* 2, no. 2: 106–29.

BIBLIOGRAPHY

Galliéni, Joseph. 1885. *Voyage au Soudan français.* Paris: Hachette.

Gans, Herbert J. 1967. *The Levittowners: ways of life and politics in a new suburban community.* New York: Random House.

Geertz, Clifford. 1963a. *Peddlers and princes: social change and modernization in two Indonesian towns.* Chicago: University of Chicago Press.

———. 1963b. *Agricultural involution: the processes of ecological change in Indonesia.* Berkeley: University of California Press.

———. 1965. *The social history of an Indonesian town.* Cambridge, Mass.: M.I.T. Press.

———. 1968. *Islam observed.* New Haven: Yale University Press.

GGAOF (Gouvernement Général de l'Afrique Occidentale Française). 1921. *Annuaire de l'Afrique Occidentale Française.* Paris: Larose.

Grandet, Claude. 1957. Les sédentaires du cercle de Tombouctou (Territoire du Soudan). In *Cahiers d'Outre-Mer* 10:234–56.

Grundy, Kenneth W. 1963. Mali: the prospects of planned socialism. In *African socialism,* ed. W. H. Friedland and C. G. Rosberg. Stanford: Stanford University Press, pp. 175–93.

Hargreaves, John D. 1963. *Prelude to the partition of West Africa.* London: Macmillan.

———. 1967. *West Africa: the former French states.* Englewood Cliffs, N.J.: Prentice-Hall.

Hazard, John N. 1967. Mali's socialism and the Soviet legal model. In *Yale Law Journal* 77 (pt. 1):28–69.

Hill, Polly. 1963. *Migrant cocoa-farmers of southern Ghana.* Cambridge, England: Cambridge University Press.

Hobsbawm, Eric. 1959. *Primitive rebels.* New York: W. W. Norton.

Hodgkin, Thomas, and Morgenthau, Ruth Schachter. 1964. Mali. In *Political parties and national integration in tropical Africa,* ed. J. Coleman and C. Rosberg. Berkeley and Los Angeles: University of California Press, pp. 216–58.

Hopkins, Nicholas S. 1964. The social structure of Mali (Kita and Bamako) in the 1880s. M.A. paper. University of Chicago: Department of Anthropology.

———. 1965. The modern theater in Mali. In *Présence Africaine* 53:159–93 (English edition).

———. 1969a. Leadership and consensus in two Malian cooperatives. In *The anthropology of development in Sub-Saharan Africa,* ed. D.

Brokensha and M. Pearsall. Monograph no. 10 of the Society for Applied Anthropology, pp. 64–69.

———. 1969b. Socialism and social change in rural Mali. In *Journal of Modern African Studies* 7:457–67.

———. In press. Maninka social organization. In *Mandé Studies,* ed. C. Hodge. Indiana University Press.

Jaeger, Paul. 1951. Légendes et coutumes au pays de Kita. In *Notes africaines* 52:103–6.

Janzen, John M. 1969a. The politics of apoliticality: form and process in a Lower Congo regional council. In *Cahiers d'Etudes Africaines* 9:570–99.

———. 1969b. The cooperative in Lower Congo economic development. In *The anthropology of development in Sub-Saharan Africa,* ed. D. Brokensha and M. Pearsall. Monograph no. 10 of the Society for Applied Anthropology, pp. 70–76.

Jones, William I. 1969. The Keita decade: economics of the coup. In *Africa Report,* March-April 1969, pp. 23–26, 51–53.

Kamian, Bakary. 1959. Une ville de la République du Soudan: San. In *Cahiers d'Outre-Mer* 12:225–50.

Kanya-Forstner, A. S. 1969. *The conquest of the western Sudan: a study in French military imperialism.* Cambridge: Cambridge University Press.

Keita, Fodéba. 1957. La danse africaine et la scène. In *Présence Africaine* 14–15:202–9.

Keita, Madeira. 1960. Le parti unique en Afrique. In *Présence Africaine* 30:3–24.

Kluckhohn, Clyde. 1951. Values and value-orientations in the theory of action: an exploration in definition and classification. In *Toward a general theory of action,* ed. T. Parsons and E. Shils. New York: Harper, pp. 388–433.

Labouret, Henri. 1934. Les Mandings et leur langue. In *Bulletin du Comité d'Etudes Historiques et Scientifiques de l'Afrique Occidentale Française* 17:1–270.

Labouret, Henri, and Travélé, Moussa. 1929. Le théâtre mandingue (Soudan français) . In *Africa* 1:73–97.

Leynaud, Emile. 1961. Les cadres sociaux de la vie rurale dans la Haute-Vallée du Niger. Ms., Bureau pour le Développement de la Production Agricole. Paris.

———. 1966. Fraternités d'âge et sociétés de culture dans la Haute-Vallée du Niger. In *Cahiers d'Etudes Africaines* 6:41–68.

BIBLIOGRAPHY

Lissagaray, Prosper Ollivier. 1967. *Histoire de la commune de 1871.* Paris: Maspéro.

Little, Kenneth. 1965. *West African urbanization.* Cambridge: Cambridge University Press.

Mage, Ernest. 1868. *Voyage dans le Soudan occidental.* Paris: Hachette.

Marcot, Père. 1892. Kita. In *Bulletin de la Congrégation du Saint-Esprit* 16:299–307.

Marty, Paul. 1920. *Etudes sur l'Islam et les tribus du Soudan.* Vol. 4, *La région de Kayes; le pays Bambara; le Sahel de Nioro.* Paris: Larose.

Mauny, Raymond. 1959. Evocation de l'empire du Mali. In *Notes africaines* 82:33–37.

Mayer, Adrian. 1966. The significance of quasi-groups in the study of complex societies. In *The social anthropology of complex societies,* ed. M. Banton. London: Tavistock, pp. 97–122.

Meillassoux, Claude. 1963. Histoire et institutions du 'kafo' de Bamako d'après la tradition des Niaré. In *Cahiers d'Etudes Africaines* 4:186–227.

———. 1964. La farce villageoise à la ville (le 'kotéba' de Bamako). In *Présence Africaine* 52:27–59.

———. 1965. The social structure of modern Bamako. In *Africa* 35:125–42.

———. 1968. *Urbanization of an African community: voluntary associations in Bamako.* Monograph no. 45 of the American Ethnological Society. Seattle: University of Washington Press.

Méniaud, Jacques. 1931. *Les pionniers du Soudan.* Paris: Société des publications modernes.

Miner, Horace. 1965. *The primitive city of Timbuctoo.* Garden City: Doubleday-Anchor.

Monteil, Charles. 1929. Les empires du Mali. In *Bulletin du Comité d'Etudes historiques et scientifiques de l'Afrique occidentale française* 12:291–447 (also published separately by G.-P. Maisonneuve et Larose, Paris, 1968).

———. 1932. *Une cité soudanaise: Djenné.* Paris: Société d'Editions géographiques, maritimes et coloniales.

Monteil, Vincent. 1964. *L'Islam noir.* Paris: Editions du Seuil.

Montrat, Maurice. 1935. Notes sur les Malinkés du Sankaran. In *Outre-Mer,* 1935, pp. 107–27.

Morgenthau, Ruth Schachter. 1964. *Political parties in French-speaking West Africa.* London: Oxford University Press.

Niane, Djibril Tamsir. 1960. *Sounjata, ou l'épopée mandingue.* Paris: Présence Africaine.

Nicholas, Ralph W. 1965. Factions, a comparative analysis. In *Political systems and the distribution of power,* ed. M. Banton. Monograph no. 2 of the Association of Social Anthropologists. London: Tavistock, pp. 21–62.

Pageard, Robert. 1958. Ségou (Soudan français). In *Annales africaines,* 1958, pp. 293–304.

Pâques, Viviana. 1954. *Les Bambara.* Paris: Presses Universitaires de France.

Parsons, Talcott. 1963. On the concept of political power. In *Proceedings of the American Philosophical Society* 107, no. 3:232–62.

Penel, Julien. 1895. Coutumes soudanaises (Malinké, Sarakollé, Khassonké). Ms. in Bibliothèque Nationale, Paris.

Pérignon, A. 1899. Notice sur le cercle de Kita. Ms. in Archives of Senegal, Fonds de l'A.O.F. File 1–G–124.

Piétri. 1885. *Les français au Niger.* Paris: Hachette.

Pitt-Rivers, Julian. 1961. *People of the Sierra.* Chicago: University of Chicago Press.

Porter, David L. 1968. Workers' self-management: Algeria's experiment in radical democracy. Paper presented at the 1968 annual meeting of the African Studies Association.

Robinson, Kenneth. 1960. Senegal: the elections to the territorial assembly, March 1957. In *Five elections in Africa,* ed. W. J. M. Mackenzie and K. Robinson. Oxford: Clarendon Press.

Roos. 1903–4. Le cercle de Kita. Ms. in Archives of Senegal, Fonds de l'A.O.F. File 1–G–311.

Sidibé, Mamby. 1932. Coutumier du cercle de Kita. In *Bulletin du Comité d'Etudes historiques et scientifiques de l'Afrique occidentale française* 15:72–177.

———. 1959. Soundiata Keita, héros historique et légendaire, empéreur du Manding. In *Notes africaines,* 82:41–51.

Smith, Pierre. 1965a. Les Diakhanké. Histoire d'une dispersion. In *Bulletins et mémoires de la Société d'Anthropologie de Paris.* 11th series, 8:231–62 (Cahier no. 4 du Centre de Recherches Anthropologiques).

———. 1965b. Notes sur l'organisation sociale des Diakhanké. Aspects particuliers à la région de Kédougou. In *Bulletins et mémoires de la Société d'Anthropologie de Paris.* 11th series, 8:263–302 (Cahier no. 4 du Centre de Recherches Anthropologiques).

BIBLIOGRAPHY

Snyder, Frank Gregory. 1965. *One-party government in Mali*. New Haven: Yale University Press.

———. 1967. The political thought of Modibo Keita. In *The Journal of Modern African Studies* 5:79–106.

———. 1969. The Keita decade: an era ends in Mali. In *Africa Report*, March-April 1969, pp. 16–22.

Southwold, Martin. 1964. Leadership, authority and the village community. In *The king's men: leadership and status in Buganda on the eve of independence*, ed. L. A. Fallers. London: Oxford University Press, pp. 211–55.

Strasfogel, S. n.d. Gouni, étude d'un village soudanais et de son terroir. *Mémoires et documents du Centre de Documentation Cartographique et géographique de l'Institut de Géographie de l'Université de Paris* 1:9–106.

Suret-Canale, Jean. 1964. *L'Afrique noire occidentale et centrale: l'ère coloniale (1900–1945)*. Paris: Editions sociales.

Suttles, Gerald D. 1968. *The social order of the slum: ethnicity and territory in the inner city*. Chicago: University of Chicago Press.

Swartz, Marc J., ed. 1968. *Local-level politics*. Chicago: Aldine.

Swartz, Marc J.; Turner, Victor W.; and Tuden, Arthur, eds. 1966. *Political anthropology*. Chicago: Aldine.

Sy, Seydou Madani. 1965. *Recherches sur l'exercice de pouvoir politique en Afrique noire: Côte-d'Ivoire, Guinée, Mali*. Paris: Pédone.

Tardif, Jean. 1965. Kédougou: aspects de l'histoire et de la situation socio-économique actuelle. In *Bulletins et mémoires de la Sociéte d'Anthropologie de Paris*. 11th series, 8:167–230 (Cahiers no. 4 du Centre de Recherches Anthropologiques).

Tellier, G. 1898. *Autour de Kita*. Paris: Henri Charles-Lavauzelle.

Traoré, Issa Baba. n.d. *Koumi-Diossé*. Bamako: Editions populaires du Mali.

Traoré, Seydou. 1959. Les associations d'âges à Sofara (au Soudan). Ms. in the Ecole Nationale de la France d'Outre-Mer, Paris. Mémoire no. 170.

Vogt, Evon Z. 1955. *Modern homesteaders*. Cambridge: The Belknap Press of Harvard University Press.

West, James. 1945. *Plainville, USA*. New York: Columbia University Press.

Whyte, William Foote. 1955. *Street corner society: the social structure of an Italian slum*. 2d ed. Chicago: University of Chicago Press.

Wolf, Eric. 1956. Aspects of group relations in a complex society: Mexico. In *American Anthropologist* 58:1065–78.

———. 1966. Kinship, friendship and patron-client ties in complex societies. In *The social anthropology of complex societies,* ed. M. Banton. Monograph no. 4 of the Association of Social Anthropologists. London: Tavistock, pp. 1–22.

Wylie, Laurence. 1958. *Village in the Vaucluse.* Cambridge, Mass.: Harvard University Press.

Zaleznik, A.; Christensen, C. R.; and Roethlisberger, F. J. 1958. *The motivation, productivity and satisfaction of workers: a prediction study.* Boston: Division of Research, Graduate School of Business Administration, Harvard University.

Zamiti, Khalil. 1970. Les obstacles matériels et idéologiques à l'évolution sociale des campagnes tunisiennes: l'expérience de mise en coopératives dans le Gouvernorat de Béja; et la signification sociologique de l'effondrement du système coopératif dans les campagnes tunisiennes. In *Revue Tunisienne des Sciences Sociales* 21:9–55.

Zghal, Abdelkader. 1967a. Système de parenté et système coopératif dans les campagnes tunisiennes. In *Revue Tunisienne des Sciences Sociales* 11:95–108.

———. 1967b. *Modernisation de l'agriculture et populations semi-nomades.* The Hague: Mouton.

Zolberg, Aristide R. 1964. *One-party government in the Ivory Coast.* Princeton: Princeton University Press.

———. 1965. The political revival of Mali. In *The World Today* 21:151–60.

———. 1967a. Patterns of national integration. In *The Journal of Modern African Studies* 5:449–67.

———. 1967b. The political use of economic planning in Mali. In *Economic nationalism in old and new states,* ed. H. G. Johnson. Chicago: University of Chicago Press, pp. 98–123.

Index

INDEX

Bambara. *See* Bamana
"Big men," as leaders, 28–30, 221
Birgo, 42–43, 121
Birthplace, and identity, 67
Blacks, as term for leaders, 205
Bribes: accusations of, 134, 195; in past, 36, 144
Brigades de Vigilance, xv, 88; and puritanism, 192; and wards, 102; at work, 88, 179–80, 197
Broker, 130, 143–44, 201, 206–7; involved in factions, 153; in Kita, 97, 145, 150, 215; in Mali, 149 n, 206; in the United States, 215–16. *See also* Intermediary
Budget, of municipality, 81
Bureaucracy, 6, 21, 76, 153, 179
Bureaucratization, 31
Bureau Executif de la Jeunesse (BEJ), 87–94, 164, 167; and Brigades de Vigilance, 197; and Bureau Politique Local, 91; and dispute settlement, 174, 175, 180–81; membership of, 80, 93; and orchestras, 173; and sports, 88, 90; tasks of, 87–88
Bureau Politique Local (BPL), 80, 82–87; and Brigades de Vigilance, 89, 179; and Bureau Executif de la Jeunesse, 87; and Consumers' Cooperatives, 107; functions of, 159, 173–74, 177, 178, 180–81; governs Kita, 83, 112; membership of, 77, 86, 87, 128, 131–33; permanent secretary of, 84–85; and town council, 79; and villages, 138; and wards, 63–64, 95, 97, 107
Bureau Politique National (BPN): in party organization, 16; visits Kita, 85, 134, 136, 164; visits villages, 138, 153

Canton, xviii, 32, 33, 37, 51
Cards: for Bureau Executif de la Jeunesse, 92; for Consumers' Cooperatives, 104, 106; for RDA, 85, 99, 100, 160, 164
Castes, 48, 52, 56; attacked, 225. See also *Dieli; Nyamakala*
Catholics, 55–57, 61, 64; relations with Muslims, 55, 56; status of, 52, 57. *See also* Saint-Félix
Centre d'Education Populaire, 92
Chief: as broker, 32, 215; canton, abolishment of, 123, 225; canton,

attitudes towards, 36; canton, during colonial period, 31–36, 59, 118–23; canton, Fatogoma as, 35, 57, 105; canton, and politics, 117, 146, 209–10; canton, during precolonial period, 27–28, 48, 59; canton, selection of, in 1942, 27, 34; ritual (*dugu kolo tigi*), 27; village (*dugu tigi*), 32, 63, 82; ward (*dugu tigi*), 81–82, 174
Circle, and party organization, 82
Cissé (lineage), 46, 49, 54, 60, 63, 65, 131
Citizenship: and Islam, 54; as a personal quality, 115, 206; as a status in Kita, 65, 67, 142; as a status shared by all Malians, 20
"Civilized," notion of, 52, 193, 205
Civil servants, 61, 64, 68, 71; and merchants, 106–7; occupy posts, 99, 105, 111; and politics, 44, 71, 106–7, 194; as strangers, 66–67, 69, 219
Clientele, 143, 145, 146. *See also* Patron-client relations
Cliques, 116, 128, 130, 132, 145
Clubs, 62, 90
Collective fields, 19
Colonial rule. *See* France, colonial rule by
Comité d'Entreprise, 110
Comité Directeur, 83, 86
Commandant de cercle: in politics, 55, 56, 87, 139, 143, 174, 176; tasks of, 69, 76–77
Commerce law, 69, 160, 164
Committee of party in ward, 63–64, 85, 94–103, 127, 128, 168
Commune of Kita. *See* Kita town, government
Communication: between Kita BPL and capital, 126; between Kita BPL and people, 16, 86, 91, 95, 100, 113, 158, 165–66; between state and party, 112; blocked, 150, 204; and national integration, 184, 223; with women, 102
Competition: description of, 62, 115, 149, 211; functions of, 148, 154; nonpolitical, 62, 89, 90, 174–75, 195; values concerning, 128, 187, 192, 194–95. *See also* Rivalry
Compromise, 170, 173, 175, 179, 181, 184, 187
Conférence des cadres in Kita, 158

INDEX

Favors, 35–36, 97, 143–44, 147, 149, 150, 152–53, 154
Finances. *See* Expenditures; Revenues
Flirting, 178
Following. *See* Clientele
Force: attitudes towards, 188, 203–4; use of, 31, 154, 156, 180, 221, 223, 224
France: colonial rule by, 4, 13–15, 24–25, 28–29, 31–33, 36–38, 40–41, 55, 76; neocolonial role of, 14–15; revolutions in, 215
Frankness, valued, 160, 200, 206
Friendship. See *Teriya*
Fula, ethnic group, 12, 13, 25, 46–47, 50, 51, 70

Game: politics as a, 151; theory, 147
Gare. *See* Kita-Gare
General assemblies. *See* Assemblies; Meetings
Generations, and factions, 146
Generosity, valued, 142, 198, 206
Ghana, 215
Gossip, 109, 151
Government. *See* Mali, national government
Grantors, 143–44, 153
Guests and hosts, 48, 143. See also *Diatigi*

History, as a political idiom, 118, 209
Household, as economic unit, 36
Human investment. See *Fasobara*

Ideal types, 184–85
Identity: and Catholics, 62; ethnic, 45–52; and Islam, 52–53, 54, 58, 72; and marriage customs, 48; national, 225; and stereotypes, 49; town, 12, 45–52, 52–53, 72, 90, 113, 155, 218; ward, 58, 61–62, 64, 72, 113
Ideological orientation, 183–84, 186–94, 208, 211, 220, 221
Ideology, 127, 183, 184
Idiom, political: and integration, 184; and Islam, 58; and kin, 25; the past as, 118, 209; and rivalry, 115–16; shift in, 7; of socialism, 18, 148
Income. *See* Revenue
Independence, national, 13, 14, 44, 74, 117, 214
Individual, as political unit, 153, 219
Informants, 24, 117

Integration: of Kita, 155, 184, 219; of Mali, 16–17, 217, 223
Intermediaries, 144, 201; examples of, 32, 35, 41, 65, 79, 143–44, 151. *See also* Broker
Intrigue, 129, 149, 150, 199
Iraq, 215
Islam: in Java, 214; in Kita, 52–54; linked to RDA, 60; in Moribougou, 54, 60; in precolonial period, 26; social role, 49, 52, 58; values, 53–54, 192
Israel, 215
Issues: in Kita's history, 119, 124, 127, 131, 135, 136; in politics, 7–8, 116, 149, 154, 166, 168; and processes, 157, 160, 163

Java, 214, 220
Jordan, 215
Judge: activities of, 170, 172, 205 n; uses court for education, 171, 193

Kamara, Mamadou, 120, 126, 130, 131, 137–39, 167, 177, 178
Kasonka, ethnic group, 46–47
Keita (lineage), 25 n, 26, 27, 49, 50, 59–60, 63, 126, 136 n, 161 n, 218
Keita, Abraham, 120, 124–25, 142, 196
Keita, Aliou, 120, 123, 137, 160
Keita, Fatogoma: as chief, 34–36, 51, 59, 118; as politician, 119, 120, 122, 123, 125, 126, 127, 129, 131, 132, 140, 145, 146
Keita, Garan, 33–34, 118, 120
Keita, Modibo (president of Mali), 15, 50 n, 85, 122, 173, 198
Keita, Moussa, 119, 120, 123–31, 139, 140, 142, 145, 146
Keita, Soundiata (emperor of Mali), 13, 26, 48, 50, 142 n
Keita, Tokontan, 28–31, 34, 36, 59, 118, 221
Kin, favored for posts, 198
Kita canton (*diamana*), 25
Kita town: as arena, 115, 163, 208; and BEJ, 91; and BPL, 82–83; description, 4, 11, 24–25, 45, 58–64; economics, 38, 43, 68–70; government, 78–82; history, 29, 38–39, 45, 53, 65; and identity, 45–52, 58; politics, 72–73, 128, 165; as urban-style center, 48

242

INDEX

Militia, 88
Mobilization, 112, 212, 221, 222, 225
Modernity, and ideological orientation, 185
Modernization, favored by government, 3–8, 215, 225
Mogoba (leaders), 204
Moors (ethnic group), 12, 38, 46–48
Morality, encouraged, 88–89, 192
Moribougou (ward): consumers' cooperatives in, 103, 106, 166; description of, 60, 62, 63, 65; mosque in, 54, 60; political role of, 60, 118, 125, 130, 146, 172
Mosques, in wards, 54, 60
Municipal organization, of Kita, 78–82. *See also* Kita town, government
Muslims, disputes among, 223 n
Mythical charter, of Kita, 25–27
Myths, of PSP and RDA, 209–12

Na (newcomers), attitudes towards, 66, 67. *See also* Strangers
Names, 55, 57
Naming ceremonies, xix, 56, 57
Nationalism, 212
Nation-building, 213, 221–27
Natives: political role of, 64–68, 72, 76, 98, 99, 124, 131, 137, 206, 220
Naturalization: of individuals, 67; of institutions, 16, 22, 109
Neighbors: in quarrels, 81, 171 n, 172
Network, created by factions, 153
Nonlocals. *See* Strangers
Nyamakala: modern situation, 20, 57, 161, 189, 206; traditional situation, 25, 35, 60, 65, 143, 198. *See also* Castes; *Dieli*

Obstructionism, as tactic, 150–51
Occupation, 68–73, 146
One-party system, 215, 218
Orchestra, 92, 173. *See also* Dances
Order, valued, 191
Orientations, 183–208
Overseers' Committee of Consumers' Cooperatives, 103

Pagan religion, 52, 57
Parades, 88, 111, 179
Participation, 3, 7, 16, 220, 226; and legitimacy, 220; necessity for, 218, 222; in processes, 116, 142, 153, 165

Parti Soudanais du Progres (PSP), 13, 136, 146, 173; history of, in Kita, 51, 71, 79, 119, 127; version of past held by, 209–12
Party: branches, 22; cards, 85, 92, 99, 100, 160, 164; functions, 75, 112–14, 180, 187. *See also* Rassemblement Démocratique Africain
Patron-client relations, 22–23, 40–44, 114, 143, 146, 152, 221, 223. *See also* Broker; Clientele; Intermediary
Peanuts, 38–40, 69, 148–49, 161
People: object of concern by government, 4; in political process, 154, 159, 201, 226
Persuasion: use of, 18, 19, 21, 100–101, 162, 187, 224; value on, 186, 188, 205
Petitioners, 143–44, 150
Pioneers, 62, 63, 89, 102, 175, 179, 193
Police, 79, 177–78
Police chief, 79, 84, 139, 143, 161–62, 170, 172, 176, 180
Political bureau. *See* Bureau politique local
Political commissioners, 132, 135, 204
Politics, negatively valued, 195–96
Popular government, 4, 6–9, 23, 155, 156, 212, 218–21, 227
Populistic government, 4, 23, 227
Pork-barrel politics, 222
Possession cult (*djiden*), 57
Posts, political, 75, 141, 155, 195, 220; and prestige, 115
Power: in colonial period, 123; divided between factions, 147; in government, 226; of government, 21–22; in precolonial period, 28; suspicions of, 207. *See also* Authority
Pragmatic orientation, 184, 186, 194–208, 209, 211, 220
Pragmatic politics, 221
Prestige, sought and gained, 71, 72, 142, 148, 152, 166, 167, 194
Principle, as a basis for action, 200
Production, change in the basis of, 19, 189
Profits, in consumers' cooperatives, 109
Progressiveness, 130, 146
Public opinion, 7, 29, 147, 158, 180–81, 182, 218, 220; in Kita, 165
Puritanism, value on, 192

INDEX

Structures and events, 117
Style: national, 11; urban, of Kita, 48
Subsections: for central arrondisse-
ment, 94, 135–37; of party, 82, 85,
137
Sudan, Western, 219
Support: basis of, 7–8; of government,
21; political role of, 116, 144, 147,
153, 156, 197, 212, 219
Suspicion, of others, 199, 202, 207
Switches, of alliances, 146, 148
Sylla, Moussa, 51, 120, 124, 126–38,
140, 145, 150, 165, 168, 182, 221

Tall, Mamadou, 120, 134
Taxes, 32, 35, 42, 81, 85, 164, 174, 176,
210
Teachers, 71, 111, 126, 177
Teriya (friendship), 41, 143. *See also*
Patron-client relations
Territory, as basis for social units, 16,
58
Theater: Catholic, 56–57; finances, 92;
and Kita identity, 90; organization
of, 66, 77, 85, 89, 90, 174–75; themes,
171 n, 189, 190, 200; values concern-
ing, 190, 193; and women, 102
Toucouleur (ethnic group), 13, 29,
46–47, 51, 60
Tounkara (lineage), 25 n, 26, 27, 50,
59, 63
Tounkara, Douga, 120, 135, 136
Town clerk, of Kita, 78, 82, 143
Town council, of Kita, 78–80, 129
Towns, in Mali, 11, 49, 51–52
Trade routes, precolonial, 37, 38
Traoré, Paul, 120, 125
Tunisia, 216–17, 225 n

Uganda, 215
Understanding, cultural, 186, 188
Uniforms, for parades, 92, 179
Unions, 110–12
Union Soudanaise. *See* Rassemblement
Démocratique Africain
United States, 215–16
Unity of town, symbolized, 52, 54, 128
Urban particularism, 218

Vallière, 32
Values: and orientations, 184, 194;
political, 22, 208; traditional, 25, 51,
214; in Tunisia, 216
Villages: attitudes of, concerning politics, 196; attitudes of townspeople
towards, 48, 52, 53; autonomy of,
172; relations with Kita, 24, 35, 42,
43–44, 46, 53, 65–66; relations with
Kita party, 23, 65, 66, 84, 85, 132,
134, 136, 137, 158; wards as, 62, 98
Voting, 169

Wards, 58–64, 172; as political units,
64, 72, 88, 97, 98, 137, 146
Warfare, precolonial, 29, 51
Wealth, and position of chief, 29
Wolof (ethnic group), 50
Women, political role of, 20, 63, 95,
96, 99, 172, 193
Wulu den (native-born), 65, 67, 124
Wulu den ton. See Kita Natives' Asso-
ciation

xenophobia, 124, 127

Yere wulu (well-born), 206
Youth: organization, 63, 87–94, 101,
164; traditional activities, 93–94

246